RESEARCH
AND THE
MANUSCRIPT TRADITION

· Frank G. Burke ·

The Scarecrow Press, Inc.
Lanham, Md., & London
and
The Society of American Archivists
Chicago
1997

SCARECROW PRESS, INC.

Published in the United States of America
by Scarecrow Press, Inc.
4720 Boston Way
Lanham, Maryland 20706

4 Pleydell Gardens, Folkestone
Kent CT20 2DN, England

British Library Cataloguing-in-Publication Information Available

Library of Congress Cataloging-in-Publication Data

Burke, Frank G., 1927–
    Research and the manuscript tradition / Frank G. Burke.
        p.   cm.
    Includes bibliographical references and index.
    ISBN 0-8108-3348-4 (alk. paper)
        1. Archives—Research—United States—Methodology.   2. Archives—
Research—Methodology.   3. Archives—Administration.   4. History—
Research—Methodology.   5. United States—History—Research—
Methodology.   6. History—Research—Methodology.   I. Title.
CD3021.B87   1997
020'.973—dc21   97-15729
                                                                CIP

♾ ™ The paper used in this publication meets the minimum requirements
of American National Standard for Information Sciences—Permanence of
Paper for Printed Library Materials, ANSI Z39.48–1984. Manufactured
in the United States of America.

Dedicated to

BOB ROSENTHAL
DAVID MEARNS
DAN REED

CONTENTS

PREFACE

It is not possible to have a work such as this come to fruition without the author soliciting the help of many colleagues. So it was in this instance. Each of the chapters, and often more than one chapter, was sent to a person whom I felt had the best perspective on the topic covered. My readers came from the ranks of manuscript and special collections curators and librarians, archivists, historians, and government officials. Those who lent direct assistance through comments and suggestions on individual chapters were Daniel Meyer, University of Chicago; Linda Matthews, Emory University; Lawrence Dowler, Harvard College Library; Mary Giunta, Nancy Sahli, and Roger Bruns of the National Historical Publications and Records Commission; and Kathleen Roe, New York State Archives. I was provided important technical information for the chapter on law and curatorial ethics by Richard A. Jacobs and Mary Ronan of the National Archives, and Steven Garfinkel, director, U.S. Information Security Oversight Office. The entire manuscript was read by Raymond Smock, historian for the U.S. House of Representatives. His comments and suggestions were of great value during the creation of the manuscript. The final organization and contents are, of course, mine.

The College of Library and Information Services at the University of Maryland provided me with graduate assistants who assisted with a number of research, clerical, and instructional chores during their tenure. Especially helpful for the creation of this work were Kristi Mashon in the initial research stage, Kate Dillon for bibliographic searching, Stacy Finley, who, among other tasks, labored over the index, and Jennie Anne Levine, who memorized most of the *Chicago Manual of Style* and also solved some of the agonizing problems of WordPerfect 5.1.

This work, and my career, are gratefully dedicated to three

men who taught me to inquire, question, and understand, but most importantly to relish the human insights learned during the career of an archivist. Robert Rosenthal and David Mearns are both now gone, but at the University of Chicago and the Library of Congress, respectively, each introduced me to the "so what?" factor when looking at the lasting importance of prospective collections of personal papers, and the need to build from strength when assembling collections into a meaningful whole. Both taught me to appreciate the turn of a phrase when presenting one's case. Dan Reed at the Library of Congress and later the National Archives provided a lesson in how to manage staff and researchers through understanding, courtesy, and an appropriate injection of Irish wit. My wife Hildegard and our five children deferentially limited their demands for my domestic assistance throughout the process of creating this work.

Introduction

Why is there both a Library of Congress Manuscript Division and a National Archives? Why are the Hemingway papers in a Presidential Library, and why aren't the Presidential libraries centralized instead of being scattered all over the country? Why don't archives have library-style catalogs of their collections? Why aren't the papers of former congressmen in the Library of Congress? Why can't I get at the papers of the U.S. Senate through the Freedom of Information Act? How in the world can I ever find letters of Roy Knabenshue?

Over the past thirty years and more I have heard these questions repeated, with variations, from researchers, students in my classes, interested relatives, and professional colleagues. Over those same three decades my archival co-workers and I have attempted to respond with reasonable-sounding answers, only to see our questioner sometimes give a frustrated shake of the head. Academic departments frequently send their budding scholars off to do "original research" in "documentary sources" without preparing them for the challenges they can expect to encounter once they leave the familiar library setting, with its card or computer catalogs, bibliographies, tables of contents, indexes, and all the supporting mechanisms that can lead to the publication that will provide the desired answers. The use of documentary sources is not taught in most academic departments, including history, English, American studies, and journalism. Over and over, studies of research methodology among scholars reveal that they learn by some sort of collegial osmosis and general fumbling about until they figure things out.

Through those years it was clear to me that researchers who were approaching the use of documents for the first time needed considerable direction, and that as they became accustomed to the structure of archives and then had to use personal papers, their education began all over again. For the most part they approach these exotic materials without understanding the traditions and practices that archivists and manuscript curators have developed for their administration, which then determine what researchers must deal with. My target audience therefore is the beginning researcher—academic, professional or amateur.

This work is an attempt to rectify that gap in research education and training. It is not a manual, although it may have some attributes common to manuals. Nor is it a text, although teachers may want to assign readings from it. It is, in fact, a professional reflection on using manuscripts for research, practical advice on administering manuscript and archival collections and institutions, and is based on what was learned during more than twenty years of teaching a course on manuscripts administration at the University of Maryland, College Park.

This work, then, is a culmination of those experiences. I have aimed it at researchers rather than at budding archivists, because researchers are not likely to become familiar with texts on manuscript use in their career, whereas archivists are. The chapters that follow are, in effect, a tour behind the scenes of a manuscript repository, explaining what is done and why, using anecdotes and examples in an attempt to convey the joy of working with these materials, and, I hope, dispersing the mists that shroud much of this kind of research. Many of my examples come from my own experience, but perhaps the reader will find relevance in some of what I say.

As readers—and especially young scholars—delve into the following pages, I hope that they are inspired to experience the excitement of the chase for facts, the vicarious participation in the lives of the great, near great, and no-account, and the recognition that history is a seamless encounter of human beings acting very humanly as they go about expressing and living their hopes, joys, fears, frustrations, and sorrows, all poured out in letters, diaries, reports, and creative compositions that communicate their personalities to all posterity.

· 1 ·

YUAN SHIH-KAI, HARRIET MONROE, AND THE MANUSCRIPT TRADITION

> For the historian *history* becomes only that part of the human past which can be meaningfully reconstructed from the available records and from inferences regarding their setting.
>
> Louis Gottschalk[1]

On December 28, 1911, William J. Calhoun, American Minister to China posted in Peking, wrote a long letter to his sister-in-law in Chicago, Harriet Monroe. Calhoun's wife was the former Lucy Monroe, and her sister Harriet was preparing to persuade one hundred notable Chicagoans to contribute $5 each so that she could fulfill her ambition to start up a monthly magazine. *Poetry: A Magazine of Verse* made Monroe and American poets such as T. S. Eliot, Edgar Lee Masters, Carl Sandberg, and many others famous.

The letter of late December spoke of dramatic events taking place in China, and Calhoun described many of them to his sister-in-law: "I have been trying for some time to get a letter off to you. . . . Our work is very heavy these days . . . we are so busy, that I have little time for private correspondence." But Calhoun pressed on: "Conditions here, since our return, have been somewhat strenuous. We never know what is going to happen. Rumor, with a thousand tongues, is very busy."[2]

What the rumors were about was the overthrow of the Manchu dynasty. It was the end of an era that Calhoun was witnessing, and he memorialized it in his correspondence, including this letter of more than nine pages.

The "man on horseback" in the 1911 revolution was Yuan Shih-Kai, a former viceroy, called out of retirement by the regent of the infant emperor, and, by a tangled series of events, to become Provisional President of the Republic, but ultimately to be suc-

1

ceeded by Sun Yat-sen and the Kuomintang, or the Nationalists. Yuan was a figure who intrigued Calhoun, and he wrote of him to Harriet: "I have only seen him twice. . . . He is big, burly and fat—heavy looking. . . . He is past the prime of life, not so much in years as in living . . . he doesn't look much like a statesman. For that matter, none of the Chinese do." He added: "There are varied estimates of the man. Some think he is much overrated: that he is merely a crafty politician, an opportunist. . . . Whatever may be said of him, he appears to be the strongest, the ablest man that China has today."

This and other letters from Calhoun and his wife Lucy are in the collection which was bequeathed by Harriet Monroe in 1936 to the University of Chicago.

Since Calhoun was an American minister, one would expect to find correspondence of his in the records of the Department of State at the National Archives. To do so, it is necessary to consult Microcopy 329, Roll 9, for Records of the Department of State Relating to Internal Affairs of China, 1910–1929.[3] There, under the date January 16, 1912, is a six-page typewritten letter from Calhoun addressed to:

> The Honorable
> The Secretary of State [Philander C. Knox]
> Washington
>
> Sir:
> I have the honor to report that ever since my return here the situation has been so confused and so obscured with doubt and uncertainty that it has been impossible to make any satisfactory estimate of it. It seems to change every day. Rumor with a thousand tongues is always busy. . . .

And further:

> There are various estimates of Yuan. He is generally regarded as the ablest man that China has today. Some think he is only an astute politician, that his success heretofore has been due to political intrigue, and that he is an overrated man. But he has a record for achievement, and the general estimate of him is, that he has character, force and capacity to do things; wherein he is to be differentiated from any other official or public man in this country of whom I have any knowledge.

The long paragraph continues:

> He is big, fat and burly. He is evidently past the prime of life—
> not so much in years, perhaps, as in fast living; and it is thought
> he has lost much of his former strength. He impresses me as
> being intelligent and resourceful, but like all Chinese he is more
> of a schemer than a man of action.

These two letters, written nineteen days apart, illustrate the essence of the difference between archives—corporate or government records—and manuscripts, or personal papers. The differences between the two genres have been obscured in much of the archival literature, which has led to complications as archivists have attempted to merge the two forms into single systems of arrangement, description, application of standards, and automated structure. The confusion has carried over to the education of archivists and the preparation of standard manuals, with some notable exceptions.

Researchers using documentary sources should be aware of these distinctions when evaluating the documentation before them, and when planning their research strategy. They should also be aware of the way in which archivists identify such materials for saving, how they are acquired, what archivists and manuscript curators do with such materials, and the different methods used for locating and using them. The following pages are meant to reveal some professional techniques and traditions which could aid researchers in their evaluation and use of original sources.

Perhaps it all began with T. R. Schellenberg, professionally raised in the National Archives, and concerned mainly with government records. Schellenberg has been considered the major exponent of archival theory and practice in the United States, dating from his teaching and writing years, which began in the 1940s. In his *The Management of Archives*, where he addresses the question of personal papers for the first time, he states:

> In what respects are private records actually different from pub-
> lic records, and in what respects are they similar? Are their simi-
> larities more important than their differences? In what ways
> should one deal with them differently? In what ways similarly?
>
> Most private records have the organic quality of public
> records and are therefore archival in character. This is the case
> with all records produced by corporate bodies, such as busi-

nesses, churches and schools, and all records produced by persons in relation to extended activities. Only small groups of
personal papers . . . lack organic characteristics. Even when they
lack such characteristics, private records have all the other qualities of public records. . . . They consist of the same types as
public records: letters, reports, and the like. They are physically
similar to public records. They are far more like public records
than they are like publications.[4]

Schellenberg seems to be mixing definitions here, comparing
public *records* with private *records*, with personal *papers*, and even
with *publications*. The validity of his argument with private and
public *records* cannot be denied, since it is clear that he means the
records of corporate bodies—businesses, churches and schools, to
which one could add institutions, organizations, and structured
groups, all of which have the character of an existence beyond the
life or role of any individual, and have a mission and function.
However, his argument comparing *records* to personal papers is
confusing, if not faulty. Schellenberg slips when, in his next sentence after referring to personal papers, he then goes back to use
the term *records*, muddying the issue. He compounds the confusion
with the gratuitous comparison of private records (or did he mean
personal papers?) with publications.

Canadian Dominion Archivist (1968–84) Wilfred Smith,
writing on "total archives" in 1986, defending the Canadian practice of collecting personal papers in a national archives, echoes
Schellenberg,[5] using as his examples those papers of corporate bodies or public officials whose papers may indeed be quasi-public
records, and not the private outpourings of an author, artist, or any
individual in private correspondence of a personal nature.

Temporarily granting both Schellenberg's and Smith's arguments in the comparison of public and private records, and even
conceding that corporate records are organically comparable to
government records, I would like to approach the question of records of any kind compared with personal papers, and use the two
Calhoun letters about Yuan Shih-Kai as the starting point for the
comparison.

First, let's look at the motivation for creation of the two Calhoun letters. Perhaps Calhoun felt it obligatory as a social, familial
function, to write to his wife's sister. The fact that it was the
Christmas season may have added to his motivation. He knew that

Harriet was an intelligent, worldly-wise woman to whom he could write of substantive matters, and not just social niceties. In any case, although there may have been subtle pressures on him to pen the letter, there is no indication that he *had* to do so. His excuse in the opening paragraph for not writing sooner indicates that he did not feel duty-bound to write, and certainly there was no imperative to convey to Harriet the impressions that he had of Yuan. We can thus conclude that the letter was a personally motivated, spontaneous act.

The letter to the secretary of state fulfills a professional obligation of a government employee to a superior officer. Or, as one source states it: "as the result of organic functions of an institutional bureaucracy."[6] Calhoun obviously had such an obligation to inform his superior of matters within his official purview. This, then, is not so much a letter as a report, and as such can be classed as an official document.

DOCUMENT OWNERSHIP

When Harriet Monroe received the letter from her brother-in-law she immediately owned the physical item, if not the means of expression that Calhoun used in it. The nine pages were hers to do with as she pleased. She could therefore destroy the document, paste it in a scrapbook in whole or in part, keep it, will it to someone, sell it to a collector of such things, bequeath it to a library, or take any other action that one can take with a personal possession. She could have done nothing, and the papers might then have been administered as part of her estate, sold on the manuscript market, and broken up into small lots for resale to collectors. She probably placed it with other letters, perhaps mixed in with correspondence from poets and other writers, in some sort of a home-devised filing scheme. Perhaps it remained in an unorganized condition until processed by the institution that received it some twenty-five years later.

Ownership of the letter by Harriet Monroe, however, does not imply her ownership of the contents or substance. The property rights in his literary effort were owned by William Calhoun, even though he sent the document to Harriet and she then owned the letter. That literary property right would be owned by Calhoun until and if the letter was published, at which time he or his assigns would own the copyright on the content for a term of years. If not published, the contents would be owned by Calhoun, his heirs or assigns, in perpetuity, and in equal measure. Since 1978 the issue of rights has shifted from common law to statutory copyright.

When Secretary of State Knox received Calhoun's report, he could legally do none of the things that Harriet Monroe could. The letter did not belong to him, but to the Department of State, and thus to the federal government. Knox was constrained by whatever regulations existed relating to government documents in general and State Department documents in particular. The only thing that he could do was to place it in the hands of a secretary who would deal with it according to the routing and filing manuals of the Department of State. At that time the staff would refer to the department's *Classification of Correspondence* manual, and classify it according to the decimal system then in use.[7] In fact, the document contains a hand-written designation at the top ("893.00/1038"), which translates from the *Manual* as:

8 = Internal Affairs of States
93 = China
.00 = American Consular Office (originator)
/1038 = document number in the file.

Indeed, it is pure conjecture to assume that Secretary Knox even saw the letter, since communications are always addressed to the person in authority, but reviewed for importance or pertinence by staff members lower in the bureaucracy. If Knox were away from the department at the time, it would have been reviewed by a subordinate, who might recommend a reply and have the document filed. Knox *could* see the letter anytime he wished, but whether he did is uncertain. If his initials were on the letter (they are not), it would lead one to believe that he had personally read it.

The literary ownership question is much simpler in the case of the letter to Knox. Since it is an official letter of a federal employee to a superior in his agency, copyright does not apply. The text is in the public domain and may be cited, quoted, or otherwise copied and reproduced without attribution or permission. I need not claim fair use in quoting the letter to Knox, since all use of texts in government documents is fair.

With the two letters in the hands of the recipients, we have already settled two legal questions. One letter belongs to the people of the United States through the medium of the State Department, the other letter belongs to Harriet Monroe. From the letter to Knox I can reproduce the phrase "he is big, fat and burly" without attribution, but in the Monroe letter I must be careful that in using the phrase I am not violating someone else's rights to first publication under the Copyright Act. But let's go on to other attributes of these two documents to see where else they differ. We will come back to copyright in chapter 11.

The letter to Harriet Monroe became part of a mixed group of correspondence, business papers, diaries, notebooks, clippings and personal papers that she accumulated and held until her death at age 76 in 1936, when her will stipulated that the lot should go to the University of Chicago. Assuming that the transfer was legally valid, the collection now belongs to the university. Although Harriet Monroe may have included in her will the disposition of *her* literary property rights, she could make no disposition of the literary rights that William Calhoun, his heirs or assigns held in his letters to her, unless they had been assigned to her by him. Since the university now owns the Monroe papers, they presumably can do what they wish with them, within the terms of the gift. Institutions have been known to dispose of collections, and Chicago may have the right to do so with the Monroe papers, including the Calhoun letter. But, unless Calhoun's rights have been transferred, his heirs still retain them, and will until at least the year 2003.

We have already seen that the secretary of state had no recourse in what he could do with the Calhoun letter. It went into the decimal file, lived out its life in the State Department in Washington, and in due course was transferred to the National Archives according to a legally drawn schedule, as part of a file considered to contain records of enduring value. There it rests today, and will remain "in perpetuity."

As to access, we saw that Harriet Monroe could provide access to her brother-in-law's letter immediately upon receipt. It could be shared with family, friends, colleagues or anyone else who wanted to read it. The letter to Knox, however, was subject to State Department access restrictions, which at the time mandated that the letter, indeed the whole file, not be public for fifty years; which meant that a researcher would have to wait until 1962 to see the 1912 letter. Although one might say that the more valid source for what Calhoun was writing would be the "official" rather than the "personal" document, we have seen that not only was the personal letter written first (when, presumably, Calhoun was closer to the events that he describes), but that it contains essentially the same information, even using the same words that later are in the official report. A skilled researcher, blocked from access to an official source, would do well to seek alternative sources for the information sought.

Now, let's really fantasize and consider what might have happened if the ship or ships that the letters were on were boarded and searched by Chinese officials as they sailed from their Chinese port. Could they take umbrage at the comments Calhoun makes to Knox about Yuan? Could they consider this an international affront to their highest official of state, and ask that Calhoun be reprimanded, or even recalled? Milder provocations have sometimes caused such diplomatic dustups, and the Americans would be forced to respond in some manner. It would be quite different, at least in an international tribunal, if the Chinese government took affront at the letter to Harriet. The Americans could claim that Calhoun was not writing in an official capacity, it was not the government's affair to intrude in his personal correspondence to a family member, and, since it was a personal communication, the most that it could be construed as would be "hearsay evidence" of Calhoun's sentiments. Any "incident" could thus be played down by the American officials. Yet, Calhoun did call Yuan "big, burly and fat," "heavy looking," and "past the prime of life," and slurred the Chinese as statesmen.

THE NATURE OF RESEARCH MATERIALS

If we enlarge the context from these two letters to all research materials, the institutions that hold them and the professionals who maintain them, we can acknowledge that research materials come in all types, shapes and sizes. When we think of libraries we think of books—pages of printed material bound between covers. But merely a glance at any library shows that it also contains magazines and journals, printed government documents, photographs, film, sound and video recordings, newspapers, and, depending on the size and affiliation of the library, personal papers, archives, digital tapes and other "machine-readable" or electronic documents. We will also see the same forms of material in archives, but in different proportions.

These forms listed above can be divided into two broad categories: those that are produced in quantity for distribution or sale, which we can call "commercial" materials; and those produced individually for some private or corporate reason, usually pragmatic in nature, which, conversely, could be called noncommercial materials. A basic professional distinction between librarians and archivists is that librarians, for the most part, deal with items that are produced or attained commercially; archivists work with noncommercial materials. These noncommercial materials then fall into two categories: corporate and private.

Corporate materials are created by or for corporate bodies, and corporate bodies can be defined as those which produce materials in pursuit of their corporate aim, and not the private aims of the individual members. Corporate bodies, therefore, can be PTA groups, governments, businesses and corporations, organizations and societies of all kinds, churches, clubs, and many other institutional structures. Any materials produced or received by such a corporate body in pursuit of its corporate aim are its *records*, and those records that the corporation considers to be of permanent, enduring, or long-range value are its archives. Calhoun's letter to Knox is a record, among the archives of the Department of State now deposited in the National Archives.

Personal materials are those created by individuals that have not attained a commercial state, or were never intended to be either commercial or public, all characterized by their personal significance to the individual. Calhoun's letter to Harriet Monroe is a "manuscript" or "personal papers" item.

With these definitions in mind, we can investigate some of the characteristics of archives and personal papers. By definition, archives are:

> the documents created or received and accumulated by a person or organization in the course of the conduct of affairs, and preserved because of their continuing value. Historically, the term referred more narrowly to the NONCURRENT RECORDS of an organization or institution preserved because of their continuing value.[8]

These records may be contracts, agreements and transactions; they could consist of legal documents showing corporate responsibilities: mortgages, union contracts, production contracts, payroll lists, etc. They could also be records of policy decisions: minutes of meetings of directing boards; internal regulations, policy manuals, etc. The rationale for creating such documents is to communicate to the corporation members what the policies, practices and procedures of the corporation are, or to document agreements and obligations in the form of contracts entered into, or to register decisions, transactions, progress towards goals, or an analysis of failure.

Personal papers, on the other hand, are created for personal, individual or private reasons, and may consist of such things as household accounts, family correspondence, documents collected as a hobby (for education, curiosity, fun, or profit), diaries, letters, photographs, film, sound and video recordings, poetry, musings, professional correspondence—such as that of a scholar or a politician; the working papers of an author, or lectures, class materials, experiments, writings, and similar products, personal computer disks and literary manuscripts not submitted for publication, or the drafts and versions of literary manuscripts prior to the final version. Personal papers may also contain commercial items that have attained personalized attributes, such as books with annotations or inscriptions, newspaper clippings, journal reprints, or film, sound or video recordings in which the person appeared, as on a news program.

Corporate records are produced to document an activity of the corporation, either to explain, advertise, justify, or prove those activities. Such documents have intrinsically long-lasting value because the corporation is not confined by physical age. It must keep a record of its policies and activities in order to document economy and efficiency, avoid confusion, defend itself against legal actions, and maintain standards in its product line or even in its dogma. Therefore, large corporations of long duration produce great quantities of records. The records of the U.S. government extend back in time more than two hundred years and consume some 1.5 million cubic feet of storage space. It is from such records that one can study global trends, long-range historical changes in society in the areas of demography, health, economics, etc. Those slow, evolutionary changes over centuries can be perceived only in a broad retrospective view, or an analysis of what one author calls "latent events."[9]

Many personal papers, conversely, are produced for the moment. The family letters are written to convey precise information about ephemeral events: the rain, the car, activities of members, the wedding. Love letters tell even less, in that they convey emotions, which, by definition, are subjective and transient. Having conveyed the message, of success, despair, news, or gossip, they have no further "value," except for reminiscence or reference. Even personal diaries, which may indicate the daily pattern of life and comment on current events, do so for only one individual and for only so long as that individual is actively engaged in maintaining a diary. A person's life span may see many changes—think of someone (like comedian George Burns) born in 1896 and alive and active into the early 1990s, witnessing the first production-model automobile and the Indianapolis 500; the Wright Brothers and the Boeing 747; Roman candles on July 4 and the Apollo rocket; the manual typewriter and the personal computer. But a nonagenarian does not begin commenting on society at age one and continue until death. The more common span of documents may stretch forty-five or fifty years, which is but a blink in time—a contribution to "manifest" history, or current events.[10]

In between these two definitions lie those documents that have characteristics of both genres. The "personal papers" of an activist, a politician, a military figure, or a patron of the arts may tell us much about events in society, and illuminate the official record, as Calhoun's letter to Harriet illuminates his official remarks to Knox. A personal diary kept during significant events can expand our understanding of the formal record of those events. There also are many corporate archives that contain the personal, unofficial papers of individuals associated with the corporate body, and, conversely, many collections of personal papers include fragments of corporate records. Indeed, in American society the line between official records and personal papers is sometimes very thin, and open to interpretation. It is in these "personal papers" of former officials and staff at various government levels that one finds "official" but "nonrecord" materials, or retained carbons or photocopies of "records" created in the performance of official duties.

We see, therefore, that the two forms of noncommercial research materials differ considerably. Archives are methodical, organized and structured, stretching over many generations, and pragmatic in their subject matter and the intent of their creation. Personal papers are subjective, idiosyncratic, emotional, contemporary, and narrowly focused. As the historical microcosm, however, they provide us with a view of society from the perspective of the individual—in love, in battle, in family circumstances, on the frontier, in confrontation with the bureaucracy.

These two views of society—the archival and the personal—could be equated with two forms of history popular over the past century. One, what we might call the Carlylian, comes from Thomas Carlyle's statement that history is "at the bottom the History of Great Men."[11] It is the theory that people are the center of history, and by studying their lives we will understand what happened in the past. Carlyle, as biographer of Frederick the Great and Oliver Cromwell, felt that one could perceive life in eighteenth-century Prussia or seventeenth-century Britain through a study of the papers of the individual who ruled it at that time.[12] His materials were personal letters, diaries, accounts of court life by courtiers—in short, personal papers.

Leopold von Ranke, on the other hand, thought that most court histories that told of activities at the top in the areas of war and diplomacy were faulted by their heavy dependence on personal materials, and therefore revealed very little about the society that supported the regime. "We can accomplish something only through exact research, through step-by-step understanding, and through the study of documents."[13] "Rankean" history operates on the premise that one can understand man mainly by studying man's institutions—i.e., government, the church, and social organizations—through their records. Only by looking at these records can the historian begin to understand the politics and compromises of statesmen, pressures external to the state, the conditions of the people, traditions, and other factors relevant to the development of policy and military affairs. "The subject matter of history is living individualities, persons, institutions, cultures."[14]

It is these two traditions—the biographical and the archival—that have led to the two traditions of collecting personal papers and archives. One school of historians contends that there is no one way to study the past because each generation makes its own journey backward from the social, moral, political, religious or other positions that they occupy at the time. Thus, what is history to one is myth to another, and the concept of "mythistory" is born.[15] And there are others who consider that no history is complete without looking at the lives and the records of the inarticulate.[16] These may be found in the so-called "inarticulate" public's letters to government agencies or elected officials. Researchers who study the inarticulate depend on oral interviews and also the records kept "about" people, rather than by them. These latter materials, however, are mostly archival, where people's existence, if not lives, are documented in census, church, military, health, welfare and other records. In many cases, however, these records tell the historian "what" happened to individuals or groups, but not necessarily "why" such things happened or the consequences of their life events. A number of examples from such sources will be cited throughout this work.

In summary, we could say that commercial or mass-produced material, archives, and personal papers all may be comprised of the same media; that the important differences between them is not the form they are in, but the reason for their creation, the rationale for keeping them, the methods of handling them, the provisions for access to them, and their legal implications. Thus, although the basic physical attributes of these various materials may be the same or similar, the intellectual and legal attributes of each are different. I would like to continue the discussion of those differences in the context of most of the processes followed by manuscript curators and archivists. Perhaps the easiest way would be to describe the ways open to researchers to deal with manuscripts as well as curatorial processes that affect the availability of documentary sources. With some anecdotal assistance I hope to be able to describe the delight of dealing with these materials.

But before going on to that, let us return for a minute to the Calhoun letter to Harriet Monroe. In a passage not repeated in the letter to Knox, Calhoun writes:

> A day or two after our return, Yuan Shih-Kai arrived. His coming broke the terrible strain; everyone gave a great sigh of relief; expectancy succeeded apprehension. It is strange what influence the personality of one man—his mere presence—will have upon a great mass of people. The city not only quieted down with his coming but it has so remained ever since. Occasionally we hear rumors of an impending outbreak. Somebody is going to throw bombs or storm the palace or assassinate Yuan. But still nothing happens. The life of the city seems normal. There is no interruption to, no change in, the continuous processions of men, women and children; of carriages, carts, rickshas and wheelbarrows; of camels, horses, mules, donkeys and dogs; of funerals and weddings, which are ever winding their

way through the city streets. And we foreigners go about the streets, the shops, walls and temples as before. We go on dining, dancing, drinking and singing as though no hoary old empire was dying, as though one of history's great tragedies was not being enacted around us, as though no sound of the war and rumble of a great revolution was heard.

Who needs Pearl S. Buck when we have civil servants who can write like that?

NOTES

1. Louis Gottschalk, *Understanding History* (New York: Alfred A. Knopf, 1950), 48.
2. Personal Papers of Harriet Monroe, box I, folder 3, "Personal Correspondence—C." University of Chicago, Regenstein Library, Department of Special Collections.
3. Citation for the original letter is: U.S. National Archives [DNA], Record Group [RG]59: General Records of the Department of State; Decimal File, 1910–1929, file no. 893.00/1038.
4. Theodore R. Schellenberg, *The Management of Archives* (New York: Columbia University Press, 1965), 65–66.
5. Wilfred I. Smith, " 'Total Archives': The Canadian Experience," in Tom Nesmith, ed., *Canadian Archival Studies and the Rediscovery of Provenance* (Metuchen, N.J.: Scarecrow Press, 1993), 147.
6. Richard W. Hite and Daniel J. Linke, "A Statistical Summary of Appraisal during Processing: A Case Study with Manuscript Collections," *Archival Issues* 17, no. 1 (1992): 25.
7. U.S. Department of State, *Classification of Correspondence*, prepared by the Division of Communications and Records (Adopted August 29, 1910) (Washington: GPO, 1910).
8. Lewis J. Bellardo and Lynn Lady Bellardo, *A Glossary for Archivists, Manuscript Curators, and Records Managers*, Archival Fundamentals Series (Chicago: Society of American Archivists, 1992), 3.
9. Bernard Bailyn, "The Peopling of British North America: Thoughts on a Central Theme in Early American History—A Working Paper," in Michael Kammen, *The Past Before Us* (Ithaca: Cornell University Press, 1980), 38.
10. Ibid.
11. Thomas Carlyle, *On Heroes, Hero-Worship, and the Heroic in History* (Garden City, N.Y.: Dolphin Books, Doubleday & Company, Inc., n.d.), 9.
12. Thomas Carlyle, *History of Friedrich the Second, Called Frederick the*

Great, 8 vols. (Chicago: Belford, Clarke & Co., n.d.); *Oliver Cromwell* (Boston: Houghton, Mifflin, 1879) et al.

13. "On the Character of Historical Science," in Georg G. Iggers and Konrad von Moltke, *The Theory and Practice of History. Leopold von Ranke*, trans. Wilma A. Iggers and Konrad von Moltke (New York: The Bobbs-Merrill Company, Inc., 1973), 44.

14. Iggers and von Moltke, xli.

15. William H. McNeill, "Mythistory, or Truth, Myth, History, and Historians," *American Historical Review* 91, no. 1 (February 1986): 1–10.

16. Jesse Lemisch, "The American Revolution Bicentennial and the Papers of Great White Men," *American Historical Association Newsletter* 11 (1971): 7–21 et al.

· 2 ·

THE RECOVERY OF REALITY

> It is as original sources for the reconstruction of the past, for
> the interpretation of parallel experience, for the impeachment
> of false or mistaken or perverted testimony, for the
> clarification of blurred report, for the detection,
> identification, and dismissal of fable, and the recovery of
> reality that they [manuscripts] are sought and brought
> together.
>
> David Mearns[1]

This enumeration of the reasons for collecting manuscripts also
serves as an explanation of who uses manuscript collections. It
stems from the author's overview of the Manuscript Division at
the Library of Congress, where he was chief from 1951 to 1967,
consulting with researchers in his office, visiting them in the reading room, having lunch with those who sometimes stayed on for
months working on their book or doctoral dissertation, their nas-
cent Pulitzer prize, their definitive analysis of the poet's work, their
unraveling of the mysteries of an incident shrouded in the tightly
woven cloth of time past. In his enumeration Mearns touched on
most of the reasons why people use original sources, expanding
our horizons beyond the belief that they are the tools mostly of
historians and genealogists.

The reconstruction of the past remains the most prevalent
motive for the use of manuscripts. The contents of the documents
relate to what once happened, was thought, or was planned. But
the past is documented spasmodically, in condensed time and in
various media. The video camera, the newspaper, the diary or correspondence, the report, minutes, summary of events, chronology,
and family tree all illustrate some small portion of events, and none
will in itself provide a comprehensive view of what happened, and
often not even why it happened. Historical researchers consult as

many of these media as necessary to piece together the life or the event being studied, and ultimately turn to the primary sources held in a manuscript repository. It is doubtful, and certainly not advisable, that a researcher start with a search of manuscripts. In themselves they tell us little of the big picture of one's life or the progress of events. Vital statistics of a person's existence are better found in biographical sketches, obituaries, census, state, county, church, or military service records. Basic documentation of events is best searched for in journalistic reports, secondary histories, encyclopedias and other compilations. From all of these sources the researcher can sketch out the chronology and the highlights of *what* happened, but not often *why* it happened. For motivation, involvement of others, rationalizations of actions, and the view from the subject's perspective—that is, a reconstruction of the past—the researcher must go to autobiographies and biographies, and the personal papers and archives collections from which they are written.

The reconstructive process can be, and usually is, a great maze of interconnecting relationships and ideas. Rarely does an individual act or create alone. A study of President Kennedy's decision to launch American science on a project to go to the moon, or to invade Cuba, demands that the researcher look at the evidence created by others—advisers, detractors, political supporters, financial consultants, international sources, and even family members. On a lesser scale, the decision of a local official to oppose the policies of his or her party require similar sources. History is the compilation and interpretation of evidence in order to document events or decisions, but because of the nature of human activity, which involves interaction with others and reaction to events outside of one's self, that evidence can lead the researcher down many paths. This human linkage is what impels manuscript curators to collect the papers of people whose lives crossed or whose influence on each other was significant.

It may be true that the war looks different to each of those who observe it, because some are behind trees being attacked, some are leading cavalry charges, some are tending the wounded in hospitals, but each account is valid and it is the cumulation of accounts that makes the historical story vivid. Thucydides himself sets as his criterion for his history the assemblage of information from many sources about the same event. Perhaps the comments of one who was in the proverbial smoke-filled room will lend a perspective that is unavailable elsewhere. It is the person on the scene who provides the most credible report, even if that person could not view the event from all angles. Thucydides knew this, and when writing *The History of the Peloponnesian War* in fifth-century B.C. Greece, declared that he was interviewing a number of people who may have seen the same event from different perspectives, so that he could verify what really happened. This process marks the first historical application of the concept of "realistic analysis" in treating past events.[2]

Secondary reports make good summaries, but not necessarily good history. In the papers of Ulysses S. Grant relating to his participation in the siege of Vicksburg, there are daily muster rolls, dispatches, telegrams, orders, and action reports, each representing the limited views of the person on the scene. To read them provides dramatic evidence of the usual complications, confusion, brilliance, mistakes, valor and ignorance of the men in the field, but it also provides a vivid picture of military men in action. Grant's telegrams to generals Sherman, Herron, McPherson and others, on troop movements, the nature of the opposition, etc., cannot be construed as being written for effect. They are straightforward communications, indicating dates, time, locations, and other elements of information that specifically place the principals without beclouding the issue with historical rumination. While providing us with specific information on geography and time, the Grant telegrams and documents present us with personal experience, which may be distorted because of the perspective of the viewer.[3] Then, on a regular schedule, Grant reported to headquarters in Washington, with ten or twelve pages of text describing the activity for the period. There is little comparison between the daily documents and the summary report; at times one would not think it was the same campaign.

The Grant/Vicksburg documents further illustrate the points made in chapter 1 and the complexities researchers face when rushing to establish historical "truth." Daily communications from "near Vicksburg" begin on May 19, and there is a draft summary report of July 6, with an expanded version created over the next few weeks. The July 6 draft is in the Grant papers at the Library of Congress; the final is in the National Archives. There is thus a separation of Grant's draft, as a personal manuscript located in the Library of Congress, from his officially submitted (after extensive editing) formal report, as a *record* located in the National Archives.

History in the true sense depends on the unvarnished evidence, considering not only what happened, but why it happened, what succeeded, what went wrong. Was it incompetence, lack of military acumen, or the loss of a shoe that made the horse stumble and ultimately cause the loss of the battle? For some researchers the summary report may be sufficient evidence; for others the microhistorical documentation provides needed detail. A long summary report leaves out details but provides motivations, rationales, and explanations not found in microdata. Thus, the "reconstruction of the past" may merely imply defining what part of the past the researcher wishes to reconstruct.

Manuscript curators know that just because a definitive biography of a person has been written, the repository holding the personal papers cannot expect only incidental use of the collection. As historian John Garraty points out, it is not surprising to see different biographers use the same collections to paint different views of the subject.[4] In most large manuscript collections there is enough material to permit the biographer to select what the planned interpretation needs. Selection is done by ignoring aspects of the subject's career, or at least reducing their importance, while emphasizing other material which, of course, is also considered a "primary source." Thus, the emphasis by the biographer is what makes the biography, and a different interpretation by another biographer would provide a different view. There is also the prospect, especially when working with relatively recent subjects, that new material will become available as the papers of contemporaries are opened for research use. The long-term renewal of the sources by the revelation of new collections provides enough substance for new interpretations, and the old, well-researched collection is once again studied in the light of new evidence. Therefore, the use of a collection for a biography may well lead to increased demand for it, rather than a decline in such demand.

It is impossible, of course, for any institution to provide all of the connections between the people whose papers are collected. We all have too many tentacles going out and touching others that make up our life experience, and curators therefore concentrate to a large extent on topical collecting rather than personality assemblage. The holdings may reflect the push and pull of local politics and local issues, but not the lives of the individuals involved except as they are incidental to those politics and issues. Conversely, an institution that has built its collections around individual authors, poets, religious figures, scientists or entrepreneurs may seek out the papers of others for their communications but not the full corpus of their life's activities. The poet Wallace Stevens, for instance, earned his living as an insurance executive, and there are many other examples of such dual lives, yet a collection dedicated to Stevens and his work is essentially unconcerned about his nine-to-five weekday existence, and does not aim to collect the records of his insurance firm. In the magnificent accomplishment of Arthur Link in editing and publishing sixty-five volumes of the papers of Woodrow Wilson, he testifies at one point that it is Wilson the man that he is after, not the history of his presidency.[5] Rather than documentary histories, most such compilations should rightfully be termed documentary biographies. In a sense, then, the past is reconstructed in the form and within the boundaries determined by the historian or biographer, and the manuscript curator attempts to assemble materials that will most likely serve the purpose of the researcher.

In the reconstruction of the past each historian is his own architect. The raw materials housed in the manuscript repository can be used to construct many histories, but unlike the materials in a lumber yard, once used they are not consumed; they may be used again in different combinations to produce another history. A manuscript collection that can be used only once and for one historical purpose is probably unworthy of retention, but in the nature of historical writing it is also an anomaly. A single diary of a survivor of the *Titanic* disaster may seem to have been exhausted when published as an example of the experiences of a single human, but it may also be used by others weaving it into a narrative of general events on the eve of the calamity, the association of the subject with others who perished, commentary on the class of people who were passengers, a study of the attitudes of merchant seamen toward life-threatening situations, and details of the architectural or engineering features of the ship. Manuscript curators always consider the range of historic pasts that can be reconstructed from what appears to be material limited to a single subject.

A few years ago I was browsing in a bookstore and picked up a copy of John Flower's *Moonlight Serenade*, a biodiscography of the Glenn Miller civilian band.[6] In the volume Flower listed every appearance of the band, which, in the days of its existence (1938–1942 for the civilian band), meant multiple appearances on the same day. A typical schedule for a New York visit might involve

an appearance at a matinee at the Paramount Theater, an early
evening broadcast of "The Chesterfield Hour" for the eastern audience, a second show at the Paramount in the evening, a re-
broadcast of the earlier program sent live to the West Coast, and
then, perhaps, a late-night recording session for the Victor or Blue-
bird record labels. Because of contractual obligations, musical arrangements, and other characteristics of a performance, there were
often changes of musicians between performances—perhaps not
involving the first chairs, but certainly among the sidemen.

What struck me was Flower's precision at noting who was at
what performance. I could understand the listing of those on a
recording date, since there is often a listing of the musicians either
on the record or, if it is in an album, on the album jacket. It was
the listing of who was at the Paramount, but not on the early
broadcast, and then again on the late broadcast, that puzzled me,
so I turned to what most of us turn to at some point in a book
when seeking clarification—the Author's Preface. In the section
called "Physical Layout of the Recording Sessions" (no page numbering), Flower gave the usual credits for those who helped him
with his research, and one of the credits was to the Glenn Miller
estate, for providing access to the band's payroll records. Naturally!
If any notations about performance are going to be accurate they
would be the payroll; it was those mundane, routine listings that
most researchers except economic historians generally ignore that
provided the clues for Flower to complete his task.

This may not be the clue for general researchers into corporate
records, or the records of a university, for instance, but it makes
great sense for performing groups. Indeed, the recently organized
business records of the Duke Ellington orchestra, held by the Archives Center of the Museum of American History at the Smithsonian Institution, devote considerable descriptive space—113
manuscript boxes—to the organization's business records. One
could imagine that future researches into the appearance of Harry
Carney or Juan Tizol on a certain on-the-air performance could
follow the Flower example in researching the question. The Ellington organization's documentary record, however, is reputed
not to be of high auditable quality.[7]

The interpretation of parallel existence, cited by Mearns, can
be traced back to Plutarch, the first-century biographer who
spanned both the Greek and the Roman worlds and was the first,
and greatest, exponent of parallel existence. In his *Lives of the Noble*

Grecians and Romans he consulted hundreds of sources and wrote parallel lives of men who held parallel positions in the two civilizations: Alcibiades and Coriolanus, Demosthenes and Cicero, Lysander and Sylla, Demetrius and Anthony. While few biographers since Plutarch have adopted that pattern, many biographies have been written to illustrate the parallel existence of people separated by geography or chronology.

Examples of the little-known life experiences of the famous and infamous are legion. The love letters exchanged between Woodrow Wilson and Edith Bolling Galt while he was courting her from the White House provide the interloper (i.e., the later reader of those intimate letters) with the view from the Pennsylvania Avenue house and from her residence at Twentieth Street and New Hampshire, ten blocks away. The correspondence of John and Abigail Adams, from the Adams papers at the Massachusetts Historical Society, are not those of a courtship, but of husband and wife, separated by four hundred miles as she writes from Braintree or Boston, Massachusetts, and he from Philadelphia, York, Passy, Paris and a host of other cities.

The delay in delivery (some ten days from Philadelphia to Braintree) leaves each writing in response to ten-day old news. Thus, while he is discussing the decision on "the greatest Question" in a letter of July 3, 1776, she is writing on July 13 of local affairs and the family health, just before she receives his letter with its discussion of the Declaration of "Independency." Thus, the researcher (who knows how it all will come out) is made privy to the historical sense of time and place. Today, we are all aware immediately of what major events are occurring, and many can relate exactly where they were and what they were doing when Pearl Harbor was bombed and when President Kennedy was assassinated. Lag time between the event and the knowledge of it has been reduced to a matter of minutes, and thus history has speeded up for most of us. It is difficult to appreciate the lapse of time in the past, and its impact on people's actions, unless one reads of these parallel experiences. We are but an audience that knows what is happening to characters in a performance, while in their roles they are oblivious to the events affecting the other, sometimes leading to tragical results stemming from ignorance. Such is the foundation for high drama.

The Cormany diaries of a husband and wife keeping parallel accounts during the Civil War present a similar circumstance, but in the form of diaries rather than correspondence. Rachel Bowman Cormany and Samuel Cormany began their diaries before they met, she beginning hers in 1858, he in 1859, and both extending through the summer of 1865. As the diaries progress they meet, marry, move to Canada and back, have a child, and settle in the Cumberland Valley of Pennsylvania, Samuel's home. Samuel enlists as a volunteer in the Sixteenth Pennsylvania Volunteer Cavalry, which ultimately sees action at Gettysburg, and Rachel settles in a rented room in Chambersburg, which is twice occupied by the Confederate army and burned by the Southern troops.

On July 2, 1863, on the eve of the Battle of Gettysburg, Rachel writes:

> At 3 A.M. I was wakened by the yells & howls of this dirty ragged lousy trash—they made as ugly as they could—all day they have been passing—part of the time on the double quick. At one time the report came that our men had come on them & that they were fighting—the excitement was high in town— but it was soon found out to be untrue—but the shock was so great that I got quite weak & imagined that I could already see My Samuel falling—I feel very uneasy about him—I cannot hear at all—They had quite a battle with Stuart—I almost fear to hear the result in who was killed & who wounded—still I want to know.[8]

On the same day, twenty-five miles east, Samuel was describing the battle already in progress:

> We were aroused early, and inspection showed a lot of our horses too lame and use up for good action—So first, our good mounts were formed for moving out, and were soon off—with the Brigade and took Reb. Genl. Steward by surprise on the Deardorf Farm. . . .[9]

And so the researcher receives a "stereoscopic" vision of events, and the drama of history is played out.

The report of a civilian watching troops march down the main street may be biased depending on whether they are friendly or enemy troops, with the general description colored by adjectives. Were the troops "dirty ragged lousy trash" or "our glorious men"? Did they march "brave and determined, but tiredly" or did they "shuffle dejectedly and obviously beaten"? Were they "confused and bewildered in their heroic retreat" or did they "slink away from the overwhelming forces facing them"? The best that a manuscript institution could do to offer balance to researchers would be to collect and provide to the researcher these contrasts in all cases, but the plethora of sources denies such luxury.

These are a form of interpretations of parallel existence, which need not be exclusively the writing of parallel lives, à la Plutarch.

The Cormany diaries may be exemplary in their genre, but in other instances it is easy to be fooled by diaries. *The Diaries of George Washington*, now published in six volumes, generally tell us very little about national or world affairs. Washington was a farmer, and his diary entries concentrate on those things in which farmers are interested: weather, crops, prices, agricultural experiments. At one point he indicates that friends suggested that if he is to keep a diary, it should contain political, military, social and worldly entries, not just meteorologic notations. Researchers must go as far as the end of volume three before reading the following entry:

> May 1781. I begin, at this Epoch, a concise journal of Military transactions &ca. I lament not having attempted it from the commencement of the War, in aid of my memory and wish the multiplicity of matter which continually surround me and the embarrassed State of our affairs which is momentarily calling the attention to perplexities of one kind or another, may not defeat altogether or so interrupt my present intention, & plan, as to render it of little avail.

He then shifts to such entries, but the effort pales, and at the end of the period he is back to weather and crop conditions.[10]

Archival records provide the greatest amount of evidence. Records of births, marriages, divorces, military service, prison terms, contracts, financial transactions, and deaths are high forms of legal documentation, sought after by journalists and lawyers as evidence, proof, or suspected implication. So, too, however, are letters, diaries, notebooks, records of telephone conversations, appointment calendars, and personal financial records which help to establish facts.

If the documents do not carry national security or other classifications, these "personal papers" often contain the types of evidence useful for the impeachment of false or mistaken or perverted testimony, and are sought by prosecutors. A prominent U.S. senator contests court actions that would provide access to his "personal" diary that is sought in connection with charges of unethical and perhaps illegal actions while in office. White House officials argue for destruction of their electronic mail, which they proclaim is "unofficial." On the other hand, people defending their views and actions do so in memoirs, where the abused take pen in hand and provide their version of the "truth" in rebuttal. For the most part, these counterclaims are published and there for all to read, but they are sometimes to be found among the personal papers of the great and near great, and reach published form only through the efforts of later researchers. In other instances they are still in the form of diaries or journals, from which a future memoir was to have been written but never came to fruition.

The value of these recountings of events to revise the reader's prior opinion comes generally from those who were on the losing side—of a court case, a scandal, a political campaign, or a war. Sometimes they stem from one of the victors who has been cast as a villain. The series of translations of diaries of Hessian soldiers during the American Revolution by Bruce E. Burgoyne are attempts to replace the "mistaken testimony" of these mercenaries in a more human light.[11] A similar effect is sought by Richard Harwell and Philip N. Racine in their publication of a Union officer's account of Sherman's last campaigns. The summation of the volume is that "He was continually fascinated by the destruction—the actions of the 'bummers,' for example, and the recurring fires—yet his description remains objective, almost impersonal."[12]

Another illustration of impeachment of perverted testimony comes to us from a Confederate general, Edward Porter Alexander, whose personal memoir might not be so special in light of the many other Confederate officers who attempt to "put the record straight." But Gary W. Gallagher, the editor, saw it differently:

> Remarkable as it may seem in a field that has been studied so exhaustively, the 1,200-page manuscript lay virtually unknown for more than eight decades—a good part of that time at the most famous of all repositories of southern primary materials [the Southern Historical Collection, Wilson Library, University of North Carolina-Chapel Hill].[13]

That statement alone should give counsel to the historian in search of a subject, but very few of these "undiscovered" documents are really "unknown." One can expect that the University of North Carolina manuscript curators at the Southern Historical Collection know what they have in their stacks, and the existence of the 1,200-page manuscript was more than likely noted in various reports of holdings issued by the collection over the years, in an attempt to bring it to the attention of researchers.

The consideration of manuscripts as "testimony," when looked at closely, calls for the *correction* of the historical record through discovery, and thus emphasizes that earlier testimony must have been false, or mistaken, or perverted if it is to be impeached. Such actions lend nobility to the role of the keepers of the "truth," whatever that may be.

The papers of state and local officials make up the bulk of the thousands of historical societies dedicated to the preservation of the history of communities throughout the country, and it is through these papers of public figures that researchers seek clarification of blurred reports from newspaper accounts, official documents, and even rumor.

A striking case of an individual who attempted to clarify blurred reports and correct false testimony is that of Leland Stowe. When he was a journalist during World War II, Stowe made some complimentary remarks about the courage and character of Russian soldiers. That stance seemed to be enough to have the FBI create a file on him, and the file grew as Stowe's later career appeared to the FBI as grounds for continuing its coverage of his activities. As a result of the agency's suspicions, Stowe found himself unable to interview any FBI staff for journalistic purposes on any subject. When he retired, and when he became aware of the federal Privacy Act, Stowe asked to see his file, which was provided to him. In it he discovered many factual errors and petitioned, under the act, to expunge them, but he learned that his file had been declared by the National Archives to be "archival," that is, of enduring value, and could not be changed. Stowe then attempted to add to the file a 400-page explanation and elaboration of the information in the file, which the FBI was willing to accept, but the National Archives was not; he was, however, given the option of having the file destroyed. Stowe agreed and the file was destroyed. Stowe then decided to place his 400-page defense in a research library, and it was accessioned into the collections at the Bentley Library at the University of Michigan, Ann Arbor.[14]

The Stowe case is rather interesting for a few reasons. First, it illustrates the fact that once an agency record is declared to be "permanent" by the National Archives, it can neither be added to nor have material removed from it. The archival argument is that any changes after it leaves an agency would no longer qualify the document as a "record" of agency activities. Admission of ex-post facto evidence into archived records would open the doors for innumerable "corrections" to information, and there is no guarantee that the correction is any more sound than the original information. Researchers are very quick to point out to archivists that names are spelled wrong, dates are inaccurate, and facts are skewed in the documents that they examine, but to permit emendations would, in effect, destroy the document as a "record" kept by the government. Had Leland Stowe agreed to leave the original FBI file intact at the National Archives, and then deposit his corrections elsewhere, future researchers would have the "complete" story, according to the principals. As it now stands, researchers can only read the clarification of a record that no longer exists, thus perhaps perpetuating questions about the FBI's case, rather than burying the whole affair. The "impeachment of false or mistaken or perverted testimony" stands, but the testimony itself is now mute.

The feminist movement, spawned in Seneca Falls, New York, in 1848 in the Victorian era, but hatched in the Friedanian, has attempted to clarify the blurred if not invisible reports of the role of women in the progress of history. Starting out as a few courses in the history departments of a few liberal universities, the academic manifestation of the feminist movement has developed full departments and degrees in institutions of (almost) every philosophical persuasion. With the discussion of feminism stepping down from the soapboxes and taking its place behind the lectern, the search for sources to legitimize scholarship has moved forward.

Jesse Lemisch, Peter Stearns,[15] and the other "New Social History" proponents fired their intellectual Very pistols in the 1960s to create some cultural pyrotechnics and light up what they saw as a barren landscape of sources for the study of the ignored, oppressed and inarticulate, and they challenged archivists and historians to leave the lush fields of "great white men's" history and plod out into the desert to discover and mine gems of minority and women's history. In many ways the "new" historians were right—the "old" historians had neglected those elements of society too long. In other ways they were wrong, in thinking that the sources had not been discovered, and were not waiting to be mined. Archivists and manuscript curators had for years been gathering the documentation from which the new history could be written. This should not be surprising, because if they had not—if they had blindly ignored the world of their day as sources for the history of tomorrow—there could be no "new" history, or as the French historian Fustel de Coulanges noted: "Pas de documents, pas d'histoire."[16] In most cases the sources were there, but the historians themselves had passed them by in pursuit of topics in the mainstream of their contemporaries and of the elusive publishing contract, the "acceptable" doctoral dissertation, the peer recognition necessary to climb the professional historical ladder to tenure or the Bancroft or other national prize.

These so-called blurred reports sometimes were quite clearly marked, but sometimes innocently buried amid the papers of the "great white men." In the former case one can cite the acquisition by the Library of Congress of dozens of "women's" collections before World War II, including the not very obscure Jane Addams, Clara Barton and Susan B. Anthony, all accessioned in 1940. Julia Lathrop, Sophinisba Breckinridge and other women of the Social Service Movement of the 1920s were also at the library, and were complemented by the collections of Grace and Edith Abbott, their professional colleagues, at Chicago's Harper Library. The Schlesinger Library at Radcliffe College noted the need for such materials and began to assemble its magnificent collection of women's papers in 1944. The National Society of Daughters of the American Revolution holdings in its Washington headquarters spread beyond the purely genealogical materials necessary to prove membership eligibility, and collected the papers of women whom they felt were of historical importance to add to their holdings. Even such lesser-known organizations as the Society of Women Geographers, founded in 1925, which felt isolated from the male-dominated National Geographic Society, began assembling materials related to members who were geographers (Annie Smith Peck), explorers (Elizabeth Knowlton), aviators (Amelia Earhart) and activists in other manly pursuits.

In other collections there was also the possibility of mining material collateral to the major collections. The Julius Rosenwald Papers at Chicago, dedicated mainly to the philanthropies of the director of Sears, Roebuck Company, includes documentation of support for Hull House and the women of the Social Service Movement, and the correspondence of Felix Frankfurter touches on the same organizations. The papers of Booker T. Washington contain considerable material on women philanthropists, the faculty of Tuskegee Institute, and female educators such as Mary McCloud Bethune and Ida B. Wells Barnett. A study of women's diaries embedded in the collections, mostly of men, in the Library of Congress has revealed hundreds that apparently have gone unused or greatly underused in historical and biographical research.[17]

But, Lemisch might argue, many of these are but the papers of Great White Wives of the Great White Men, and justifiably so—their papers were kept because their husband's or family's papers were kept, and they happened, incidentally, to be included. But that does not explain away the propensity of manuscript curators and archivists for gathering the curious, the atypical, the interesting, the poignant, the revealing, the incisive, and the homologous along with the traditional documentary research source. How, otherwise, to explain the sudden "discovery" by recent writers, of the papers, diaries and records needed to document the new history? These documents, like this continent, have been here all the time, and their "discovery" merely attests to the lassitude of earlier researchers to consider them worthy of discovery, or to chart the proper course to them.

Once the quest goes beyond personal papers, or manuscript collections, the Lemisch charge loses even more validity, because it is in the official records of governments, organizations, labor unions, churches, and estates that one finds literally tons of unmined historical ore for the new social historians. Over the past two decades the National Archives and the Library of Congress have been attempting to assemble in the two institutions descriptive lists of records of the federal government relating to African Americans and women. The National Archives has been quite successful, because of the relatively easy identification of federal agencies or the military services that dealt with the "colored," "negroes," "blacks," "Afro-Americans," or "African-Americans."[18] The records of the "Colored Troops" are prominent in the military records, and for the immediate post–Civil War era there is the million-document collection of the Bureau of Refugees, Freedmen, and Abandoned Lands at the National Archives (RG 105). These records, shunned by researchers for a century, were finally pried open and held up to them by one long-tenured and dogged staff member who convinced society that it needed to know the thousands of life stories revealed in the letters, petitions, depositions, and claims of former slaves in the Reconstruction era.[19] One of the results has been the launching of the landmark publication of the documentary series, *Freedom: A Documentary History of Emancipation, 1861–1867*.[20] The Records of the American Colonization Society, not a government agency but a private organization, are in the Library of Congress, documenting the establishment of Liberia and the movement to return former slaves to their native continent. This collection, dating back to 1816, has been described in Register 53: *The American Colonization Society* (1979).[21] Hundreds of other collections have existed in archives and manuscript collections and, like the women's papers, are suddenly being "discovered" by researchers. African-American records have ironically been fairly easy to find *because* the race was segregated!

One must, however, consider that while much of this material of interest to historians of the mid–twentieth century has been in the manuscript and archival stacks for a century or more, the archivists and curators themselves did not always consider it of significant value for research, and quite frequently underreported it. Finding guides stressed the main features of the collections, from the curators' point of view, and it often was only after a realization that researchers thought something was important that the curators went back and described their collection in terms of that new importance.

The attempt of the National Archives to prepare an analysis of holdings relating to women is proving to be more difficult than analyzing some other groups, not because of a paucity, but rather an abundance of such materials, often difficult to define or to discriminate out of the masses of material relating to activities and occupations in which women *may* have been engaged, without having them specifically identified. Thus, one could root about for them in the records of the Labor Department, or the Department of Agriculture, or the various agencies, bureaus and departments in which the health, welfare and education functions have been placed. There is also the military, where the women's service units (WACS, WAVES, WAFS, etc.) are easily isolated, and, indeed, a guide to those records has been published,[22] but the role of women in the civilian workforce during war is not so easily assembled. Nor is it easy to segregate materials relating to women in the old-line agencies, such as the Treasury, State, War and Navy Departments, and even the Bureau of Indian Affairs or, more recently, the Department of Transportation, Housing and Urban Development, or the intelligence agencies. If women did not hold key positions in many of these agencies prior to 1945 (women like Frances Perkins being but one of the exceptions), many were employed by them, communicated with them, were provided services by them, or were dealt with in legal matters by them. Women paid taxes, collected Social Security, served in the military or related service such as the nurse corps, rendered public health services, taught in Indian and other federally sponsored schools, administered post offices, tended lighthouses and operated as air traffic controllers. They wrote letters requesting services, sat on committees, served in Congress (easy to identify!), sat in judgment of their male peers as jurists, gathered and processed the census, and served as librarians and archivists in the federal service. Where does one begin, and where does it all end?

In the next chapter we will explore some of the guides and catalogues that attest to the avidity with which research materials nationally have been collected and preserved at the personal, the federal and even international level. Should there ever be a cry that we, as a nation, have ignored the history of our household pets, researchers will probably find the sources waiting for them in collections husbanded by archivists and manuscript curators.[23]

A recent, unpublished study of sources for the writing of the new social history reveals that if one uses the criteria for sources that such historians say they require to do their work, and applies those criteria to the holdings reported by the *National Union Catalog of Manuscript Collections* (*NUCMC*)[24] since 1959 when it began gathering information, and by other aids, there is little doubt that the materials are already in the manuscript repositories, and have been there for many years, awaiting "discovery." [25] The records of the labor unions and the papers of national and local officers are in the many labor archives of the country, from the George Meany Center in Silver Spring, Maryland, to the Labor History Center at Wayne State University;[26] the immigrant American is represented in collections such as those at the Balch Institute in Philadelphia and the Center for Immigration History in Minnesota, with specific reference to Jewish immigrants from Eastern Europe in such institutions as the YIVO Institute for Jewish Research in New York and others.

If historians, biographers and other researchers feel that history of their subject has been distorted by blurred reports, or even by the existence of fable, they will find focus and reality mostly attainable in the underused collections in thousands of existing repositories throughout the country.

David Mearns himself spoke from experience when he referred to researchers' use of manuscripts for the detection, identification and dismissal of fable, since he had been involved in such dismissal himself. The papers of Abraham Lincoln were secretly deeded to the Library of Congress by son Robert Todd Lincoln in 1919. A 1923 deed of gift stipulated that they not be opened until 21 years after his (Robert Todd's) death. He died in 1926 and the papers were therefore sealed until 1947. The closure itself spawned many rumors about their content, and, as with the undisclosed papers and records of another assassinated president a century later, volumes were written based on various surmised plots, and the adherents to the conspiracy theory were confident that the opening of the Lincoln papers would reveal all, and history would have to be rewritten in consequence of the revelations.

When the day of revelation came Mearns himself presided at the removal of the veil of secrecy in which the plots and political machinations were most certainly shrouded. But the day was anticlimactic. There was no plot, no seditious conspiracy, and no history-revising events were revealed. The broken seal on the manuscript containers did not loose the ghosts of past schemes.[27]

Fables, of course, have a life of their own, and, as a century later, those who believed the conspiracy theory were not put off by "no evidence." After all, they rationalized: No evidence is NO evidence;[28] it is neither negative nor positive, and they turned their sights on other sources for the elusive "truth." Every researcher should know that fable is, to paraphrase Henry James, fueled by the absence of biography, that if we know more we suspect less.[29]

Many collections do not relate to external events but provide inner reflections of a person through a diary such as those of the Cormanys, or confiding letters. The importance of such inner reflections may not be a consideration in the case of a textbook author, but if the writings of a literary or political figure stem from these inner musings they are of value to future researchers. Similarly, the writings of an individual, collected over many years, can indicate intellectual development. The letters of the Marquis de Lafayette that were written soon after his arrival in America reveal an uncertain young Frenchman, struggling with the English language. In a letter to George Washington from Lafayette's camp near Albany, New York, the syntax, grammar and spelling are so distorted that it may well have caused the commander in chief to wonder what was happening there.[30]

As time goes on, however, Lafayette's letters display a mastery of the language and apparently of himself, as his confidence grows.[31] The man and his character are better understood by looking at his writing style, his vocabulary, and the obvious intelligence that enabled him to grasp the essence of this foreign language in such a brief span of time.

There is, however, also a long tradition of the uses of historical facts for the *creation* of fables. Poets, playwrights, and writers of fiction have for centuries used the documented human condition as a basis for their artistic elaborations on life and the mores of humankind. Shakespeare had obviously read Plutarch when composing his *Antony and Cleopatra*; Pierre and Natasha were woven by Tolstoy into the historic actions of the French and Russian armies; Stephen Vincent Benet had at least read and absorbed the information from Civil War newspapers when creating his epic *John Brown's Body* in order to place Clay Wingate and Sally DuPre from Appleton in the appropriate dramatic setting. In recent years Herman Wouk employed an assistant working full-time as a records researcher in the National Archives documenting the background into which Captain Victor "Pug" Henry would most appropriately fit, and Alex Haley devoted years of his own time at the National Archives, the Maryland Hall of Records, and other sources in order to dig up material for his largely fictionalized *Roots*. The Colonial Records of Maryland in the Maryland Hall of Records also provided the basis for much of John Barth's *The Sot-Weed Factor.*[32]

The genre here is the recognized historical novel (or play, in the case of *Antony and Cleopatra* or *Amadeus*). Other authors depend not so much on placing their fictional charges in real-life historical events, as on weaving truth and fable to create a "realistic" dramatic effect, and perhaps even to promote a cause.

In the Federal Records of the Farm Security Administration (FSA) (RG 96), located in the National Archives branch facility in San Bruno, California, there are a series of reports from Thomas Collins, an FSA employee who was director of some of the FSA migratory camps. In an eight-page report from the Kern Migratory Camp, and a fifteen-page report from the Arvin Migratory Camp, Collins reports on conditions during 1936, when the great dust bowl migrations were delivering poor farmers to the waiting prosperity of California.

Kern Migratory Camp

Report for week ending February 22, 1936
Labor Situation:

> This week there was no demand for labor. The heavy rains throw more heads of families out of employment. Those employed were engaged in the following classifications of labor:

(a) Pruning, irrigating, ditch cleaning, tree spraying, burning brush. Rates of wages 25c an hour. Average weekly earnings of campers for this work $10.00. Outlook for work of this kind is nil. All operations have closed down until early in May.

(b) Wood cutting. Average earnings for the week, $10.00. Prospects for next week are very poor.

(c) Olive picking. Average weekly earnings $3.00 for six days. Another week of this work is available.

> In all it has been a very discouraging week for the campers. Men, accustomed to hard work, willing to work, have been thrown out of employment. They all agree that work will not be available until the latter part of April or the first week of May. Those eligible for relief have refused to make application so long as there are beans and sow belly in the family larder. The very thought of relief bows down the head of the biggest and the strongest. Evenings, as they gather around for counsel with the camp management they discuss this problem. On their way to bed they are determined to go to town and make relief application. The morning finds them again undecided and they burn the now precious gasoline supply and roam the country in search of work at any price. In the evening they again go through the same ordeal only to start out again in search of work the following morning.
>
> Today, February 22, 1936, they have agreed to go to town. Said a group last night "jest as well haf all our teeth yanked out as ter go sit down, tell our life's histry and ask for relief. Culd we only git a job for thats all we wants. We's able ter wuk and wants to wuk."

Thomas Collins[33]

The records were researched by John Steinbeck when writing *The Grapes of Wrath*, and the story of the camp encompasses all of chapter 22.[34] Not only did art imitate life, but life can be used to substantiate art. The camp director, Thomas Collins, shows up as Jim Rawley in the book, in Steinbeck's frontispiece dedication:

"To Tom, who lived it," and again in the credits for the 1940 Twentieth Century-Fox film production as "Technical Director."

Thus, the records substantiate Mearns' "identification of fable," in sort of reverse order, since it does not turn out that the truth is fable, but that fable is the truth.

In a sense, all of the examples used so far in this chapter have been devoted to one aspect or another of recovering reality, but not all manuscripts deal with reality in the sense of "true facts." We have seen how Steinbeck used reality to create fiction, but many collections contain fiction without reference to reality. Poetry has meaning, but may be abstract or impressionistic, and not "real." Illinois journalist Hi Simons probed for the reality behind the abstractions of Wallace Stevens's poetry by asking the poet what he meant by certain lines, phrases or illusions. Stevens was kind enough to reply, and so the reality behind his abstractions has been recovered for the journalist and for those who study the rather amazing exchange of correspondence between the two, beginning in February 1937 and continuing spasmodically until just before Simons's death in April 1945.[35]

For some researchers reality consists of a record of their own existence, often blurred by the inefficient oral tradition among families, the lassitude of many family members in compiling appropriate records of their generation, or the loss of such data through natural disasters, fire, and family mobility. I say *compiling* such data because their initial retention is, in fact, the obligation of others—in records kept by the community, religious organizations, the state, the federal government, and many other public agencies. This information is naturally scattered in a wide variety of geographical and archival locations, so some individuals have taken it upon themselves to assemble this mass into some rational order that will satisfy *their* needs, and pass it on to the next generation—which may elect to ignore it and let three or four more generations pass before an individual in the line of descent picks up the trail and continues the compilation.

Genealogy is a major activity of the American population, and one may sometimes wonder why. It is understandable why people who live in a society that rewards descent from royal, noble or otherwise important ancestors would be interested in associating themselves with the lineage of those ancestors. Titles, land, income or prestige may be the prize, and therefore worth the time and effort to establish the links.

It is understandable why people whose religion provides an opportunity for them to welcome their ancestors into an after-life Elysium, as does Mormonism, to devote considerable effort to identifying those ancestors in order to reassemble those souls in the ever-after.

It is understandable why Americans search their own ancestry in order to prove that they are descended from some family member who participated in a major historical event, such as being transported to these shores on the Mayflower, or participating (perhaps only neutrally) in life in the Colonial period or the American Revolution or the short-lived glories of the Confederacy.

But these three categories of interest in genealogy—financial or social reward, religious reward, or a reward in prestige—are not the backbone of Americans' search for the reality of their own lives through genealogy. Yet the "pastime" has infected every level of American society, especially with the appearance of *Roots*, which began a boom in African-American genealogical research. One could well ask "why?" Is there something in the human psyche that makes us all historians, looking at the past in order to better understand the present, and perhaps the future? Is this inclination universal, shared with the Kurds, the Tlingits and other branches of the human race? Is it our tradition inherited from our forebears, who often *did* have good grounds for establishing kinship for the reasons cited above? Ancestor worship may be a human trait common in many primitive as well as modern societies, but tracing the progeny of the generations back into primordial time is not so much veneration, but rather construction of a familial jigsaw puzzle. Perhaps we were all imbued with the "Genesis syndrome" from our youthful Bible studies.

Whatever the reason or the rationale, genealogy in the United States consumes a considerable amount of the leisure time of the American population, especially the senior population. The Library of Congress has a large and active genealogy section. At the National Archives in Washington there is a genealogy search room (formally designated the Microfilm Research Room) with over one hundred microfilm and other photocopy readers and printers, a full staff, and a supporting reference library, that accounts for well over 50 percent of the researchers using the institution's facilities at any one time. These facilities and staffs are emulated on a smaller scale in the National Archives' eleven branches throughout the country and in every state archives and most state libraries. County and municipal libraries would be greatly under-attended if they did not provide genealogical services. With the shift in American age-group populations upward toward the older citizen—a general aging of the country—one can anticipate more retirees, more leisure time, and more genealogical activity in the libraries, archives and historical societies.

Genealogy is pursued most frequently in archival records, with records of birth, death, marriage, and divorce as the four primary documents needed to ascend the hierarchical progression. Since many of the original documents on these four phases of life have been lost to natural and man-made disasters, genealogists have turned to other records that are perhaps not as reliable, but at least provide solid leads to the truth. These supplemental vital records are censuses, migration, military, and other service records from schools, penal institutions, hospitals, the courts and the whole legal and public service community. Documentation of ownership and occupation of land and structures, and therefore proof of locus, comes from city directories and plats, land grant documents, tax lists, and similar rural and municipal rolls. In searching out the person, the genealogist most often stumbles upon the community, and genealogy branches out into family history as well as community or local history. It is in these two subfields that the manuscript collection comes into play.

There are certain circumstances in which a collection of family papers will provide the basic data sought by genealogists. The validity of the information depends to a large extent on its closeness in time to the action and the actors. A family Bible in which entries are made on the day of happening—a birth, a death, a wedding—is probably the most trustworthy record in family papers. Such facts may be suspect if a series of chronologically separated actions appear in a single hand with the same ink, indicating, perhaps, a later "catching up" by a family chronicler. A notation of a marriage by one of the partners is probably more accurate than from a third party, ex post facto. The social status and literacy level of a family may make a difference in the validity of a notation. Louis Armstrong, the Louisiana-born jazz musician, always claimed that his birthdate was July 4, 1900. He told people that information came from his mother. The church records from the parish in which he was born indicate, however, that a Louis Armstrong was baptized in August 1901, probably indicating birth a week or two earlier. When the local church official admitted that the notation was well known but never made public, he reasoned that it must be another Louis Armstrong, because someone so famous as the musician would certainly have known his own family vital statistics![36] It has been said that among Armstrong's kin it was not uncommon to provide a holiday or notable historical date as the celebrated birthday for easy later remembrance. If the Queen of England can have an "official" and an "actual" birthday, egalitarianism decrees that the same should apply to an African-American descendant of southern slaves!

For the most part, family papers are not the primary source for genealogical statistics, but they are the source for fleshing out relationships, for discovering motivations for formal liaisons, causes of death, property transfers, geographic migrations, feuds, community involvement, aspirations, education, political preferences, military service, and all of the other life experiences that extend our horizons far beyond the entries in a church register or an obituary notice. Thus, family papers complement not only the official record, but the "other" lives of the principals. The unexpected decision of a politician not to run again, of a corporate magnate to throw it all over and go live in a shack on the Outer Banks, of a government lawyer to retire early and enter private practice in his or her home town may have nothing to do with their careers and may therefore leave no clues in their official records or correspondence, but the family papers may make everything perfectly clear to the eye of the perceptive biographer or historian.

To attain this clarity, the biographer is not just looking at events, but is searching out materials that provide insight to the individual's psychological make-up, motivation, inner strengths, compelling forces, external influences, and the ever-present impact of chance. Whereas the historian studying the Bay of Pigs may take interest in a Kennedy appointment calendar, noting discussions with military and political leaders, a biographer of the president may be just as interested in a personal diary documenting the president's *angst* about the weight of such decisions on the lives or fortunes of others.

There are few major collections of personal papers that do not in some way or another reveal the inner person, or perhaps more than one level of inner person—that which is merely unknown and that which may be completely unsuspected both attest to the power of the personal document to provide insights to a life previously unsuspected. For recovering the reality of controversial figures such as General George Patton it is often necessary to go beyond the myth, the movie or the official reports.

The papers of George S. Patton at the Library of Congress are replete with the military and biographical details relating to his education, career, and brilliant military professionalism. Correspondence with peers and superiors reveals what one would expect in the way of details about Patton the military officer. Two parts of the collection, however, take the biographer deeper into the Patton psyche. His letters to his wife Bea reveal his cynicism about and mistrust of many of his superiors and major political leaders of the time. One of the devices used by Patton to expose this attitude is his use of nicknames that he applies to others, and by which they are almost invariably identified. It took a Manuscript Division staff member knowledgeable about World War II military history to decode the sobriquets and provide a key to their identities, which ranged from "Destiny" (Eisenhower) and "toddy" (General Charles P. George) to "the tent maker" (General Omar Bradley).[37]

At a deeper level are Patton's poetry and his comments on his photography. His poems indicate an almost Wagnerian preoccupation with the heroic—with Duty, Honor, and Pride, with an occasional barracks coarseness.[38]

His comments about photographing such things as enemy dead reveal another trait—sanguinity, in the full dictionary sense of the word. On January 24, 1945, just after the defeat of the Germans in the Ardennes Battle of the Bulge, and the Allied thrust towards Germany with Patton leading the charge, he wrote to his wife:

> I think I wrote that the other day I found a lot of frozen corpses in queer positions all a weak claret color. I wish I had my color camera. That is going to be a hell of a stink come warm weather now we can't find the bodies due to the snow unless a foot or hand happens to stick out.[39]

Who needs Norman Mailer when we have military officers who can write like that?

To the biographer looking for the motivations and attitudes of the inner man, these are the important parts of the Patton collection, whereas the military historian concerned about strategy, tactics, tank warfare and the drive from the beaches of Normandy to the bridge at Remagen might possibly mention these aberrations in a footnote.

The Greek *thymos*, expounded upon as a basis for man's actions beyond nature and economics by Francis Fukuyama in his *The End of History and the Last Man*, [40] may best be sought in the collections of personal papers in the nation's manuscript repositories. Thus "reality," as far as one can discover it at all, rather than "statistics" is probably more recoverable from personal papers than from archival records.

NOTES

1. David C. Mearns, "Historical Manuscripts, Including Personal Papers," *Library Trends* 5, no. 3 (January 1957): 316.

2. Thucydides, *History of the Peloponnesian War*, trans. Richard Crawley (London & Toronto: J.M. Dent & Sons, Ltd., 1914). Everyman's Library ed., chap. 1, bk. 21.

3. For the Vicksburg campaign daily communications and the summary report, see John Y. Simon, ed., *The Papers of Ulysses S. Grant* (Carbondale: Southern Illinois University Press, vol. 8, April 1–July 6, 1863). Daily communications from "near Vicksburg" begin on May 19 (p. 237), and the draft summary report of July 6 is on pp. 485–508, with an expanded version on pp. 509–519.

4. John A. Garraty, *The Nature of Biography* (New York: Vintage Books, 1957), chap. 1; also Ian Hamilton, *Keepers of the Flame: Literary Estates and the Rise of Biography from Shakespeare to Plath* (New York: Faber & Faber, 1994), especially the chapter "Froude's Carlyle, Carlyle's Froude," 158–176.

5. *The Papers of Woodrow Wilson*, ed. Arthur Link, vol. 27, *1918* (Princeton: Princeton University Press, 1978), xvii.

6. John Flower, *Moonlight Serenade; a Biodiscography of the Glenn Miller Civilian Band* (New Rochelle, N.Y.: Arlington House, 1972).

7. My source is the typescript of the business records portion of the finding aid to the Duke Ellington Collection housed at the Archives Center, Museum of American History, Smithsonian Institution, and produced by David Jellema in May 1994, 66 pp.

8. James C. Mohr and Richard E. Winslow III, eds., *The Cormany Diaries. A Northern Family in the Civil War* (University of Pittsburgh Press, 1982), 339.

9. Ibid., 324.

10. *The Diaries of George Washington*, ed. Donald Jackson (Charlottesville: University of Virginia Press, vol. 3, 1771–75, 1780–81, 1978), 356.

11. Among the soldiers whose diaries have been translated by Burgoyne are Carl Philipp Steuernagel, Philipp Waldeck, Jacob Piel (or Biel), Karl Friedrich Rueffer, Johann Ernst Prechtel, Georg Adam Stang, Johann

Conrad Doehla, and two whose diaries are anonymous. Johann Conrad Doehla, *A Hessian Diary of the American Revolution*, trans. and ed. Bruce E. Burgoyne (Norman: University of Oklahoma Press, 1990), ix.

12. Richard Harwell and Philip N. Racine, eds., *The Fiery Trail. A Union Officer's Account of Sherman's Last Campaigns* (Knoxville: The University of Tennessee Press, 1986), dust jacket notes.

13. Gary W. Gallagher, ed., *Fighting for the Confederacy. The Personal Recollections of General Edward Porter Alexander* (Chapel Hill: The University of North Carolina Press, 1989), xiv–xv.

14. James Gregory Bradsher, "We Have a Right to Privacy," in Mary Boccacio, ed., *Constitutional Issues and Archives* (n.p., Mid-Atlantic Regional Archives Conference, 1988), 11–20.

15. Jesse Lemisch, "The American Revolution Bicentennial and the Papers of Great White Men," *AHA Newsletter* 9 (November 1971): 7–21; Peter N. Stearns, "Toward a Wider Vision: Trends in Social History," in Kammen, *The Past Before Us*, 205–230.

16. "No sources—no history," attributed to Fustel de Coulanges and quoted in Ernst Posner, *Archives of the Ancient World* (Cambridge: Harvard University Press, 1972), 12.

17. Janice Ruth, "Women's Diaries: a Draft Guide to the Holdings of the Library of Congress Manuscript Division" (unpublished typescript, 1988, in the Manuscript Division).

18. Debra Newman (Ham), comp., *Black History: A Guide to Civilian Records in the National Archives* (Washington, D.C.: National Archives Trust Fund Board, 1984); Newman, comp., *List of Black Servicemen Compiled from the War Department Collection of Revolutionary War Records* (Washington, D.C.: National Archives and Records Service, 1974); Newman, comp., *List of Free Black Heads of Families in the First Census of the United States, 1790* (Washington, D.C.: National Archives and Records Service, 1973); Newman, comp., *Selected Documents Pertaining to Black Workers Among the Records of the Department of Labor and Its Component Bureaus, 1902–1969* (National Archives and Records Service, 1977); Debra (Newman) Ham, comp., *The African-American Mosaic: A Library of Congress Resource Guide for the Study of Black History and Culture* (Washington, D.C.: Library of Congress, 1994).

19. The staff member was Sarah Dunlap Jackson (1919–1991). She has had more books dedicated to her by thankful historians than the proverbial "long-suffering wife."

20. *Freedom: A Documentary History of Emancipation, 1861–1867*, ed. Ira Berlin, Series I, 3 vols.; Series II, 1 vol. (Cambridge: Cambridge University Press, 1982–1993). To be completed in eleven volumes in five series. Current editor, Leslie Rowland.

21. Library of Congress, Manuscript Division. Register 53: *The American Colonization Society* (1979), 34 pp; and in the *National Union Catalog of*

Manuscript Collections (Washington, D.C.: Library of Congress, 1961–). Thirty-four vols. of catalog, plus indexes published either in volumes, separately, or both. Two index series published commercially are: *Index to Personal Names in the National Union Catalog of Manuscript Collections, 1959–1984* (Alexandria, Va.: Chadwyck-Healey, Inc., 1987), 2 vols.; and *Index to Subjects and Corporate Names in the National Union Catalog of Manuscript Collections, 1959–1984* (Alexandria, Va.: Chadwyck-Healey, Inc., 1994) 3 vols., 69–2026.

22. *American Women and the U.S. Armed Forces. A Guide to the Records of Military Agencies in the National Archives Related to American Women*, comp. Charlotte Palmer Seeley. Revised by Virginia C. Purdy and Robert Gruber (Washington, D.C.: NARA, 1992), 355.

23. For example, there is a collection of cat stud books available for research at the Glendale, Calif., Public Library. See *Directory of Archives and Manuscript Repositories in the United States* [DAMRUS] (National Historical Publications and Records Commission, Phoenix, Ariz.: Oryx Press, 1988), entry CA290-280. The Oakland, Calif., Public Library has the papers of poet and librarian Ina Donna Coolbrith, which contain the "pedigree papers of her cat" (*NUCMC* 61-923), and other *NUCMC* entries such as the following appear: Baskervill Family (61–2647) breeding papers for dogs (hounds?); the Osman B. Gilman (64-1297) collection is that of a cocker spaniel breeder; Herbert Charles Sanborn's collection (69-1635) contains "stuff on dogs"; Sherman Shumway Hanks' Papers (70-333) contain "materials relating to the borzoidox"; Gertrude Van Rensselaer Wickham's Papers (74-1807) consist mostly of "letters about dogs"; etc.

24. *NUCMC.*

25. Timothy J. Mahoney, "The Impact of 'New' Social History on American Manuscript Collections as Reflected in *The National Union Catalog of Manuscript Collections, 1959–1991* (unpublished typescript, fall 1993), 27 pp. with charts.

26. Daniel J. Leab and Philip P. Mason, eds., *Labor History Archives in the United States: A Guide for Researching and Teaching* (Detroit: Wayne State University Press, 1992).

27. David C. Mearns, "The Lincoln Papers," *American Library Quarterly* 4, no. 8 (December 1947): 369–385; Mearns, "He Had Nothing, only 'Plenty of Friends.' The Story of the Long-awaited Abraham Lincoln Papers," *New York Herald Tribune Weekly Book Review* 24, no. 25 (8 February 1948): 1–2.

28. David Hackett Fisher, *Historians' Fallacies; Towards a Logic of Historical Thought* (New York: Harper and Row, 1970), 62.

29. James' original quote in Ian Hamilton, *Keepers of the Flame*, 28: "Henry James's suggestion is that bardolotry [idolatry of Shakespeare] is fueled by the absence of biography, that if we knew more we would worship less."

30. Marie Joseph Paul Yves Roch Gilbert du Motier, Marquis de Lafayette, *Lafayette in the Age of the American Revolution: Selected Letters and Papers*, ed. Stanley J. Idzerda (Ithaca, N.Y.: Cornell University Press, 5 vols., 1977–1983), Lafayette to Washington, 9 February 1778, vol. 1, 287–288.

31. See Lafayette to the American Commissioners, Paris, 8 April, 1785. Ibid., vol. 5, 315–316.

32. Stephen Vincent Benet, *John Brown's Body* (New York: Reinhart & Co., Inc., 1927). Herman Wouk, *Winds of War* (Boston: Little, Brown and Company, 1971) and *War and Remembrance* (Boston: Little, Brown and Company, 1978). Alex Haley, *Roots* (New York: Doubleday & Company, Inc., 1976). John Barth, *The Sot-Weed Factor* (Garden City, N.Y.: Doubleday, 1967).

33. U.S. National Archives, Pacific-Sierra Region, San Bruno, Calif. Records of the Farm Security Administration, RG 96. Report for Week Ending February 22, 1936, doc. no. 716286, p. 3. See also Ann M. Campbell, "Reports from Weedpatch," *Agricultural History* 48, no. 3 (July 1974): 402–404.

34. John Steinbeck. *The Grapes of Wrath* (New York: The Viking Press, 1939), chap. 22.

35. Papers of Hi Simons. Department of Special Collections, Regenstein Library, University of Chicago.

36. Remarks of Michael Cogswell, Louis Armstrong Archives, Queens College, New York, in a presentation at the "New Orleans Jazz in Archives" session, Annual Meeting, Society of American Archivists, Sheraton Hotel, New Orleans, La., September 5, 1993.

37. The Papers of George S. Patton, Jr., *Register* (Washington, D.C.: Library of Congress, 1964, with additions to 1976), 5.

38. Ibid., 4 folders, in Box 60, "Writings."

39. George S. Patton, Jr., to Beatrice Patton, January 24, 1945. Ibid., "Family Correspondence," Box 35.

40. Francis Fukuyama, *The End of History and the Last Man* (New York: The Free Press, 1994).

· 3 ·

Opening the Doors to Scholarship

In offering a critique of the NUCMC one is immediately impressed with the purpose, scale, and complexity of the undertaking. It suggests—no less—an ordering of the total manuscript resources of our nation. Its effect on the writing of history and national self-awareness is manifest. One must also remain sympathetic to the fact that it is a pioneering effort with unusual intellectual and organizational problems. This work also has lessons for this profession since it has touched, and has the potential of continually touching, all of us as philosophical and technical issues arise from its efforts.

Robert Rosenthal[1]

Research in manuscript collections can be a daunting process to an inquirer new to the medium. The Library of Congress, even with its ten thousand manuscript collections, represents only a minor segment of the collections in the country that are available for research. In addition to manuscripts, there are also thousands of archival collections in government, corporate, institutional, and organizational archives. Although it might seem reasonable to expect that the records of the Grumman Aerospace Corporation would be in the corporation's History Center in Bethpage, New York (they are), it is less obvious that the papers of World War I ace and president of Eastern Airlines Eddie Rickenbacker are in Auburn University, Alabama. Researchers are also confronted by the problem of locating materials *about* Grumman Aerospace or Rickenbacker in other collections around the country. Since 1959, however, many tools have appeared that can help researchers locate the corporate records that have strayed from their origin, or the papers of individuals. Access to these resources can expand the researcher's horizons, while shortening the time and drudge work associated with locating pertinent documentation.

The logical place to begin a search is at the repository level. With an estimated 9,000 to 10,000 archival and manuscript repositories in the country it would be impossible to go directly to the correct ones without some professional help. In 1988 the second edition of the *Directory of Archives and Manuscript Repositories in the United States (DAMRUS)*[2] appeared, containing general holdings statements for 4,225 U.S. institutions. In addition, it lists another 335 repositories in abbreviated entries for which collection information was not received, but which may be found in the *National Union Catalog of Manuscript Collections* (NUCMC) or the *Guide to Archives and Manuscripts in the United States.*[3] *DAMRUS* is indexed to collection names and names or subjects mentioned in the "Holdings" and "Materials Solicited" paragraphs of each entry. *DAMRUS* is organized alphabetically by state, then by city thereunder, and then by institution name. It is a simple matter to consult it for any institution in Michigan or just those listed from Detroit. The major difference in coverage between *NUCMC* and *DAMRUS* is that the latter includes archives *in situ*, and, indeed, begins each state entry with a brief analysis of the state archival program.

Two editions of the *Directory* were published before funds ran out to continue the project. Chadwyck-Healey, Inc., has stepped in, however, and has produced a World Wide Web (WWW) and a CD-ROM retrieval tool called *ArchivesUSA* that contains an updated version of *DAMRUS*, plus other materials.

A typical entry as it appears in *DAMRUS* is:

MI230-165
Detroit Public Library
Burton Historical Collection
5201 Woodward Avenue
Detroit MI 48202

(313) 833-1480

OPEN: Tu, Th, F, Sa 9:30-5:30, W 1-9; closed Sundays, Mondays, and holidays
COPYING FACILITIES: yes
MATERIALS SOLICITED: Materials relating to the history of the Old Northwest, Michigan, and Detroit; automotive history; black music and musicians; and fine arts.

HOLDINGS:
Total volume: 10,000 l.f.
Inclusive dates: 1700 -
Description: The Burton Historical Collection at the Library includes over 6,500 l.f. of letters, papers, ledgers, and other documents relating to the history of

Detroit, Michigan, and the Old Northwest, including papers of pioneers, officeholders, businesspersons, traders, and organizations, as well as non-current records of the city and county. Other collections include papers and photographs regarding black music and musicians, literature, fine arts, and automotive history.

SEE: Hamer; NUCMC, 1966-73, 76, 79, NUCMC, 1967 (as Detroit Public Library, Automotive History Collection).

SEE: Beers - Southwest; Hinding; Robbins; Parkinson; Spalek; Ingram; Allard, Crawley, and Edmison; Bean and Vane; Hines.

[This is followed by three short paragraphs of citations to finding guides in the library]

A check for other entries under "Old Northwest" in the index of the *DAMRUS* volume leads to a number of other institutions reporting material on the topic.

The *DAMRUS* entry is obviously not very detailed about the "letters, papers, ledgers, and other documents" but provides a guideline for the use of the next level of national guide— *NUCMC*.

In 1958, after almost two decades of wishing and planning, and with a grant from the Council on Library Resources, the Library of Congress began gathering material necessary for the production of an annual catalog of manuscript collections in the United States. The project had long been promoted by members of the historical and archival professions, and was urged upon the curatorial community in 1955 by a joint committee of the Society of American Archivists and the American Association for State and Local History.[4]

In 1961, the first volume of the *National Union Catalog of Manuscript Collections* (*NUCMC*) came off the press and covered material sent to the Library since 1959.

NUCMC was to be a catalog of personal papers collections, not archival records if they were in the place where one would expect to find them. Therefore, the Michigan State University Archives, located at Michigan State University, would not be included because the archives were in a predictable location; but they would be included if they were in the Detroit Public Library or at the Bentley Historical Library.

The purpose of *NUCMC* was to inform the public of the location of collections that are important for specific research. An additional goal was to bring together (through the index) collections relating to the same subject, person, or other common factor. The *NUCMC* index provides references to "Hospitals," the "Republican Party," "The Breckinridge Family," "Politics," and many other subjects or topics. Institutions entered their collections in the catalog in order to attract researcher attention.

In its volumes *NUCMC* compiled descriptions of 72,300 collections at 1,406 institutions. Each of the descriptions provides title, dates, size, source (provenance), form, occupation (of the collection subject), biographical information, and a brief analysis of the contents of the collection and key correspondents. The researcher can therefore use the indexes to locate not only specific collections by title, but also references to individuals, subjects, and topics within collections, and the repository where they are housed. A typical entry is the Edith Dolan Riley Collection at the University of Washington.[5]

MS 65–1049

Riley, Edith Dolan, 1885–
　　　Papers, 1909–64.　4 ft. (ca. 5000 items)
　　　In University of Washington Library (Seattle)
　　　Politician and chairman of the Democratic Central Committee, Spokane Co., Wash.　Correspondence, 3 vols. of reminiscences, speeches, writings, audiograms with typed transcriptions related to the reminiscences, photos., memorabilia, and other papers.　The reminiscences are of Democratic Party work in Washington and focus upon Lewis B. Schwellenbach for whom Mrs. Riley handled patronage, James M. Geraghty, and Clarence C. Dill.　Other papers are concerned with her official work with the Democratic Party, the League of Women Voters, and the Federation of Motion Picture Councils.　Correspondents include Homer T. Bone, A. Scott Bullitt, Mary W. Dewson, Clarence C. Dill, and Franklin Delano Roosevelt.
　　　Unpublished inventory record in the library.
　　　Information on literary rights available in the library.
　　　Gift of Mrs. Riley, 1964.

In order to gather the information it needed for each collection, the *NUCMC* staff posed eleven questions, one of which was "Description of Content and Scope of the Collection." Everything asked for in the *NUCMC* data sheet could be supplied from an institutional descriptive tool known as the manuscript register. If the information were not yet in a register, the content and scope of the collection could be supplied by listing the document clusters, or "series," that made up the collection. Thus, one could provide information that the Edith Dolan Riley Papers, illustrated above, contained:

Correspondence, 3 vols. of reminiscences, speeches, writings, audiograms with typed transcriptions related to the reminiscences, photos, memorabilia and other papers.

To a trained archivist the above statement implies that there are at least seven series in the Edith Dolan Riley papers, and a fair estimate of the research potential comes from the register statement that the size of the collection is 5,000 items.

Unfortunately, few researchers are aware of this. The concept of series is esoteric; the fact that a *NUCMC* entry describes or lists the series in a collection is probably abstruse, and even the fact that *NUCMC* exists may not be known to many graduate students. The lack of instruction in the sources for research materials is one of the great shortcomings of modern education in research methods. The young researcher, therefore, often is faced not only with masses of material, but also with a lack of training in how to get to those resources and understand them.

In the case of *NUCMC* confusion is compounded by the erratic way in which it is indexed. In the early volumes an index is included in each volume. Later, separate indexes were published (in addition to the internal one) for every three successive volumes. Ultimately, the indexes to each volume were printed in paperback, with a cumulated hardback version appearing for each five volumes (thus permitting librarians to dispose of the paperbacks and save shelf space).

In 1983 a commercial publisher simplified the process. For the volumes covering entries from 1959 to 1984, Chadwyck-Healey, Inc. produced a two-volume name index and a three-volume subject and corporate name index to *NUCMC*.[6] They are traditional index formats, derived from *NUCMC*, and therefore using the *NUCMC* authorities. The reference is not to volume number and page, but, as in the original volumes, to the year in which *NUCMC* received the information, followed by the entry (or card) number. Thus, reference to Learned Hand, as it appears in the 1959–62 index volume, is:

Hand, Learned, 1872–1961. *59–12*, 59–152, 62–2431.

The interpretation is that there is a collection of Hand's papers cited in the volume for 1959, entry 12, which is underlined, plus two other collections that contain something of Hand's in collections listed in the 1959 and 1962 volumes.

The Library of Congress announced that the 1993 volume of *NUCMC* would be the last in book form. The Library of Congress then began entering information from data sheets sent to it in the library computer utilities (Research Libraries Information Network—RLIN, and Online Computer Library Catalog—OCLC; see chapter 6), but initially only covering those years when the Library of Congress used electronic means to produce *NUCMC*, beginning in 1980. Chadwyck-Healey's *ArchivesUSA* meanwhile has replicated on one CD-ROM and a WWW version the complete *NUCMC*, 1959–94, with a complete index. Future researchers, therefore, may discover a full set of the printed volumes in their library, may locate entries that have been entered into the computer utilities since 1980, or may seek out the Chadwyck-Healey Web site or CD-ROM that can provide diverse search configurations.

As significant as *NUCMC* is in its coverage of collections, it includes only 1,406 repositories. Other sources, however, provide some indication of collections in institutions that are not included in the catalog.

The *Guide to Archives and Manuscripts in the United States*, referred to as the *Hamer Guide*, after the compiler, is long out-of-date and out of print, since it is a 1961 imprint. As with *DAMRUS* it is a product of the National Historical Publications Commission, predecessor to the National Historical Publications and Records Commission. The commission attempted to update the *Hamer Guide* in the 1980s by first producing the directory of repositories, to be followed by a collection listing of the holdings for each. Because of lack of funding the project never got past the first stage. The *Hamer Guide*, however, remains largely valid for the material that it contains, since repositories rarely dispose of collections. It is arranged in the same order as *DAMRUS*, by state, then city, then institution, and then continues with a brief listing of the collections in each. The index is comprehensive. A researcher might, therefore, find in *DAMRUS* an institution whose "Holdings" statement indicates the possible presence of collections in a researcher's field; a quick check of *Hamer* might then indicate that the repository has specific collections of interest; and a search of *NUCMC* might then provide greater details about each collection. The search could be completed by consulting *The National Inventory of Documentary Sources in the United States* (*NIDS-US*),[7] for the complete finding aid to the collection in order to analyze what material is in each box. *NIDS-US* is also incorporated in the *ArchivesUSA* package.

ArchivesUSA does not include *Hamer*, but brings together *DAMRUS*-like entries, a complete *NUCMC*, and the *NIDS-US* index, thus short-circuiting the search process and taking the researcher directly to the finding aid reference.

Other, specialized, guides and directories exist for researchers, although most of them are now becoming dated, with more recent information showing up in the computerized systems rather than in print. Automated systems will be discussed in chapter 6, but researchers should be aware that many of them are not retrospective in that they do not include material from earlier published versions. It is often necessary, therefore, to consult older reference tools in print form in order to perform a thorough search.

Two of the specialized guides that cover more than one institution are Andrea Hinding's *Women's History Sources*[8] and the Burton *Guide to Manuscripts in the Presidential Libraries*.[9] The latter combines some of the features of *DAMRUS* and *NUCMC*. The introduction lays the groundwork for the seven Presidential libraries covered, the conditions for research, and the general holdings of each of the seven Presidential libraries. The 4,603 collection entries, although in a straight alphabetical order by name, are convenient because of the interrelationships and crossovers between libraries. They are patterned after the entries in *NUCMC* and, if they duplicate them, the *NUCMC* catalog entry number is provided. The index is complete and accurate and provides easy access to the body of the catalog. Entries in the Burton *Guide* and index have been verified against Library of Congress authority lists. The limitations to the Burton *Guide* are the usual ones: it covers only seven of the Presidential libraries and does not include material received after 1985.

Andrea Hinding's *Women's History Sources* includes 18,026 "collections" in 1,586 repositories. However, some of the entries are for only one item, such as entry 340, a single letter from Clara Barton located at the Bancroft Library. The collections represent a mixture of women's papers and papers of men that contain women's material, such as letters and diaries of wives. There are also family collections as well as records of associations, institutions, businesses and corporations that contain women's records or letters. The Hinding volume covers more repositories than *NUCMC*, but one-quarter the number of collections. The volume includes repositories and collections not in *NUCMC*, to some extent because the work did not depend on volunteer submissions but resulted from visits to the repositories by project staff analysts. Additionally, the inclusion of single items as "collections," and records collections *in situ*, adds some entries that *NUCMC* would have excluded. The index consumes all of volume 2 and refers not just to collection names, but also to correspondents or subjects mentioned in the entries, similar to the *NUCMC* indexes.

All of these guides, directories and indexes except *Archives-*

USA suffer from the same shortcoming: they are dated and none is scheduled for reissuing or updating.

NIDS-US is continuing to expand and update its information, but is not a *guide* in the strictest sense, since it goes deeper than the collection level. The ongoing project makes it possible for internal repository descriptive tools (registers and inventories) themselves to be available through microcopy to subscribers. *NIDS-US* brings together microfiche of finding aids in the Library of Congress, the National Archives, the Smithsonian Institution, state archives, state historical societies, Presidential libraries, and university collections. An index to the microfiche is also included in *ArchivesUSA*, and all of the material is both on CD-ROM and in an on-line database. *NIDS-US* has finding aids available on 34,800 microfiche, with each fiche containing approximately seventy page images, or up to 2,436,000 inventory and register pages.

It is uncertain what the researcher will find when searching for collections in the catalogs of an automated archives/manuscript repository. At this writing not enough institutions have automated their documentary collections for a pattern to emerge. There also are few if any institutions where the researcher can search the locally automated archives/manuscript system unassisted. Indeed, many of these systems are proprietary, and require operator training before they can be used. Fortunately, this picture is changing, as programs become more user-friendly, but it is not changing very fast, and in an institution where there is both a manual and a computerized access system the researcher will probably find that the manual system will be available for direct access and have more information in it than the computerized system. In the coming years, as more standardized systems are adopted from repository to repository, and as data input grows, or as all new collections are entered only in the automated system, the tide will begin to turn, and the researcher may have better and more direct access to the documentary resources in archives and manuscript repositories.

The implications of automation on descriptive methodology will be discussed in chapter 6, but one may wonder why archivists have not adopted across-the-board descriptive standards for their finding aids and are only now confronting the problem. Essentially, archivists and curators felt no need to adopt processes that were compatible with those of other institutions, since each archives or manuscript repository holds unique papers collections. The library imperative for shared cataloging of titles that were to be found in hundreds or even thousands of libraries was not pertinent for archivists. Descriptive processes used at the National Archives or the Library of Congress might be emulated, or staff moving from those institutions to others might carry such processes with them, but many institutions felt that their homegrown formats served their purposes and need not match or be compatible with those of others. The missing factor in that thinking, however, was the researcher.

Not every important document is in the Library of Congress or the National Archives. As stated earlier, *NUCMC* cites 1,406 institutions; the NHPRC's *DAMRUS* lists 4,560 repositories containing manuscripts or archives in fifty states. While dramatizing the problem facing the researcher doing comprehensive studies, these publications also illustrate some of the attempts being made to minimize the problem by institutions and curators cooperating in reporting their holdings to national guides in order to assist researchers looking for scattered documentary sources.

Many researchers who do broad research visit numerous repositories looking for related material. Most find it necessary to learn the system of the institutions visited before they can knuckle down to searching the collections. Thus, intensive use of archival or manuscript materials requires that researcher and curator participate in verbal communication. Even if a researcher visits a repository and reads the finding aid to one or more collections, the necessity for person-to-person communication exists because the finding aid provides only clues to the collection contents. Library reference service and manuscript reference service therefore differ significantly. In a typical library situation the researcher is looking for the *source* to be consulted for information. The reference librarian is an interpreter of sources, and, in effect, is interpreting the catalog for the user. Simple advice, such as a suggestion to look under the heading "Prussia" or "Bavaria" or "German Democratic Republic" when the item sought cannot be found under "Germany," is probably no longer the main service of the reference librarian, and even amateur researchers probably can figure it out by interpreting the added entries of the catalog. More complex advice, such as understanding that a publication series changed its name, or that a government function was moved to a different agency, might be more of a challenge to the reference librarian. But more and more the reference librarian is becoming an interpreter of on-line information sources of very specialized topics, subjects and research areas. There is also the growing diversity of CD-ROM sources, which may be confusing and even unknown to researchers, and with which reference librarians try to keep current.

Archivists who deal with corporate or government records find it necessary to inform the neophyte researcher that a name-search in government files is rarely possible. Instead, the researcher is led through the maze of citizen/government relationships in order to arrive at the location of documentation. Doing a biography of Amelia Earhart? What did she have to do with the federal government? If she traveled overseas, there may be some files in the State Department's passport records. If she was a licensed pilot, one may find a record of her license application in the records of the Civil Aeronautics Administration, or the Civil Aeronautics Board. If she requested permission to land at military bases in her trans-Pacific flight, there may be correspondence relating to her request in the records of the unit of the Army or Navy that provided such clearances. If she was on a government goodwill mission, there might be records in another part of the State Department files. Indeed, the National Archives has compiled a *Reference Report* of five pages listing "Records Relating to Amelia Earhart" that describes sources in records of the U.S. Coast Guard, general records of the Department of Commerce (which administered the Civil Aeronautics Administration in the 1930s), the general records of the Department of State, records of the Office of Territories, the National Archives Gift Collection, the records of the Federal Aviation Administration, general records of the Department of the Navy, records of the Hydrographic Office, records of the Bureau of Naval Personnel, records of the Office of the Chief of Naval Operations, records of Naval Districts and Shore Establishments, records of U.S. Army Overseas Operations and Commands, records of the War Department General and Special Staffs, and records of the Office of the Adjutant General.[10]

While the reference librarian therefore stands between the researcher and the information sources, as their interpreter, the archivist stands between the source (the automated or paper finding aid) and the records, bringing a knowledge of government structure, mission, function and process to bear on the posed question. If one can equate a finding aid, not with a catalog card but with a book's table of contents, the difference becomes even more vivid. The librarian leads the researcher to the source or the work and its table of contents, but no further. The archivist begins with the table of contents and reaches into the content itself. This seems reasonable, because the researcher, given the book and the table of contents at hand, can browse through the work and its index, if one exists. The archival researcher cannot browse through a few thousand feet of records described in a finding aid, and therefore needs the assistance of the archivist to zero in on those that are most pertinent to the search.

In manuscript collections this one-on-one assistance may not be as critical as it is for archival record groups, because many collections are of a size that permits browsing, although that may not be desirable from a security viewpoint. But the manuscript curator may be able to provide expert advice to the researcher because it could have been the curator who processed the collection and prepared the finding aid in the first place. This is not at all unusual in small and medium-sized repositories with a limited number of staff members who at one time or another perform all curatorial functions. In such cases it is the curator who is providing intimate, internal knowledge of the collection to the researcher, and, therefore, the curator becomes the ultimate finding aid.

If manuscript curators are the ultimate finding aid, why do they bother to produce finding aids? Why not require that every researcher entering the institution discuss research questions with the curatorial staff and be directed into the material? Although that procedure might be acceptable for researcher walk-ins, even under those circumstances the provision of a number of seemingly appropriate finding aids to the visitor by a knowledgeable staff member, giving the visitor some time to browse before going into consultation, is undoubtedly a more efficient way of handling the situation than confronting the researcher cold, orally.

The truth is, many researchers have an idea about what they want, but are not always certain about specifics. Also, many researchers will define their needs in the narrowest terms, where a broader approach may suggest many possibilities to the staff. A request to see the papers of Ira Eaker at the Library of Congress would bring forth the Eaker finding aid and a staff request that the query be narrowed to specific areas or items in the Eaker collection. If an interview reveals a research need for material based on the development of the U.S. air forces in World War II, the staff might then suggest many other collections, from Albert Tissandier and Alfred Hildebrand for early aviation developments, to Carl A. "Tooey" Spaatz, Curtis LeMay, and many others.

But not every researcher enters the institution before making an inquiry. One of the purposes of the printed finding aid, therefore, is to provide at least minimum reference to the collections away from the repository. The registers can be mailed, in some cases sent by FAX, or in limited instances (as of this writing) accessed by computer. Many can also be accessed on microfiche at major libraries through the use of *NIDS-US.*

Although a solution to the access problem would be better indexing, that becomes prohibitive when staff is confronted with millions and millions of documents in a large archival group, or even in a large collection of personal papers. There must also be a decision about whether to index *every* name, place, event and subject in the material, or just the *important* ones. Since importance is generational and subjective, such an index may not age well, and if the comprehensive approach is used there will be thousands of names indexed to which few if any researchers will ever refer, because the nature of manuscript collections is that they consist of aggregates of material relating to unimportant people discussing unimportant things. One need only look at the lists of names indexed in the 1.2 million items in the Library of Congress Presidential Papers. It is only in that aggregation that the collection assumes historical reality and importance, as events unwind from routine daily occurrences. As Marshall McLuhan once remarked in another context, "data classification yields to pattern recognition."[11] To put a twist on that phrase, I would state it as "Accumulation of insignificant correspondence leads to recognition of significant historical patterns," or a "mosaic" effect.

In truth, the manuscript curator is not in a position to lead researchers directly to the material in which they are most interested. The curator provides guideposts, hints, suggestions, and structure, but it is the researcher who must take these maps and actually travel the documentary path.

Once the researcher locates pertinent material he or she may find access to it difficult on a number of grounds. Since we are discussing personal papers and not corporate archives there is little chance that the collections will be subject to the Freedom of Information Act (5 U.S.C 522), which applies only to government-produced records at the federal level. Nor would the Privacy Act (5 U.S.C. 522a) apply, since, once again, we are not discussing government-produced records. The two limitations on research access to manuscript sources are institutional restrictions and donor restrictions.

NUCMC provides minimal information about access to its listed collections, stating: "open to investigators under restrictions accepted by the repository," or something similar. Further inquiry by the researcher may reveal that only a small portion of a collection is restricted, perhaps just a few letters or a personal diary. Since it includes only individual collections, *NUCMC* does not address the question of institutional restrictions on access. For that information the researcher could try the entries in *DAMRUS*.

Institutional restrictions vary. Large state historical societies and public university departments of special collections tend to be quite liberal in their rules for access. If an individual shows reasonable cause for using material, and can provide some identification, access is usually granted, with few questions asked. If the institution is a private university or historical society, and especially a small regional, denominational, or local institution, many questions may be asked before a researcher is granted access. In some cases a document from a parent institution may be required, stating why the researcher needs access. If the institution is a corporate archives there may be very tight restrictions on access, requiring approval of a corporate office or committee. Some corporate archives are closed to all outside researchers. The irony is that while national directories and catalogs such as *NUCMC* indicate access restrictions where they apply, those institutions that are most restrictive do not even list their holdings in such national publications.

There has recently been an almost imperceptible movement in the archival profession to take a very conservative approach to access, even where the donor has stipulated no restrictions. There is evidence of concern for the unstated rights of the correspondents, generally referred to as "third party rights," within a collection, who may not even know that the private thoughts and ideas they shared with the recipient are now open for all to see since the recipient deposited the collection in a research repository and declared "no restrictions" on access. Some archivists, however, have taken on the conservatives and declared that the status quo ante should apply. The curator should accept the wishes of the donor.[12]

The episode of the Dead Sea scrolls over the past twenty-five years has raised controversy among scholars over restrictions on material that is reserved for use by only a select group, and also by the issue of some of the Dead Sea scholars copyrighting the portions of the scrolls that they have reconstructed from fragments.[13]

What the researcher will probably find is that access to a collection is not the most significant restriction that exists. After locating the necessary documents, and building a historical case for or against a specific issue, the researcher may find that the limitations of the Copyright Law are the real *bête noir*! The Copyright Act does not limit access to collections, any more than it limits access to printed material, but it does affect the right to publish letters or documents from collections.

The Copyright Act, Title 17 of the United States Code, was revised by Public Law 94-553 in October 1976 and became effective on January 1, 1978. In brief, the law replaced common law in the area of document copying and "literary property rights." The law includes unpublished material as a genre to be protected under copyright, and includes "manuscripts" in its definition.[14] It also takes note of the fact that "manuscripts" are no longer only written documents, produced by placing an image on paper. The law states:

> Copyright protection subsists, in accordance with this title, in original works of authorship fixed in any tangible medium of expression, now known or later developed, from which they can be perceived, reproduced, or otherwise communicated, either directly or with the aid of a machine or device.[15]

We will discuss the legal issues of copyright, freedom of information, privacy and ethics further in chapter 11.

Much of this may be irrelevant in a discussion of *access* to manuscript materials, except that access implies the intent to use, and in many cases the intention is to quote from or publish a document or a group of documents in full. Other limitations to access for researchers using manuscript material are more subtle, but can pose as much of a block to research as those already mentioned. The unique nature of documentary sources implies that they may be found in only one location—the owning institution. According to a study conducted by the NHPRC, there are between 15,000 and 20,000 research institutions that contain manuscript collections. A researcher's ability to get to the distant repository is a subtle access restriction.

In order to provide off-site access to their collections, many repositories have undertaken systematic microfilming of entire collections, and offer the film for sale, either as a complete set or by individual rolls. Much of this filming has been supported by federal and other grants. Surrogate copies such as microfilm and the emerging digital copying systems can be useful substitutes for the originals. But few researchers are content with such surrogates, which are not the same as research on the scene, especially if the custodial institution holds related collections, which most would. These auxiliary collections may not be significant enough on their own to warrant photocopying, although a researcher (with enough funds) may be willing to have them filmed for a fee. In some cases, competitive airfares may make it more economical for the researcher to travel to the institution rather than photocopy large amounts of uninspected documentary material.

A neglected tool in manuscript research is the documentary edition of the papers of an individual or of an event or activity. Through the support of the NHPRC alone, there have been 718 volumes in 47 titles of documentary book editions, 8,377 microfilm reels of 183 titles, and 1,822 microfiche produced and on the shelves of libraries, historical societies and in private holdings. These titles are for the most part historical or biographical, from the Adams family papers to the Benjamin Cudworth Yancey papers, and almost every university press has published papers, diaries, memoirs, and other documentary editions outside the scope of the NHPRC editions. The National Endowment for the Humanities has also supported many documentary editions. Each of these editions contains indexes and cites the location of the documents assembled for the edition. The citations can be clues to the location of collections from which only a handful of documents are used. Such a case might be a letter of "Andrew Johnson to Brig. Gen'l L[orenzo] Thomas, adjutant General of the U.S.A.," which identifies the repository of the Thomas letter as the Connecticut Historical Society, Tracy Collection.[16] Are there other Thomas letters there? Why is a letter from Johnson to Thomas in the Tracy Collection, when one would expect to find it in the National Archives, since it is to a military officer? Such clues set the researcher off on a hunt after new material from unexpected sources.

What all of the above implies is that the researcher should expect the manuscript curator to be attuned to the difficulties of using original sources, and to make every attempt to lessen the difficulties by providing advice as well as service to those doing research.[17] Archivists are in a position to assist researchers in ways that directories, guides, finding aids and computer networks cannot. After a few years at a repository the archivist or curator can be more knowledgeable about the people, topics and historical events in a specific area than the accredited expert researcher coming to use the collections. The major difference is that the archivist has a great deal of knowledge about a few collections or record groups, whereas most historical researchers have broad knowledge across many collections or record groups, since the nature of historical research and writing is to test evidence against other evidence.

It also soon becomes apparent to the curator that not all researchers are historians doing scholarly work. The users of manuscripts and archives come from the ranks of lawyers, genealogists, biographers, journalists, and even novelists. Some have not exhaustively consulted the secondary sources that give broad overviews before they attack the minutiae of personal papers and corporate records. Most are unaware of the mysteries of archival finding aids, provenance, and original order. Many have difficulty with handwritten documents. Human nature, however, makes it difficult for some researchers to admit these shortcomings, and it is one of the roles of the reference archivist to ease them into a receptive mood so that the processes can be explained, questions can be negotiated, answers can be provided, and research can proceed.

A researcher should expect the reference archivist, therefore, to proceed by asking open questions, rather than closed ones that can be answered with a yes or no. The questions in many instances are conversational. The object of the research may be elicited: Is this a personal search? Material for a book? An article? Are you trying to prove something legally or piece together random facts, or maybe verify a specific fact? Have you visited this archive before? Other collections? Did you find anything? How long have you been at it? Are you familiar with archival finding aids? Our finding aids? Do you live nearby? Are you staying with friends or paying for quarters someplace? How much time do you have to spend on this project? How much time per visit? Do you have a deadline? What do you know about the subject already? Have you read up on it in secondary sources? Which ones? What led you here?

Asked in a chatty, casual way, with evidence of sincere interest in the researcher and the research problem, these kinds of questions can provide answers that will determine the research methodology for the visit. A seasoned researcher on the last leg of a research excursion may know exactly what to ask for, be familiar with the finding aids, be seeking specific facts or incidents to round out previous research leads, and probably will need little attention. A neophyte, unfamiliar with procedures and terminology, just beginning to search for original sources, and with a limited schedule, might expect a completely different approach.

Researchers should also expect that the archivist/curator is able to explain the application of various federal and state laws and institutional regulations relating to access. If there are donor restrictions, how does one obtain permission? What about security clearances? Can material be copied? Can it be published? How are copyright approvals obtained, and from whom? What facilities are there at the institution for mass copying?

In sum, the reference archivist not only provides access to a collection where it is available, but also tries to facilitate access where it is not. Although a government archivist must honor his or her role to administer material according to the government's rules (local, state or federal), the archivist must also ensure "equal access" to all researchers of "equal standing." That is, all persons authorized to have access to various levels of documentary materials should be provided such access equally. A person without a national security clearance is not provided access to security classified material, but all those who do have such clearance should be provided access equally. This naturally also applies to the general public accessing open material.

Reference archivists perform an important role in an archive, perhaps matched only by those who select collections or appraise records as potential additions to the store of documentary resources available to the research public. Theirs is a knowledge-based activity, requiring an understanding of the existence of sources, but also of the meaning and relevance of those sources to the larger holdings of the institution—they are, indeed, the tour guides to the historical treasures of the past. We will have a further discussion on this topic later when we address the question of ethics in the profession in chapter 11.

NOTES

1. Robert Rosenthal, "The Minotaur among the Manuscripts," typescript, 12 pp. Unpublished paper delivered at the annual meeting of the Society of American Archivists, October 14, 1971.

2. *Directory of Archives and Manuscript Repositories in the United States (DAMRUS)*, 2d ed. (Phoenix: Oryx Press, 1988).

3. Philip M. Hamer, ed., *A Guide to Archives and Manuscripts in the United States* (Hamer *Guide*) (New Haven: Yale University Press, 1961).

4. Joint Committee on Historical Manuscripts, "National Register of Historical Manuscript Collections: A Report by the Joint Committee on Historical Manuscripts" (n.p.: Society of American Archivists, American Association for State and Local History, 1951), 7, photocopy of unpublished manuscript.

5. Edith Dolan Riley Papers, in University of Washington Library (Seattle), *NUCMC* entry MS65–1049.

6. *Index to Personal Names in the National Union Catalog of Manuscript Collections, 1959–1984*, 2 vols. Edited under the supervision of Harriet Ostroff, editor of *NUCMC* (Alexandria, Va.: Chadwyck-Healey, Inc., 1988); *Index to Subjects and Corporate Names in the National Union Catalog of Manuscript Collections, 1959–1984*, 3 vols. (Alexandria, Va.: Chadwyck-Healey, Inc., 1994).

7. *National Inventory of Documentary Sources in the United States (NIDS-US)*, pt. 1. Federal records, microfiche in loose-leaf and printed index (Teaneck, N.J., Chadwyck-Healey, Inc., 1983); pt. 2. Manuscript Division, Library of Congress, microfiche in loose-leaf and printed index (Teaneck, N.J.: Chadwyck-Healey, Inc., 1985); pt. 3. State archives, libraries, and historical societies, microfiche in loose-leaf and printed index (Teaneck, N.J.: Chadwyck-Healey, Inc., 1985–). CD-ROM Index to NIDS, National Inventory of Documentary Sources [computer file] (Alexandria, Va.: Chadwyck-Healey, ca. 1996, version 2).

8. Andrea Hinding, ed., *Women's History Sources: A Guide to Archives and Manuscript Collections in the United States* (New York: Bowker, 1978), 2 vols. Volume 2, *Index*, edited by Suzanna Moody.

9. Dennis A. Burton, James B. Rhoads, Raymond W. Smock, comps., *A Guide to Manuscripts in the Presidential Libraries* (College Park, Md.: Research Materials Corporation, 1985).

10. *Reference Report*, "Inquiry: Records Relating to Amelia Earhart." (Washington: National Archives, n.d.). Typescript, 5 pp.

11. Marshall McLuhan, *Understanding Media*, 2d edition (New York: Signet Books, 1964), Introduction, viii.

12. Mark A. Greene, "Moderation in Everything, Access in Nothing?: Opinions about Access Restrictions on Private Papers," *Archival Issues: Journal of the Midwest Archives Conference* 18, no. 1 (1993): 31–41. Among the many sources Greene cites for his argument, the telling ones relating to restrictions placed by archivists only out of deference to the letter writers are: Trudy Huskamp and Gary M. Peterson, *Archives and Manuscripts: Law*, Basic Archives Manual Series (Chicago: Society of American Archivists, 1985), 40, 53; David R. Kepley, "Reference Service and Access," in

Managing Archives and Archival Institutions, ed. James G. Bradsher (Chicago: University of Chicago Press, 1983), 166–167; Mary Jo Pugh, *Providing Reference Services for Archives and Manuscripts*, Archival Fundamentals Series (Chicago: Society of American Archivists, 1992), 56–57; Sigrid McCausland, "Access and Reference Services," in *Keeping Archives*, ed. Ann Pederson (Sydney: Australian Society of Archivists, 1987), 190–191.

13. "Judge Upholds Scrolls Copyright," *Washington Post* (March 31, 1993), B-1.

14. 17 United States Code (U.S.C.) 101

15. 17 U.S.C. 102.

16. Andrew Johnson, *The Papers of Andrew Johnson*, ed. LeRoy P. Graf, vol. 7, *1864–1865* (Knoxville: University of Tennessee Press, 1986), 417.

17. Douglas Greenberg, "Get Out of the Way if You Can't Lend a Hand: The Changing Nature of Scholarship and the Significance of Special Collections," *Biblion: the Bulletin of the New York Public Library* 2, no. 1 (fall 1993): 5–18.

· 4 ·

GATHERING THE EVIDENCE

Besides a lawyer-like care in the watch he keeps over his
biases, the historian finds his chief bulwark against error in his
passion for direct, reproducible evidence

Jacques Barzun[1]

Why are the Ernest Hemingway papers at a Presidential library? Why are the papers of former congresswoman Helen
Gahagan Douglas at the University of Oklahoma instead of in California, her home state? Why are Louis Armstrong's papers in
Queens, New York, rather than in New Orleans? Is there any logic
to the location of manuscript collections by which researchers can
figure out where to look for them? Archival practices, traditions
and quirks of fate have scattered collections all over the repository
landscape for reasons as diverse as the lives of the subjects represented in them. The task of the researcher, therefore, is to be aware
of the idiosyncrasies of the collecting process, but even moreso to
understand the tools that can be used to pry collection locations
from the multitude of directories, guides, catalogs, and databases in
which they are embedded. These sources are too diverse to be
labeled as a "system," but they possess enough characteristics to
hint of general guidelines for their use. I will therefore try to delve
into the curatorial experience and rationales for placing collections
where they are.

Archivists, recognizing the human need to understand the
past, and also understanding that the past is reflected in art, crafts,
physical monuments, and the capturing of the words used by the
past to describe itself, promise only to do their best to bring that
evidence to the present, leaving its interpretations to the practitioners of realism, pragmatism, relativism, and any other "ism"
proponents who wish to take a turn at it. Archivists also recognize
that what one says in writing in a corporate setting of governmen-

tal, institutional, business, or religious pursuits does not always reflect the inner thoughts, biases, enthusiasms and passions of the individual dispensing information, and they therefore look for those views in the personal writings and musings of the noncorporate person. Assembling or collecting history, then, is undertaken only after there are decisions about what should be added to the existing corpus of materials in order to expand the boundaries of understanding: the decision must also relate to the ability of the collecting institution to house, care for, and make available the material that it collects.

The first question relates to an acquisition policy, which defines the collecting areas: American history? modern poets? military heroes? The second question, which is more difficult, relates to the scope of collecting. Should there be an aggressive acquisition policy? A limited one? Acquisitions by purchase only? Hovering in the background may even be an element of "need," which may be dictated by the client community.

Since 1960 there has been considerable growth in the number of institutions of higher education in the United States, from 2,021 to 3,638.[2] There has been a concomitant increase in advanced degree programs in the humanities, with history master's and Ph.D. degrees rising from 2,136 in 1960 to 3,194 in 1991, and English and literature advanced degrees rising in the same period from 3,328 to 7,394.[3] In many cases new institutions that offer these degrees are campuses of a growing state university network, and many of those campuses have progressed from normal schools to teachers' colleges to state university branches. Although not all consider themselves "research" institutions, their expansion has been accompanied by a natural growth in graduate libraries and in departments of special collections throughout the country.

Let us imagine, therefore, that the Springfield Community College was elevated to be a branch of the state university, and that the new administrators felt that the institution could not rely on the regional libraries, archives and historical societies for its scholarly resources, and that it had to have its own library and research collections. It might not be difficult to establish a well-stocked library, since the school could develop an acquisition policy based on its academic department needs—let us say humanities, journalism, architecture, practical science, and mathematics—thus eschewing law, medicine, and the theoretical sciences. Although it might take years before it could place on its library shelves most of the classic works in these fields, except through recent editions, it could begin building a modern collection through book jobbers, blanket orders with certain university presses, and continuing orders of journals and serial publications. After deciding on an acquisition policy and appointing bibliographers to select pertinent titles, the only limits to growth would be shelf space and funds.

But what about the department of special collections? With nearby institutions collecting personal papers and even other organizations' archives in the humanities, sciences and mathematics fields, how would State University at Springfield build its research collection? Certainly with an acquisition policy, but acquisition policies in manuscript collecting are fraught with uncertainties. (We will assume that the S.U.–Springfield *Archives* will be a few years off, since the new school has not yet created any administrative materials, and it will be a while before those of continuing or enduring value will be retired.)

The establishment of an acquisition policy for manuscripts generally follows the axiom that institutions collect first and foremost in accordance with their institutional purpose. A municipal historical society concentrates on material relating to the city, even if not exclusively. An ethnic museum or archives collects related ethnic material. State and federal repositories collect in state and federal interest areas. The only repositories that have free choice of any dimension are universities and private research libraries. This is an exaggeration, as we will see throughout this book, but it has a lot of truth to it.

Even in universities, however, choice is traditionally limited to fields of institutional specialization. The purpose of the manuscript collection is not to collect manuscripts, but to serve the research public. At a university the research public may be eclectic but may still be defined in terms of the faculty, the curriculum, the ethnic, religious or other base, or the region in which the institution is located. Over time faculty and curriculum may change, and with them the collecting policies for the manuscript collection, leaving a residue of collections in an area no longer active. The collection then becomes attractive to outsiders who are pursuing research in a field where the university may have significant holdings but little institutional interest. When this phenomenon occurs in the book collections of a university library, the library may feel free to "weed" the collections of printed materials that are no longer pertinent to its acquisition policy. Manuscript curators and archivists rarely feel free to follow the same course.

The reason for this hesitancy has much to do with donor relations. Libraries, for the most part, buy their books with funds allocated for that purpose. It is a normal business transaction between seller and buyer that brings the materials into the stacks, regardless of the thought and effort that went into the selection of the titles in the first place. Manuscript curators, however, acquire their collections mostly through solicitation and personal contacts with individual donors. The form of transfer is not normally a sales agreement, but a contract between the donor and the institution that stipulates terms of the gift and is not taken lightly.[4]

The contract is often the end result of a long process engaged in by manuscript curators to acquire collections by donation. A few institutions purchase entire collections, but most cannot afford to do so, and they therefore seek donations, a process providing benefits to both giver and receiver. For the donor, masses of material documenting a life's activities and felt to be of research value to others can be deposited in an appropriate scholarly setting, and, if it can be established that these materials have monetary value, in the context of the collectors' market, then such value can be considered the value of the gift. As with any other gift to an educational or cultural institution, it has value as a deduction from taxes. For the receiving institution there is the benefit of a gift of research materials at little or no initial cost.

Often the initiative begins with a curator who recognizes the research potential of the papers of an individual or family. This pursuit of a donor by a collecting institution implies a panoply of procedures and postures that will lead to the eventual acquisition of the prize. The repository already knows its own acquisition policy. The curator then seeks information about what collections might become available within the range of that policy. Acquisition policies can be broad or narrow, and may be closely adhered to or, at one's peril, ignored. The 1978 *Directory of Archives and Manuscript Repositories in the United States* (*DAMRUS*) was the first national directory of repositories to contain a statement of Materials Solicited, and in the second edition in 1988, 4,560 repositories are listed. These statements vary greatly in their range. The Montana Historical Society provides an example of a narrow policy, which states for Materials Solicited:

> Materials relating to Montana, the Pacific Northwest and the northern Plains, with particular emphasis on political, social and

cultural activities of the post-1910 era. Will also accept materials outside normal areas of acquisition to ensure preservation if a collection appears in danger of destruction or damage.[5]

At the other end of the collecting range is the State Historical Society of Wisconsin, which lists as its desiderata:

> Wisconsin history and government, and National materials relating to labor, industry, agriculture, socialism, civil rights, student activism, contemporary social, economic, and political movements, and mass communications. Will also accept manuscripts, maps, sound recordings, and visual documents which relate to other areas in American history, with emphasis on the upper Midwest and the Great Lakes region.[6]

This broader approach may reflect the SHSW's location, which is on the campus of the University of Wisconsin at Madison, and the fact that its library acts as the American history library of the university.

Other institutions have variations on these two approaches, with some collecting more broadly than others. West Virginia University at Morgantown, for instance, established a narrow policy:

> Materials relating to West Virginia history; the history of Appalachia and the upper Ohio Valley; the coal industry; labor history; and genealogy, including personal papers; business records; State, county, and local government records; photographs; maps; recordings; tapes; and films.[7]

The University of California at Santa Barbara extends its policy beyond its specific geographic area:

> Civil War, Reconstruction, slavery, westward movement, California and local history, birth control, and fine printing history. Will also accept materials related to all teaching areas of the University.[8]

That last statement, about teaching areas, is typical of the larger university collections. Materials are collected in support of the faculty and courses offered. Quite often it is faculty members, working on specific projects, who bring in or arrange for the curator to contact the holder of collections of books or manuscripts. For instance, after completing work on the biography of Governor Frank O. Lowden of Illinois (1861–1943; governor, 1917–1921), Professor William T. Hutchinson of the University of Chicago arranged to have the governor's papers donated to the university library in 1950. And, speaking of the University of Chicago, its acquisition policy certainly reflects the academic interests of the research departments, especially in the humanities and social sciences. The Materials Solicited statement in *DAMRUS* for the University of Chicago is:

> 20th century European and American intellectual history; South Asian cultural and social history; American sociology and anthropology; Czech and Slovak immigration history; development and social control of atomic energy; and the history of The University of Chicago and related institutions, boards, governing bodies, and individuals. Will also accept other materials supporting the teaching and research programs of the University.[9]

DAMRUS, therefore, is a good starting place for researchers looking for institutions that collect in their areas of interest. They should also look closely at the stated acquisition policies vis-à-vis the actual holdings of each repository, which are also listed in summary fashion. When asked to state their acquisition policy, it seems that many institutions merely related it to their current holdings, in effect stating that since this is what they have, this must be what they collect! The sudden intrusion of birth control and fine printing in the Santa Barbara entry above indicates an *ex post facto* acquisition statement (although I could be wrong), and the statement of the Morgantown (West Virginia) Public Library that ends with "Will also accept all historical materials," leaves one wondering if that is a policy at all! Some policies that may seem humorous or frivolous merely draw our attention to the broad interests of the research public and the collections that are out there. The Bridgeport Public Library in Connecticut, for instance, lists as its solicitation policy:

> Materials on Bridgeport and regional activities in greater Bridgeport area, pertaining to government, business, labor, ethnic groups, community organizations, health, welfare and reli-

gion. Circus materials (especially pertaining to P. T. Barnum and associates) also solicited.[10]

The Motor Bus Society of West Trenton, New Jersey, indicated that its acquisition policy was what one would expect:

> Material relating to the manufacture and operation of motor buses and trolley buses in North America, including photographs and vehicle construction/operational data. Will also accept other historical documents of a selected nature.[11]

Not all acquisition policies have the same impelling rationale of a motor bus society collecting material relating to motor buses. The Glendale Public Libraries in Glendale, California, for instance, lists as its acquisition policy: "Materials related to local history and to cats and cat genealogy. Will also accept materials related to California history."[12]

DAMRUS casts a wide net and provides information on collections of psychics and psychic readings, UFOs, the Loch Ness monster and Bigfoot, and Niagara Falls hotel registers.[13] *Archives-USA* incorporates all of these entries under the "Repository Search" facility and the name of the repository as given above.

The scattering of subject collections across the institutional spectrum is a natural result of following many paths in creating an acquisition policy and conducting a search for collections. The curator follows the professional literature to see who is producing what, and looks at the appropriate newsletters, bulletins and informational handouts to keep abreast of who is where and what is going on: who is getting promoted (demotions are never reported), who is retiring (an ideal time to begin the solicitation, but in some cases too late) and, indeed, who has just died.

Leads to new acquisitions develop from the literature about the collecting field. Who is contributing to it; who are the superstars? Who might reasonably have material of interest to the repository? It need not always be the primary figure in the field, and, in fact, it requires insight on the part of the curator to find out who the secondary figures are who have an association with the primary figures. Some of Theodore Roosevelt's political methods are revealed in the papers of a lesser known kingmaker (Lemuel Quigg) who managed a gubernatorial campaign for the great man.[14] A broader understanding of most important figures is enhanced by the papers of their colleagues or coparticipants.

The point is that if it is localized or specialized enough, an acquisition policy can be meaningful and attainable. However, if a repository decides to solicit the papers of major twentieth-century American authors there is a competitive field that has to be accommodated. There is only one John Steinbeck. If the University of Virginia gets his papers, what will Berkeley, Texas and Michigan do? They will obviously approach other twentieth-century American authors or their heirs, and there are many of them. But what if MIT, Berkeley and Chicago decide that their acquisition policies are for the papers of major atomic scientists? Each has a right to make such a claim and pursue it. If Chicago is the first to acquire the papers of Enrico Fermi, can Szilard and Oppenheimer and Teller be far behind? It may not happen, but with Fermi in hand Chicago could go to the other scientists and make the argument that for research purposes it is better to have their papers in the same facility as those of their colleagues. There is one principle that curators try to follow when building a collection, and that is the "build from strength" strategy. Chicago, however, moved towards social control of atomic energy, and built its holdings on its strength in that niche with collections such as The Association of Oak Ridge Engineers and Scientists and Related Groups, the Atomic Scientists of Chicago, the Emergency Committee of Atomic Scientists, the Federation of Atomic Scientists, the Associations of Scientists for Atomic Education, and a number of collections of similar associations.

Tracking down sources is not an off-hand activity; the curator must spend considerable time and intellectual energy on the process. It is not sufficient to read the obituaries every morning and, depending on what is reported there, decide whose papers to "go after." Contacts must be cultivated. The curator must either become intimately familiar with the field and what is happening in it, or must have the assistance of colleagues, such as faculty members or staff specialists who are interested and follow the field closely. It is perhaps the highest art of the manuscript curator to recognize greatness early and to make early contacts with those in special fields who will undoubtedly rise to greatness and produce the richest papers. That is not easy, and can just as well result in shelves and shelves of papers of unknowns who showed promise but no performance. On the other hand, the curator must also try to recognize mediocrity or trendiness, and not mistake popularity for substance. Unfortunately, repositories are full of the papers of writers, politicians, and social activists who are unrecognizable to later generations. It is in these cases that the terms of a gift, with an institutional commitment to process, protect and provide the collection forever, become a burden.

The competitive nature of collecting, however, may not be much of a factor in a local institution dedicated to collecting materials on local individuals, families, businesses or events. If there is but one collecting agency in the area, the staff there may have little concern about others outside the area taking an interest in their community or social leaders. The personal family papers of the early settlers of Springfield are probably not going to be competed for by remote repositories. The only time that conflicts might arise is if a member of the family who became a local outstanding leader has risen to greatness outside of the community, at which point others may well be interested in acquiring the great one's papers.

Building from strength is especially important if staff and space are a concern of the repository (and I know of none where it is not!), because an overextended acquisition policy can cause major disruptions in the institution. Much as the staff of a department could be held accountable for their excesses, the upper levels of administration cannot be completely exonerated. An acquisition policy cannot be made in a vacuum, and any department of special collections is still answerable to higher levels of administration. Acquisition policies must be agreeable to all in the interest of the institution. It is unlikely that an academic library would suddenly announce that it is instituting a major policy to acquire feline stud books without appropriate internal agreement. It is valid to collect anything, as long as such collecting is seen as supporting the mission, aims and goals of the institution as represented by research-in-progress, course offerings, a real or anticipated audience, and facilities to house and administer the material collected.

On the point of adequate facilities, most manuscript and archival institutions are pushing against space barriers, but one rarely sees an announcement to the effect that institution X has decided to cease adding to its holdings until its facilities for storing materials are enlarged. Archives—that is, holders of institutional records—have a more difficult time with this problem than do collectors of personal papers. Formal archives exist at the end of the chain of paperwork management, and through appraisal evaluations and scheduling they are committed to receive institutional documents at some point in that life—when they are no longer needed for administrative or other purposes and are retired. The dilemma is much like that of Lucy and Ethel (in an episode of the television program "I Love Lucy") in the chocolate factory, standing at the end of the conveyor belt, receiving the finished bon-bons and putting them in fancy boxes. As the conveyor speeds up, delivering more chocolates per minute, the two are at a loss as to how to keep up, and begin stuffing them in their mouths, pockets, blouses, and anywhere else. The solution, of course, is to control the flow, with reduction of the quantity of chocolates or the speed of the conveyor. The archival analogy is what David Mearns once cited as a "phenomenon consorting with a quandary."[15] The phenomenon is the increase of paperwork production in society, and the quandary is what to do with it.

The manuscript administrator has an option not always available to the archivist, in that manuscript materials that are peripheral to the core of the acquisition policy can be rejected. The only other alternative is to increase space, and if not in the main location of the collection, then off-site.

The Manuscript Division of the Library of Congress, whose collections have more than tripled in the past thirty years, was initially relieved of crowding by a move from the old annex, or Adams building, to the more spacious Madison building, but ultimately had to house its unprocessed backlog off-site in Landover, Maryland. The New York Public Library manuscripts overflow is located in an annex blocks from the main building, on West Forty-third Street. In increasing numbers, repositories both on and off campuses are finding expansion difficult in the vicinity of the original facility because of lack of available land. This is especially true in urban areas. Also, the pace of the production of library and archival materials has quickened to the point where growth becomes almost exponential.

The alternative to loss of historical materials by their being squeezed out of overburdened institutions is the creation of more collecting institutions, perhaps becoming very specialized in their acquisition policies. Accurate figures do not exist, but there are some indicators of such growth. When, in 1961, the National Historical Publications Commission's (NHPC's) *Guide to Archives and Manuscripts in the United States*[16] appeared, it contained information on 1,300 archives and manuscript repositories. However, a more precise indication of the national number of repositories holding manuscripts and/or archives may be projected from the example of Washington State. In the Hamer *Guide*, Washington State had 50 repositories represented. In the 1978 *DAMRUS* it had 150, but when Washington did a spin-off volume in 1981 covering only the state, it listed 500 collecting repositories.[17] It is not surprising that in the face of these figures and the sporadic means used for reporting the research materials in these publications, the researcher feels uneasy about stating that his or her quest for pertinent material has been thorough.

The implications of this growth (or at least better reporting procedures), of the space situation at the larger, older institutions, and of the increase in new institutions are important to the question of collecting policies. As stated earlier, the older institutions are forced to be more selective if they are to provide the researcher with processed collections in workable facilities that maintain collection preservation standards. Newer institutions try to shape their acquisition policies so that they are not immediately confronted with major competition from those already in the field, or they work out cooperative agreements to share the field. Some state societies, such as Wisconsin's, have agreements with the state university system to distribute the collecting activities across the state, and not try to crowd everything into the inadequate facility on the Madison campus. In some respects, the National Archives has accomplished the same results with the distribution of Presidential libraries across the nation. If one follows that rationale, it is not difficult for the National Archives to justify why, long ago (1960s), it regionalized its holdings so that it was taking care of the records of agency branches outside of Washington by housing their archives within the region of creation, with staff and facilities under the National Archives and oversight by the central office in Washington. Since most regional government offices deal with regional issues, this proved to be a boon to researchers in those regions, and the National Archives has since made a virtue out of necessity by touting the "democratic" nature of its service—bringing the research materials to the researcher. It is thus the only national research institution that has "branches," consisting of the Presidential libraries and the regional archives, distributed throughout the country.

Since they are so central to the future of scholarship, and since they impact on the space needs of an institution, acquisition policies are not among those internal affairs that are normally kept a secret. Institutions are wise to announce to the world their collecting strategies and goals. We have seen that many repositories publish their acquisition policies in *DAMRUS*, and many institutions do so in pamphlet form, to send to prospective donors and to remind the staff of what the institution is attempting to acquire. A published policy statement can also be a handy device for refusing those collections that are not wanted but are offered with varying degrees of insistence. If the prominent alumnus insists (through the chancellor or provost) that the career-long accumulation of data on Alpine flora and fauna is an absolutely indispensable collection for the institution to have, the curator's citing the acquisition policy that limits collections to material dealing with Great Lakes history and ethnology can be a great deterrent. The curator has to be prepared, of course, to suggest another institution that is avidly seeking Alpiniana, and recommend it to the donor. A cardinal rule is that one does not alienate donors, present or future, because one never knows exactly how broadly their altruistic or eleemosynary spirit extends. Should they be willing to donate a wing to the library to house their magnificent collection, the curator might have to think about consulting with the chancellor and provost, as well as the library director, before making a decision. Research rooms, wings, entire floors and buildings carry names that attest to the largess of alumni and friends. The terms of such gifts are sometimes difficult to reject, in light of the financial relief that they may provide to the administration. On the other hand, long-term care of such facilities may be a burden in disguise.

Acquisition policies, therefore, are beneficial both to attract wanted collections and to fend off those that are less desirable. Staff awareness of the policies can be important when staff members come in contact with people who have manuscript material or know of the existence and location of such collections. The importance of the social occasions that staff attend is sometimes significant. Small talk about "where do you work, and what do you do" has more than once resulted in a lead for new collections hidden in attics or old trunks. One of the ties that bind manuscript curators together is the tale of "the great acquisition," and the peculiar twists and turns of fortune that led to it. The routine cases are mentioned only in the regular "Reports of Recent Acquisitions."

THE JOYS OF SOLICITATION

Establishing an acquisition policy can be relatively easy: implementing it can be extremely difficult. A savvy curator knows where to go, besides *Who's Who*, to seek out collections. Many initial contacts are made through others. On a campus it may be a knowledgeable faculty member who provides initial contact and puts the curator in touch with a prospective donor. There may be a notice in the newspaper of a publication or even the death of a notable figure whose work fits into the acquisition policy of the institution. While obituaries may be leads worth following, there are a few things wrong with them as sources.

1) If one curator reads the notice, it can be assumed that others have also read it.

2) It is a bit late to be thinking about approaching a donor if extreme unction has already been administered, unless the death was untimely and the victim was cut down in early or midcareer.

3) With the principal gone, the curator must deal with the heirs. That implies lawyers, wills, property settlements, and just plain family pride, often leading to an overassessment by the heirs of the value of the deceased's papers. Most curators find it better, therefore, to negotiate with the creators-*cum*-donors, who often do not have such an inflated impression of their own worth and can be quite generous with their papers.

Depending on the circumstances, therefore, negotiations for papers can be delicate in some cases, and very businesslike in others. There are many stories at archival conventions of the reluctant surviving spouse, being wooed by many repositories and obviously holding out for higher stakes, which usually means peripheral perquisites, since all of the institutions are probably asking that the deceased's papers be donated. This attitude and wooing of donors sometimes results in placement of collections in repositories on the basis of old school ties rather than research appropriateness.

There is then the tale of the papers of Ernest Hemingway and his widow, Mary. Mary Hemingway gathered her husband's papers after his suicide in 1961 from a variety of locations in which he had "stashed" them over the years, including the storeroom behind Sloppy Joe's Bar in Key West, Florida, the Ritz Hotel in Paris, the Hemingway's former Cuban home, the Finca Vigia, as well as a Havana bank vault. She even got permission from President Kennedy—although they had never met—to go to Cuba to retrieve what material there was as Castro was about to make the house into a museum. This took place soon after the Bay of Pigs, when Americans could not travel to Cuba. Hemingway had thought of giving his papers to the New York Public Library, but arrangements never materialized, and meanwhile the major col-

lecting institutions, including the Library of Congress, were wooing the widow in hopes of winning, not her hand but her
husband's literary legacy. She felt strongly, however, about leaving
the papers to an institution where they would be prominent, and
not just one of a number of collections of famous authors, and also
where some mementoes and trophies could be exhibited, including an antelope head and a lion that she had bagged on a safari.

After President Kennedy's assassination Mary Hemingway met
Jacqueline Kennedy's secretary at a party in 1964, undoubtedly
learned of the plans for a Presidential library, and offered the collection to it. The rest, as they say, is history, and the papers of Ernest
Hemingway are now in their own room, with a curator, the antelope head and the supine lion, in the John F. Kennedy Presidential
Library in Boston,[18] a perfect tribute to the triumph of emotion
over logic.

Building from strength can lead to a broadened acquisition
policy, as some papers coming in for one reason contain significant
material relating to one or more different fields, and the collections
begin branching off. It is rare that individuals are so single-minded
that one does not find secondary themes. The Einstein papers, for
instance, are concerned not only with physics, but also with his
developing interest in Zionism. Felix Frankfurter, jurist, also had a
strong interest in Zionism, which is reflected in his papers. Almost
every academic has materials relating to the institution with which
he or she was associated, so that one finds faculty meeting minutes,
information about campus politics, tenure committee files, and related material, depending on how active the subject was in campus
life and politics.

Indeed, there is hardly a collection of manuscripts that does
not contain some surprises. Who knows what activities lurk in the
papers of men and women? Papers of jurists that contain materials
on Southern plantation economics;[19] papers of law firms that contain significant historical material on the Agent Orange problem in
Vietnam;[20] papers of journalists that contain significant analyses of
the works of a major poet, as in the Hi Simons papers (chapter 2).

There are surprises in corporate or government archives too.
A discussion of the physique of Yuan Shih-Kai in the records of
the Department of State may seem, at first, to be an interesting
departure from stodgy government business. But, in its context, it
is government business, or at least of that part of government dealing with foreign affairs. It should not be surprising to find letters

from Wyoming farm women relating to their health problems, or the harrowing tales of the 1938 Atlantic hurricane, preserved in oral histories taken by the WPA Writers Project.[21] One just has to rationalize the process, and know that records deal with the operations of agencies, which have defined functions. Some archivists are making a point of these relationships by promoting the concept of the rediscovery of "provenance" (who created the records in the context of what function) as the basis for archival description rather than subject description.[22] The contents of manuscript collections do not conform to a similar logic or rational order. Although one *may* know that the American minister in Peking in 1911 was Harriet Monroe's brother-in-law (which is rather esoteric knowledge), that may not immediately lead the researcher to consult the Monroe papers for a physical description of Yuan Shih-Kai!

When an institution begins the acquisition process with a prospective donor it is reasonable to assume that communication or solicitation will start with an initial letter. The letter is normally brief and to the point, states the intention of the institution to open discussions on the disposition of the subject's papers, states why it is appropriate that the collection come to X institution, and asks for a chance to talk further to the prospective donor, leading to a visit and inspection of the materials. The letter probably contains a brochure about the institution, its collections, and collection policy and discusses prospective gifts, tax benefits and other aspects of gifts. Inclusion of a well-written, professionally printed brochure could impress the donor with the seriousness of the institution's collecting program.

It may be, of course, that the prospective donor is a colleague of a faculty member, or sits on some board with a member of the manuscript institution's administration. These relationships may be points of entrée through personal contacts, after appropriate briefing sessions with the manuscript curator. There are as many ways to approach a prospective donor as there are donors, and perhaps the only totally prohibited approach is to telephone the bereaved family on the day of the obituary, and ask about the disposition of the deceased's literary remains.

This last point takes us back to the curator's stress on early contact with someone whose papers are important to the institution's collecting program. Curators often find it better to deal with the creator of the material than with heirs. Family members not only may have an exaggerated concept of the monetary value of the collection, but they rarely are aware of the research importance of a collection. Oddly enough, adult children, and even spouses, often have little idea about what the deceased did on a day-to-day basis, what issues were being addressed, decisions made, inspirations received, correspondence carried on, significant discoveries revealed, and liaisons negotiated. Dealing with the creator of the collection often provides important keys to the papers and reveals some of the undocumented scenarios that were followed. There is a term cropping up in archival studies based on one used by Max Weber called "charismatic hierarchies." The archivist sees this as meaning the power behind the throne, or the aide behind the great person. Sometimes the charismatic hierarchy is the unheralded spouse who, in reality, is providing inspiration, direction and purpose to the main player. If the curator gains an understanding of these relationships it may shift the collecting emphasis to include the papers of behind-the-scenes individuals, where the *real* story is to be found. Perhaps a retired and increasingly philosophical celebrity will reveal such relationships, whereas family or heirs may have no inkling that such political, academic or other liaisons had even taken place.

John A. Garraty, speaking in the context of a biographer, has a message for manuscript curators in his quote from Edmund Gosse: "The Widow is the worst of all the diseases of biography. She is the triumph of the unfittest. . . . She paints her husband quite smooth and plump, with a high light on his forehead and a sanctimonious droop of his eyelid."[23] This astute observation, however, is not always valid. A number of presidential widows can be credited with perpetuating the reputations of their husbands through their own efforts to keep their papers together, protect them from deterioration through proper storage, and present them to the research public by donating them to major research libraries.[24] Conversely, the "cleansing" of collections by survivors has often left future biographers and historians frustrated over the obfuscation of reality in the effort to "protect" a reputation from imagined denigration beyond the grave.[25]

LEAVING A TRAIL

At the point of writing a solicitation letter, the curator has taken the first documentable step in attracting a collection. There may be a response to the letter that requires further communication; there can be evaluations of material, lists of contents, shipping instructions, legal documents transferring title, and all of the other paraphernalia that accompany a negotiated gift. The curator prepares to handle all of this future paperwork in an orderly way by establishing a case file on the prospective collection. The case file (some manuscript people call it the "collection file," or even the "lead file," which provides leads to new collections, which further illustrates the lack of standard vocabulary in the field) will contain all or most of the documentation relating to the pursuit and, one hopes, the receipt of the collection. It has obvious utility as a management tool but also can contain the corporate memory should the solicitation drag out over years, and it can often be helpful to the researcher. There can be delays when donors are approached in midcareer and make a continuing commitment to the institution, with increments of material arriving from time to time. The case file probably also contains a vita of the person whose papers are being solicited, "memos to the file" reporting on telephone conversations with the donor, and any description of the papers that can be prepared, perhaps sketchy at first and becoming more detailed as the negotiations go on.

If the institution has an automated database of collections and solicitations, or is a member of a national database, such as the Research Libraries Information Network (RLIN) or the Online Computer Library Center (OCLC), this might seem to be the time to place the initial entry into the automated file which would announce it to interested researchers. But, since the collection probably has not yet been procured, or, if it has, is presumably unprocessed, the institution may find it unwise to advertise its existence immediately, because it could attract researchers when it is in no condition to be served to them. The general rule curators follow is: an institution does not advertise an unprocessed collection or one to which it does not yet hold title.

It is an axiom that no collection should be accepted unseen. There is no guarantee that a great person will have great papers. On inspection it may be revealed that all of the great papers that were expected were left in the office files at the agency or corporation where the subject worked, and are now part of its archives, while what remains is a collection of Christmas cards from famous people, congratulatory letters, some annotated speeches, and newspaper clippings. Interesting as these items may be, they are not the stuff that produces significant research. Collections are judged by substance, and large ones are often measured by how many books and Ph.D. dissertations can be derived from them. Not all collections measure up, especially small ones, yet even small assemblages may be supportive of the larger ones, because they may add a personal element or a counterview of the subject. None of these things can be evaluated from afar; someone has to inspect the collection, and that calls for the curator or staff to make a solicitation trip.

The solicitation trip is extremely important for the proper evaluation of offered materials. As negotiations approach a climax, the curator arranges to visit the donor or, at the very least, to have a capable, noncompeting colleague in the donor's area make the visit. The curator then tries to be left alone with the papers, be they in office, den, basement or attic, for a period of time long enough to look them over. The first evaluation, and the easiest, is the extent of the collection. How many shelves would it fill? Are all the materials of similar size, or are there a lot of things in long tubes, oversized sheets, perhaps posters or maps? What is the general condition of the documents? Are they neatly located in filing cabinets, stacked in cardboard cartons, stuffed in drawers, laid flat on bookshelves and all other surfaces around the room, or scattered helter-skelter? Is there a lot of printed matter; are there many books, photo albums and scrapbooks?

What about their physical condition? Is the room hot, cold, moist, dry? Is there the smell of mold? Do conditions seem conducive to vermin? Is there a leaky roof or dripping pipes?

Inside their containers—desk drawers, filing cabinets, cardboard boxes—are the papers and other items neatly placed in folders and labeled, or randomly shoved in? What is the preponderant form of material—personal letters, business or professional correspondence, reports of various kinds, files about other people, professional case files, lecture notes, book or article drafts, galleys and page proofs? Left alone with the collection for an hour or so, the curator should be able to sample the material, study a folder here, a scrapbook there, and get a pretty good idea of content.

Satisfied that the papers are significant enough to accession, which means a commitment to keep them in the institution's stacks forever, the curator then enters into the final negotiations to close the deal and transfer the material to the repository (or decline the offer). There is the chance, of course, that inspection will reveal a room full of insignificant material, in which case diplomacy comes into full play. How does one tell an alumnus who makes significant financial contributions to the institution that the papers are not really what the curator had in mind, and, although nice, they are not of any great research value? It is at that point that the curator may enlist the assistance of the library director, provost, chancellor, or perhaps even better, an understanding friend of the donor who can act as a mediator.

If, however, the papers are quite suitable for accessioning, it is then necessary to take steps to legally transfer them. The most common form of transfer is through a deed of gift, which conveys title to the papers from the donor to the institution. We will discuss the deed of gift and its importance to researchers more in chapter 8, but its provisions have to be clear before the repository begins doing anything to the collection.

One of the things that makes donation of valuable materials such as personal papers possible is the tax allowance permitted the donor. If someone had a Peter Paul Rubens painting it would be considered a capital asset for the market value that attached to it. If that Rubens were then given to a public institution it would be appropriate to consider it the same as a cash gift. With certain limitations, the appraised market value of the Rubens could be considered the same as a monetary gift and deducted from the donor's income tax. The same applies to personal papers. If they have intrinsic market value and can be appraised, then giving them to an institution can be equivalent to making a cash donation.

After legal and financial questions are settled, the curator is prepared to begin the process of transferring the material from the donor to the recipient institution.

Of course, all of the above is "textbook," and things rarely happen according to that infamous model, but in the case of major accessions the model is fairly typical.

Following Leads

With the safe deposit of a new collection in the repository the process of solicitation does not stop. The negotiations with the donor may well have led to the discovery of other materials in the hands of colleagues, antagonists, superiors or supporters. This new knowledge can provide leads to new collections (indeed, as noted, a solicitation file in one institution may be called a lead file in another). The contents of the documents themselves can be revealing. If there is significant correspondence, it might reveal lines of communication not previously suspected and uncover friendships and professional liaisons that could suggest complementary material in the papers of another scientist, author, composer, etc. These, then, become targets for further solicitation, with the opening statement that the repository already has the papers of their friend or colleague.

This enlargement of the circle of correspondents may even extend to the family. If, as in the example from chapter 1, Calhoun wrote to his wife's sister, Harriet Monroe, did she have other sisters or brothers to whom he would have written? How big was the Monroe family, and what other interesting lives did they lead besides publishing a significant poetry magazine in Chicago and accompanying a foreign service officer throughout China? It is these questions that lead to expanding rings of solicitation and acquisition, and no matter how definitive one tries to be, curators invariably find lines running to tempting new fields.

There is also the urge to "round out" the collection by going to the circle of friends. With whom did Harriet Monroe correspond, and what are their papers like? Was she methodical in keeping all incoming letters and copies of her letters going out? If not, one would have only one side of the correspondence—the incoming—which is comparable to sitting in a room and listening to someone hold a telephone conversation. The Harriet Monroe letters, at least the signed ones, are not to be found in Harriet Monroe's papers, but rather in the papers of the many recipients. How much does the curator want to pursue?

One method that scholars use to find those leads is to advertise. Every week, in the book review or literary supplement sections of major newspapers there appear the little squibs that say something like: "Am engaged in research on Lemuel Quigg and would appreciate information about any letters or collections of Quigg material. M.Q., Box 268, this paper."

Such notices occasionally appear in professional historical journals also, but it is rare for manuscript curators to resort to such methods of advertising. First, they know that the search for manuscript materials is global, and cannot be satisfied by advertising in a few papers read in a few cities by a few people. Secondly, manuscript curators are much more aware of traditional ways of tracking down manuscript materials. They know about *NUCMC*, the Hamer *Guide*, Hinding's *Women's History Sources*, the Burton *Guide to Manuscripts in the Presidential Libraries*, Chadwyck-Healey's *National Inventory of Documentary Sources* and *ArchivesUSA*, the variety of repository guides and finding aids, and more recently, the possibility of searching RLIN and other networks to locate names and collections. Manuscript curators also communicate on the electronic mail networks, and many belong to the plethora of "listserves" that are cropping up for the use of archivists, manuscript curators, rare book librarians, editors, and most other specialists in the information field.

On rare occasions a repository will purchase a few items to fill out its holdings, and staff members scan dealer catalogs that specialize in almost any collecting area—the Civil War, railroads, women artists, maritime history, twentieth-century authors, political personalities, jazz, etc. It is rare, however, that manuscripts are purchased with an eye to supplement existing holdings, because prices are high. Dealer catalogs do not serve the institutional collector as much as they serve the private collector. A good yardstick curators use is to ask the question "What will this one letter of a Revolutionary War leader, costing $15,000, add to the research value of my collection of that person's papers?" Manuscript collections are valuable only in the broad scope of content, in-depth coverage of events or insight into the human condition. Rarely does a single document so change a collection's research value that it would be worth the cost. Better to have a friendly philanthropist buy the $15,000 document and then donate it to the repository, although the $15,000 given directly (and unrestricted) might be of greater benefit to the institution.

A different case is often made for a particularly informative diary, or a letter book containing a run of correspondence. Some institutions buy entire collections. It is notable, however, that the power of the purse has not necessarily made them the premier collecting institutions in the country. Donors may feel more loyalty to their alma mater and give their papers for a simple tax deduction rather than sell them to another institution for immediate return, which would be taxable income. If one looks at the donors of major collections it becomes apparent that many do not want a large cash settlement, and they may even spread out their gifts by segmenting the collection and giving portions of it in successive tax years so that their single-year donation is not too large. In

Presidential libraries prospective donors are often appealed to based on that old collegiality of the administration under which the donors served. It does not always work: some administrations are less collegial than might appear in the newspapers, and cabinet members' papers may end up as collections scattered over the special collections landscape.

Finally, there is the rarest of all methods for acquiring collections—by trade. Trades happen only when two repositories find that they have each somehow assembled or accumulated collections more properly belonging to the other. Perhaps it was the result of a bad acquisition policy, or an ill-advised accession, or, more likely, an old collection brought in for good reason at one time but now isolated as a result of a shift in acquisition policy or the inability to build from strength. That odd collection of an atomic physicist at a Memphis repository might therefore be traded to Princeton for its odd collection of a Tennessee businessman.

Curators are reluctant to trade collections, or part with them in any way, however, because of the donor factor. If at the time of the gift a deed was prepared, property changed hands in good faith. The donor (and ultimately the donor's family) thought that the literary remains of the beloved family member were going to be in X university, the beloved's old school, and later they find that the remains are being unceremoniously shipped across country to an alien institution. The alumni fund takes a sudden dip in that year's gifts, and no one in the development office can figure out why.

It is also not unheard of that collections will arrive unannounced. Although this most often happens with small parcels of papers when someone is clearing out a desk and finds a group of letters that he or she presumes will be of interest to Y historical society, it occasionally happens on a larger scale. There is at least one case of a major political collection coming to a repository because the president of the university encountered the politician socially, a chat revealed the existence of a large collection of papers, an invitation to donate was extended, and when the curator showed up for work one day there it was on the loading dock, with no advance notice that negotiations were in progress. An obvious breakdown in communication between the manuscripts staff and the administration had taken place, and the staff was saddled with an acquisition that initially overwhelmed its resources and, indeed, took over ten years to schedule for processing, thus delaying researcher access.

Some of these conjectures may be exaggerated, of course, but they remain important to the curator, whose job it is to build a collection of research materials, to honor those who should be honored, to become the final resting place of the literary remains of the repository's heroes and heroines, and to woo future donors.

But curatorial concentration on saving the papers and records of "heros and heroines" should not be exaggerated. It is often the villains who have the richest collections, and the old saying, "I would rather have two minutes with the Devil than two hours with a saint," has some truth to it for researchers as well as journalists. Unfortunately, campus or institutional politics sometimes cloud the vision of those who would benefit most from bringing in controversial collections. The long and tortured search by former President Nixon to find a home for his papers was frustrated by the narrow views of faculty and administration at Duke University and the University of Southern California. In rather sanctimonious statements the faculty, including the history faculty, condemned the idea of their institution housing the papers of such a "villain." As a result, the Nixon Library is at present the only Presidential library since Hoover's that is not administered by the federal government through the National Archives, and it is located in Yorba Linda, a suburb of Los Angeles in Southern California. As it turns out, the Nixon vice presidential and presidential *materials* are at this writing at the National Archives College Park facility (Archives II) on the campus of the University of Maryland and, coincidentally, just across the campus golf course from the Spiro Agnew papers, which are located in the university's McKeldin Library. The Nixon materials were seized by the government after revelations about the Watergate tapes and after the administrator of General Services, Arthur Sampson, signed an agreement with Nixon about his papers that was not well received by the U.S. Congress.

In rejecting the Nixon materials on "political" grounds, Duke and the University of California ultimately did themselves out of a magnificent research source that documents one of the more stirring and controversial periods of twentieth-century American history. Every manuscript curator knows what I stated earlier: one measures the value of collections by the number of books and doctoral dissertations that could be written from them. Historians began mining the Nixon lode as soon as the papers were first opened to the public in 1988, and the traffic to the Archives II facility where they are kept increases monthly.

Perhaps one can take resigned consolation in the fact that it is not only the "villains" who are treated as Nixon was by university faculty. The community around Harvard fought vigorously to keep the John F. Kennedy Library from the Cambridge neighborhood, even though it was to replace a Massachusetts Transit Authority (MTA) car barn, and the library ended up far from Harvard, at the tip of Columbia Point in Boston. The change turned out to be beneficial to the University of Massachusetts–Boston, which already had a small campus there. The state then parlayed the combination of the two facilities into a mini-research center by locating the new Massachusetts State Archives between the two.

In another case, Ronald Reagan ran into difficulties with Stanford University when the faculty rose up to protest locating his library on or next to the campus, on the grounds that the "tourist traffic" would disrupt campus life. Archivists will attest to the fact that there is more "traffic" on such campuses on one fall Saturday afternoon in the football season than a Presidential library generates in an entire year. The Reagan Presidential Library is now located in Simi Valley, California, and is not affiliated with any other research or educational institution, although it is one of the libraries administered by the National Archives and Records Administration.

When the researcher is confronted with the facts of a collection's location and contents, and questions why it is where it is and why it seems to be incomplete, all of the conditions mentioned in the previous pages contribute to the archivist's answer. Much of what happens in pursuing and capturing personal papers depends on chance, which means that the researcher cannot rely on logic to explain the location. There must be extensive probing if one is to discover why certain collections are where they are and why they contain what they do. Archivists and manuscript curators have devoted considerable time and energy to the process of informing researchers of collection locations and contents. We will move on to a discussion of what researchers should know about those processes in later chapters.

NOTES

1. Jacques Barzun, *Clio and the Doctors* (Chicago: University of Chicago Press, 1974), 50.

2. National Center for Education Statistics, *Digest of Education Statistics, 1993* (Washington: National Center for Education Statistics, 1993), 168, 173, 240, 243, 290–291, 295–296.

3. Ibid., 290, 296.

4. Gary M. Peterson and Trudy Huskamp Peterson, ibid., 24–38; Edward C. Kemp, *Manuscript Solicitation for Libraries, Special Collections, Museums and Archives* (Littleton, Colo.: Libraries Unlimited, 1978), 141.

5. *DAMRUS*, entry MT530–500, p. 347.

6. Ibid., WI346–720, p. 688.

7. Ibid., WV650–520, p. 682.

8. Ibid., CA774–800, p. 56.

9. Ibid., IL170–884, p. 150.

10. Ibid., CT36–80, p. 72.

11. Ibid., NJ918–520, p. 379.

12. Ibid., CA290–280, p. 30.

13. See the entry for the Association for Research and Enlightenment for psychics and psychic readings, Virginia Beach, Va. (VA810–40, p. 640); the International Fortean Organization (INFO) for UFOs, Loch Ness and Bigfoot (MD285–360, p. 247); and the Niagara Falls Public Library for hotel registers (NY602–570, p. 451).

14. The Herbert R. Strauss Collection of Theodore Roosevelt Papers. The correspondence of Theodore Roosevelt and Lemuel E. Quigg, 1894–1919. Regenstein Library, Department of Special Collections, University of Chicago. Although the collection contains 102 letters *from* Roosevelt to Quigg, and 62 carbons of Quigg's replies, the National Union Catalog of Manuscript Collections lists this under the main entry *Roosevelt, Theodore* (MS64–812, p. 156). The University of Chicago's list of collections lists it under the Herbert R. Strauss Collection of Theodore Roosevelt Papers, whereas in reality it constitutes part of the papers of Lemuel E. Quigg.

15. Mearns, ibid., 318.

16. Hamer, ed., *Guide to Archives and Manuscripts in the United States.*

17. *Historical Records of Washington State: Records and Papers Held at Repositories* (Olympia, Wash.: Washington State Historical Records Advisory Board, 1981).

18. Megan Floyd Desnoyers, "The Journey to the John F. Kennedy Library," in "Ernest Hemingway: A Storyteller's Legacy," *Prologue: Quarterly of the National Archives* 24, no. 4 (winter 1992): 348. Additional details beyond the contents of the article were supplied by Ms. Desnoyers in conversation with the author, July 11, 1995.

19. See, for instance, Tennessee State Library and Archives, "The Jacob McGavock Dickinson Papers" (Revised). *Register Number 1.* Manuscript Section. Archives Division. Tennessee State Library and Archives. Nashville, Tenn., 1959/1964.

20. Feinberg and Associates, Washington, D.C.

21. Records of the Work Projects Administration (RG 69). Records of WPA Federal Project No. 1, Federal Writers' Project, 1935–1944. New England Regional Office Files.

22. Tom Nesmith, *Canadian Archival Studies and the Rediscovery of Provenance* (Metuchen, N.J.: The Scarecrow Press, Inc., 1993), passim.

23. John A. Garraty, ibid., chap. 8, "The Materials of Biography."

24. Ruth McWilliams, "Preparing for the Biographer: A Widow's Task," *Manuscripts* 36, no. 3 (summer 1984): 187–196.

25. For some British examples, see Ian Hamilton, *Keepers of the Flame* (Boston: Faber & Faber, 1994).

· 5 ·

Mapping the Roads to the Past

> Behind every finding aid there has to be a warm body
> somewhere.
>
> Hugh Taylor[1]

A recent book titled *Blue Highways*[2] used the term to denote the color of secondary roads on standard road maps in the United States. The book described the glories of traveling these routes if one wished to see the details of life in America, instead of the blurred view from the faster interstates. In today's analogy the electronic information networks are faster "information highways," and I would contend, then, that the traditional information paths are the slower, but often more interesting roads to the past. The maps that lead the researcher down those trails are the descriptive devices created by manuscript curators in the form of "finding aids," an arcane term that one curator declares "has no analogue in the real world."[3]

If any activity performed by manuscript curators has changed in the past decade, it is the process of describing collections. It is here that the computer has made a significant impact, and it naturally follows that it is here that professionals are waging open battles about tradition versus innovation. The literature is bringing all of the old standards out to the battlefield, where the outcome at this writing remains uncertain. But, although traditions are being questioned, there are some principles that appear immutable.

In the Fairfax County (Virginia) schools, library education begins early. In kindergarten students are taught the basics of books—what a title page is, what is meant by a binding, and other essentials. By the fourth grade they are taught the basics of library usage and how to orient themselves to the collections. One task they formerly had to perform was tantamount to cataloging books.

The students were given a sheet of paper divided in two columns. On the left were the names of authors, titles and subjects of books, in random sequence. The right column contained a list of Dewey Decimal Classification (DDC) numbers, in random sequence. The student was expected to draw lines connecting the appropriate DDC number to its matching author/title/subject entry. They were being taught how to use the library classification scheme, and, incidentally, the basics of cataloging! Today they are taught at the same age how to access catalog information through the library computer On-Line Public Access Catalog (OPAC).

It is not a quantum leap from those exercises to the students' being able to use any school or public library that employs DDC, which is probably the majority of such libraries in the country. It is also not difficult to imagine those same students entering college and learning the Library of Congress classification system or other sophisticated systems. It is also not beyond belief that by the time they are in college they will have learned more advanced computer catalog searching. It is already necessary to do automated catalog searching at most academic institutions. At some libraries there is also the option of using the "touch screen" catalog or a mouse, which do not even require a keyboard. Obviously, today's students are computer literate, at least in the library, and probably elsewhere.

However, take that same, bright student in graduate school and assign a project in the archives, or in special collections using personal papers, and he or she is probably lost. There is typically little or no training in using these special materials. There may or may not be a card catalog or card index, although some repositories now have descriptions in on-line catalogs. If there is a catalog, it does not have a classification scheme with familiar call numbers. The stacks are closed. The attendant provides something called a register, inventory, or guide that looks formidable. All of that is compounded by the problems and trials of finding and getting into Special Collections, the National Archives, or the Manuscript Room in the first place, and then finding that it is not open evenings or weekends.

When the neophyte makes the first approach to manuscripts or archives it soon becomes obvious that if the researcher moves from one repository to another there are no common systems or standards for access or for description. These limitations might well deter novices from using original sources, thereby depriving them of the joys and exhilaration of such research.

Archivists and manuscript curators know that there *are* "systems," even though they are not very sophisticated by library standards. The librarian has available a system that classifies all knowledge in the humanities, arts, sciences, technology, etc. With this universal scheme, the librarian attempts to place each work to be catalogued into its place in that scheme. It is very Linnaean in concept, in that Linnaeus classified species.

Archivists, however, rely on the system of provenance, which means that information does not reflect structures of universal knowledge as in library classification, but rather description reflects organizational structure and activities from which the information was created. The reference is not to some abstract classification of all knowledge, but to the explicit organization and function of the body that created the information, and the action that precipitated that creation. It is important, therefore, that the material or the information be structured in accordance with the structure of the creating body. Schellenberg is quite adamant about it:

> An archivist should not preestablish classes on the bases of factors other than provenance. Whenever such factors—time, place, or subject—are taken into account in establishing classes, records are likely to be arranged in violation of the basic archival principle of provenance.

He then goes on to state even more emphatically: "An archivist, in a word, should not attempt to develop a classification system at all."[4]

A wide variety of assumptions stems from that philosophy of description. The most prominent and pervading is the concept of the record group. This concept decreed that records are not formed into diverse "collections" or assemblages of material related according to some external scheme, such as universal classification, subjects, chronology, or any other that is specially devised. The record group concept, based on the principle of provenance, implies that records should remain together as true to the order of their creation as possible, and that records from one organization or function should not be mixed with records of another. The first "official" definition of the term "record group" came in the National Archives in February 1941, when it was defined as

> A major archival unit established somewhat arbitrarily with due regard to the principle of provenance and to the desirability of

making the unit of convenient size and character for the work
of arrangement and description and for the publication of inventories.[5]

This adoption of the record group by the National Archives was
aimed at creating information structures that mirror organizational
structures of agencies whose records the National Archives holds.[6]
The significance of this principle is that it turns around the traditional approach to information in that it drives the researcher to
approach information sources through the organization of mission,
function, and process, not of universal knowledge. Archivists believe that if one understands the mission and function of a corporate body, and how they are distributed or segmented throughout
an organization, information follows; and therefore, a researcher
should know the mission and functions of agencies and the processes carried out by their component parts—the offices, divisions,
and branches. The descriptive finding aid of archivists, therefore,
describes the functions and processes of each office whose records
are held, and it is up to the researcher to determine if these activities might possibly produce the documentation that is sought.[7]

THE REGISTER AND INVENTORY

The history of the archival "inventory" and its metamorphosis into
the personal papers "register" has been told often in the professional literature.[8] It is a story based on the struggles of an emerging
profession to discard nonarchival influences that were not pertinent to its needs and to develop new techniques for the records of
the nation. If one subscribes to the theories of Max Weber regarding the structure of bureaucracies and their hierarchical chain of
command, it is not difficult to understand the thinking of those
archivists who developed the archival inventory format for describing the records of a bureaucracy. Bureaucracies are structured with
each level of the government or corporation responsible and re-
sponsive to the level above, with policy decisions passed down
from the top and carried out according to the functions of the
lesser offices, each doing its part to contribute its expert knowledge
to the whole.

In such a system, the records naturally flow primarily from the
bottom up, with some lateral communications, usually for specific

purposes but ultimately adding to the overall purpose of the corporate body. Archivists express the function and purpose of the corporate body in a general statement at the highest level. The records created to express these functions and purposes are traditionally scanty but "evidential," incorporating the minutes of the highest board, the explication of policies based on actions and assumptions at the lower levels, and the statements of purpose generated to respond to those outside forces to which the corporation is responsible: stockholders, legislature, voters, or other groups.

The next level is that of initial organization for implementation, where officers are charged with formulating policy into action documents and structures for implementation, and monitoring the progress of the implementation, initiating practices, preparing procedures, and conducting oversight. The documents at this level reflect these activities, but can be understood only if the higher level of policy is understood. Policy is the driving force: management is the machinery that controls and steers it. Records at this management level, therefore, relate to procedural matters, budgets, structures, personnel practices, and communication with outside forces, such as contractors or other corporate bodies including governments, and contain the cumulated reports from lower levels on their progress towards the corporate goals.

In large organizations there are often surrogate management levels, when the organization is structured in branches or geographic regions. Although these intermediate organizations receive and generate records, and can therefore be documented, they are but microcosms of the larger management structure, carrying out its functions in smaller organizational units.

Below this management level is the operational level, where the activities involve implementing policies through application of procedures and practices established by the management team, and reporting back to management on progress, accomplishments, and problems. It is at this level that action takes place, and the records document the action of the organization, whether through sales, the establishment of case files, the number of units produced, or whatever is the measurement of the organization's product. These records are considered to be "informational."

The archival concepts of evidential and informational records, therefore, result in the production or creation of evidence of the organization's functions at the managerial level, whereas the information about the outcome and results of the organization are produced at the operational level in case files, products, and public communications. The archivist, often in association with the records manager, is responsible for determining how much of the documentation of these activities should be kept and, once kept, how best to describe the corpus of material so that information can be located and abstracted quickly. That descriptive device is known as the archival "inventory." "Inventory" implies passivity and, in many respects, is just documentation of what exists, not what should exist.

If these attributes of an organization are reflected in the hierarchical structure of an archival inventory, there are similar but quite different reasons for the development and structure of a register of personal papers.

An individual, working alone or with minimal support services, is not a bureaucracy, but an idiosyncratic entity from which many actions emanate concurrently. The person may be at the same time a son, father, brother, husband and uncle. He may also be an author, teacher, institutional officer, inventor, craftsman, bookkeeper, performer, policymaker, and worker. Actions initiated by him may have to be carried out by him, especially in the field of individualized creative action.

The "records" created by such a person are in no way hierarchical, except as the various roles relate to the individual who initiated and performs them. What is required in the case of the papers of individuals, therefore, is segmentation or compartmentalization, so that each of the activities can be studied and understood as an entity, and yet can be placed in the context of the individual's full range of activities. The structure of the descriptive device that provides access to the individual's papers is, or would seem to be, different from that describing organizational records. This is not necessarily the case.

An organizational inventory is structured so that the nature, function and policies of the organization are described first in a general, narrative statement, with some statistical information about the life dates of the organization being described, the dates of the totality of material produced and retained in the archives, and the total quantity of material making up the records.

This is mirrored in the description of personal papers by the vital dates of the individual, the dates of the papers in the collection, and their total quantity.

At the second level of description the archival inventory provides an administrative history of the corporate body: the legal authority for its founding or chartering, its development, growth, function, structure, major landmarks, officers, influences, and termination or merger with another organization if it no longer exists. If the organization still exists, the description is open-ended but there should be an indication of the date to which the inventory is valid.

A description of personal papers accomplishes much the same thing with a biographical sketch. As the term infers, the sketch indicates birth, education, professional or career development, major activities, creative products (such as books, plays, works of art, etc.), awards, and personal events such as marriages, divorces, and, if deceased, date of death. If the person is prominent enough to be listed in major biographical works the life details are given not as revelatory information that the researcher cannot find easily, but rather as landmarks that the researcher can relate to the personal papers. The sketch is often a reflection of an entry in a biographical listing, such as *Who's Who*.

The two descriptive documents next give an overview, in a narrative essay, of the entire contents of the records or personal papers. This essay is the archivist's and curator's opportunity to provide the researcher with a general picture of the records or the collection. It should note strengths and weaknesses, lacunae, peculiarities, and other information of value to the user of the papers. I say it should provide such an overview, but not all archival inventories do, whereas most descriptions of personal papers have a content and scope note in which such information is conveyed.

When Archivist of the United States Solon J. Buck left the National Archives in 1948, he assumed a position which, at that time, many would have called equally as important in the cultural community—he became chief of the Manuscripts Division (renamed the Manuscript Division in 1957) of the Library of Congress. He brought with him the concept of description en masse, embodied in the inventory, rather than the traditional item-by-item listing and indexing to which manuscript curators were accustomed.[9] The term "inventory," however, was replaced by its counterpart, the "register," which the descriptive document has been called since its importation into the division.

But the marriage was not a natural one, even though it seemed to work. The problem is that corporate records and personal papers come from two different traditions, as we have already seen. Although there can be an adherence to collection integrity in manuscripts (in archival jargon a *"respect des fonds"*), that is, keeping material from a common source, or *fonds*, together and not mixing it with material from other sources, the archival concept of "original order" goes out the window in manuscript collections. Individuals creating and keeping their own papers have no imperative to impose order upon them except for their own convenience. They are not bound by corporate rules, they probably have no secretaries consulting filing manuals, and they are not, as are corporate officers, responsible for long-term retrievability. Indeed, it is a wonder that many people keep anything at all!

The manuscript tradition is, in many ways, closer to the library tradition than to that of archives. In manuscript processing the documents at hand are analyzed for content, since it cannot be assumed that there is a defined "function" within even the functions of the individual's life and career. Since there is no function or "adequate documentation" of the person's personal existence, often the only way to describe the collection is to describe items of information within it. This process may not be carried to the degree of describing every item, but some items will defy incorporation or assemblage with others, except in a meaningless "miscellany." However, it is clear that some compaction could take place by grouping all correspondence of like nature together and forming the equivalent of the archival "series."[10] This compaction became necessary because of the nature of nineteenth- and twentieth-century collections. While the Jefferson papers number some 50,000 items in the Library of Congress, representing his life and career, those of Woodrow Wilson number 278,000; Theodore Roosevelt, 350,000; Theodore Francis Green, 500,000; William Howard Taft, 675,000; Booker T. Washington, one million; and Gifford Pinchot, two million. The tendency for personal papers is to become the equivalent of corporate records. Indeed, when dealing with the papers of any of the men just mentioned, the "corporation" would be the presidency, Tuskegee Institute, or the agriculture movement in the United States. There was thus a certain justification for moving these "personal" papers into the mold of corporate archives.

But once started, the process was difficult to stop. What about the papers of author Samuel Guy Inman (42 boxes), sculptor Vinnie Ream Hoxie (12 boxes), or minister Samuel Warren Dike (26 boxes)? These were not nearly as large nor as "corporate" as the presidents' and world leaders' papers. Yet they were subject to the same descriptive device, with its requirement for "series" listings. These series could be manufactured by bringing like materials together; for instance, all personal correspondence, all business correspondence, all diaries, etc. This, however, was a reversal of the original concept of series, which dictated that records which "naturally" fell together because of some requirement in their creation would then be classed as a series. In the manuscripts tradition this philosophy was turned on its head, with the movement of diverse materials into some rational relationship that would "create" a series.

Richard Lytle conducted a study of the retrieval effectiveness of the two approaches to documentary sources, using the archives of the Baltimore Regional Institutional Studies Center (BRISC). His study, in the form of a doctoral dissertation, was not directed at an answer to which method of research was better, but was a methodological study to evaluate which method would be best to use in order to determine which research tool was better. For the study he employed the provenance approach—structured inquiries about the records according to the known organization of the entity that created them—and the content indexing approach, which employed searching by names, subjects, and direct access points. His very preliminary findings were that there was little difference in the results, with the provenance approach perhaps having a slight edge.[11]

The Lytle thesis, however, is based on archival records, and not on personal papers, where there is little concern for the provenance approach.[12]

Over time the inventory and the register evolved into different research tools, but neither was considered a definitive analysis of the material it described. The registers of the Library of Congress are described in the traditional preface in each one published:

> A register provides the essential information about a manuscript collection: its provenance and conditions of administration; an organization or biographical history or chronology; a scope and content note; a description of series; and a container list, which generally identifies the folders in each box. A register, however, is not a calendar or index and usually does not permit its user, without reference to the collection itself, to locate individual manuscripts. It is an aid to research, not a substitute for it. Some additional information about this collection may be secured by correspondence with the Manuscript Division . . . but detailed inquiries must be satisfied through a researcher's examination

of the collection itself. This register has been prepared to assist in such an examination.[13]

The manuscript researcher, however, has an easier time with finding aids than does a researcher in archival records. The manuscript register is concise, can be elaborative in its explanation of the strengths and weaknesses of a collection, and may serve very well as an entrée to the collection. That is less likely to be the case with the researcher looking for Ira Eaker in the inventories to various U.S. Army record groups. In those it is not the name that is the key, but rather a knowledge of Eaker's position(s), the theaters of war and military units in which he served, his rank and duties, and similar organizational facts that provide the clues.

Yet all of this forematter in both registers and inventories describes the context of the collection, not the contents. The context is the life and times of the individual, or the provenance of the papers, or the administrative controls such as physical dimension or material forms, and is introductory to an actual analysis of the contents of the body of material. It is in this forematter that the documentation is put in its natural context, and where the researcher should be able to search for functional statements, authorities for action, interorganizational or interpersonal relationships, structure, mass, chronology and statements of policy. Except for the possibility of future termination dates (either organizational or personal) the statements to this point can stand unchanged, regardless of what happens down at the operational level. New functions may be added, or a new degree or prize awarded, but the basic vital statistics and contextual information should not change, since they are historical, physical or chronological fact. Once an agency, organization or corporate body terminates, or an individual dies, the contextual information becomes stabilized and unchangeable, even though more records are found or more personal papers are contributed to the repository, unless previously determined "facts" are proven untrustworthy or wrong.

Manuscript curators sometimes get so caught up in the importance of the subject whose papers they have just processed that they describe the subject's life, contemporary events, the contents and scope of papers that have strayed elsewhere, and important contributions that the subject made, even though they are not represented in the papers. This can be distracting for the researcher, who may even be misled into thinking that all of these matters will be revealed in the papers. The cardinal rule of manuscript description is that it should describe the collection at hand as an aid to research, with only passing reference to material or events not covered by the collection itself. At the series level that is easy, because series describe material physically present in the collection.

The level of description will probably stem from the level of arrangement. If arrangement stops at the series level, as is common with most archival groups, description probably will stop there too. If arrangement of manuscript material descends to the item, however, there is no certainty that the collection will be described at the item level. In a sense, the items are self-indexed if their order in the folders is mentioned in the description. "Fine tuning" a collection's arrangement is time taken away from doing anything to the backlog.

Description has essentially three purposes: to assist the staff in locating materials at a future date; to assist researchers in working their way through collections; and to add a measure of collection security by providing narrow targets for research. Staff needs are an important consideration because in any collection of noncirculating unique material much of the searching of the collections will be done by staff in response to reference requests, either verbal by telephone or written. The researcher should remember that staff does not do research: that is, does not try to find the answers to historical questions or to analyze the content and substance of collections. But the staff does research to provide guidance to distant researchers and inform them of the existence of certain materials and their apparent pertinence to the question at hand. Corporate archivists, on the other hand, may be called upon to do substantive research as a service to the corporate community. A call from the advertising department, the planning office, the legislature, the mayor, or any other official is difficult to deny. The archivist, therefore, may be the most frequent user of archival records, and the finding aids to the records are designed to aid that research. This is not as critical with the manuscript curator, who rarely provides internal, on-demand reference service.

The researcher should expect to be given every clue possible to the content and importance of the collection, and many clues will have been gained by the staff in the processing or arrangement stage. If the processor kept notes during arrangement, the substance of many of these may be incorporated into the narrative description of the collection at various levels. Negative information can be extremely useful and time-saving for the researcher. If the subject was secretary of the Navy during a crucial period for defense, but the collection has no papers from that period, the mention of that fact can save considerable searching by the researcher interested only in the subject's naval period. Precise and brief descriptions are important so that the maximum amount of information can be provided in the minimum amount of time, since time is a commodity which most researchers find in short supply.

In the age of automation curators are trying to pare down description to precise and meaningful language and avoid flowery prose. One means of searching computerized text is to do a word search or a string search, looking for word combinations from full text. It is deceptive to say, therefore, that General Henry "Hap" Arnold was the architect of the world's greatest air power and have him appear in a full-text search for architects. This kind of thing will never be totally avoided, however, and the amount of "noise" that one gets in a retrieval system (that is, the lack of precision) has to be balanced against the applicable variables. It is, perhaps, possible when searching for references to the Plymouth Compact to retrieve information about the early settlers of Massachusetts as well as the automotive industry in Detroit.

The Intervention of Automation

The profession today is concerned with two questions: (1) Should the traditional printed finding aids be converted to an automated database? or (2) Should they be discarded and an entirely new format of finding aid be devised that would use to the fullest the power of the computer?

The first approach means writing computer programs to receive, retain and manipulate information in a structure originally designed for presentation on paper. The second implies retrospective conversion of all collection information now in traditional printed finding aids, and probably reanalysis and description of existing collections, in addition to application of automated description to all new collections. The alternative, of course, is to have what one archivist calls a bifurcated system—all collections that have been described up to a certain date being left in traditional form in paper, and all new collections formatted according to the latest acceptable automated standards.[14] One difficulty with "progressive conversion" is that the number of manuscript collections in a repository does not grow very fast. If a repository receives one hundred new collections a year it is an accomplishment, and the accessioning of twenty-five large, significant collections is almost unheard of, except at a few of the mega-repositories. Therefore, for many years there will be an insignificant amount of research information in the computer, while most of it remains resident in paper.

While listening attentively to the voices calling for change, it is not surprising that archivists are only reluctantly contemplating the conversion of their present descriptive systems to automated formats. For most, the burden of redescription is too heavy. Many are of the opinion that it is better to get an old, halfway acceptable finding aid into electronic form and then work on its improvement than to either ignore it altogether or go back and completely redo the intellectual analysis of the collection. In chapter 6 we will discuss the ways that archivists are approaching these questions in automated systems.

Thus, when researchers wonder why there seem to be multiple systems—some manual, some automated, for finding aids in a single repository; and when they question delays in the progress towards total automation in these collections, it is well for them to understand what the traditions are, on what they are based, and what their strengths and weaknesses are. But the researcher (as well as the novice manuscript curator) must also have a sense of the advances in archival automation in description over the past few years.

This point is stressed because of the controversy raging in the archival community about "functional" description as opposed to "operational" description of records, especially when one begins describing records in a database. I contend that functional description is already structured into the inventory and register, even if it is not universally used. It is not difficult to imagine such description being accessible to the computer searcher on a horizontal search plane; that is, where the researcher can search across all holdings at the highest general level in order to locate agencies with similar functions or individuals with similar activities and interests. This is not a new concept. In a paper published in 1967 the idea of searching at the collection level for general information (e.g., all papers of clergymen) was suggested; then, after locating a number of collections that meet the criteria, searching vertically, or in-depth through each of them in turn for specific data.[15] The two-step process is commonly done by providing the researcher with the introductory material in brief catalog card summaries, and then having the researcher indicate which ones contain information at the macrolevel that could lead to the desired information at the microlevel in finding aids and indexes, where such tools exist. This search mechanism can be applied to well-structured automated finding aids.

The first approach to collections of personal papers is traditionally through names, whereas in archival records it is more than likely by subject or topic. Both are delimited by time period. If a researcher is interested in aviation in warfare there is little reason to search through Colonial or Revolutionary War collections (except for early ballooning). The chronological approach is even more applicable in requests for records of time-specific subjects, such as the Civil War or the Soviet-American space race.

The next intellectual sorting-out is often geographical. Information about life in nineteenth-century Boston will probably not be sought first in the papers of southwestern Indian agents (although, as one soon learns, there is no guarantee that such information will not be there).

After these major divisions researchers look for subjects (Black poets, the Depression, Indian wars) and topics (early influence, relief services, recruitment of troops), followed by personalities or individuals. At the macrolevel of description of archives or manuscripts one can be fairly precise about topics and subjects—at least major subjects—but only superficially list important individuals. In archives the important individuals tend to be officers or members of the corporate body; in personal papers the important individuals are most likely those who communicated often with the principal subject. Some institutions break up this description into sections and distribute them throughout the finding aid, where they are more closely associated with the series subsumed under them.[16]

THE SERIES

The descent below the introductory levels to the series level brings considerable change to the descriptive process. Instead of discussing context, the description now dwells on the documents themselves—their format, contents, bulk and general coverage. The series description deals with intellectual material in a physical dimension. What is being described are letters that contain specific reference to names and subjects; or photographs that show people or geographically locatable scenes, objects, buildings, or activities; or maps that represent certain specific portions of the earth, moon or planets. Series descriptions, therefore, are bounded by the material that they describe. The art of the curator or archivist is to make the material in the series as understandable as possible in as few words as possible. Good series descriptions are models of conciseness, giving direction to the researcher without an overwhelming amount of detail.

Series descriptions are structured the same for both archives and personal papers, providing series title, dates, size, a narrative description, and the order of organization. The narrative may be long or short; the dates may include those for the bulk of the series and those for its entirety; the arrangement may be simple or complex, with many subarrangements, but the five-element structure is fairly standard. It is in the series that most archivists and manuscript curators have come together philosophically and have at the same time agreed upon, if not formally adopted, a structure—one of the few in the profession.

The Series Title

Series descriptions are formal in their use of terms that describe the papers they contain. The title describes either the type of material in the series, such as correspondence, letters, reports; or the nature of the material, such as case files, subject file, etc. An example of the first might be:

> Letterbooks, Letterpress Books, and Letter Index Books 1864–1880.

An example of the latter might be:

> Subject File, 1861–1883 and undated.

Series Dates

Dates might be single, intermittent, inclusive, spanning the entire series, or indicating where the bulk of the material lies within a larger span. Some examples could be:

Letter, July 12, 1886;
Letters, July 12, Aug. 14, Nov. 28, 1886;
Correspondence, 1886–87;
Correspondence, 1828–96 with the bulk 1880–90.

Series Size

The unit of measurement of size is irrelevant except that it should be consistent. Whether a series is in inches or centimeters, linear or metric straight line measurement, it has meaning to the researcher as an indication of the effort needed to master it. Gross collection measurements can provide the researcher with an idea of the scope of the entire body of material; however, they are also given for curators to determine storage area requirements. The National Archives, therefore, measures series in linear inches or feet that are meaningful to a researcher but computes entire record groups in cubic feet that are meaningful when determining storage requirements.

Series Description

The descriptive paragraph for the series is the curator's opportunity to state concisely what the researcher will find in the papers in a general way. It is traditionally brief, descriptive, and informative. It might, like the scope and content note, indicate negative information, or a statement of what is not in the series that might be expected to be there. As an example, in the register for the Robert Wilson Shufeldt Papers at the Library of Congress one series entry reads:

5–10 Official Correspondence, 1839–1889. 6 containers.
Letters received and a few drafts of letters sent, chronologically arranged. The correspondence consists mostly of official letters and orders to duty. Correspondence concerning Shufeldt's years in Cuba, the Tehuantepec Survey Expedition, and the world cruise in the USS Ticonderoga will be found in the Subject File.[17]

Some series descriptions, especially in archival materials, do not dwell on contents, but rather on organization of the files. A typical example of this appears in the Records of the [California] Secretary of State, California State Archives Inventory No. 6, 1978:

54. Record of Incorporations. 1850–66, 1872–1935. 255 lin. ft. (617 vols. + 120 cu. ft.)

Govt. Code, Sec. 12164, provides that the Secretary of State shall record all articles of incorporation filed in his office

Indexes available. See series 56 below.

This series consists of the record of the filed articles of incorporation that, until 1929, the Secretary of State recorded in "proper books" in his office. The record copies for 1850–1929 (articles #1 through #133,270, in books A through N, 1850–66, and 1 through 602, 1872–1929) are in handwritten or typewritten form (3A, rw3); the record copies for 1929–35 (articles #133,291 through #162,394, in boxes 1 through 120) are in photostat form (2A, rw1,2). (Record copies of articles of incorporation from 1935 to the present are maintained on microfilm by the Secretary of State's Corporate Division.) Although a record copy of a very large percentage of filed articles was made, a substantial number of articles were not recorded and so are not included in this series. But where original filed articles are missing, the record copy may be the only copy available.

An untitled journal (VB144, #2534) contains a log of the recording of incorporation filings from July 27, 1905 to Dec. 31, 1906, with entries on number and name of corporation, staff member recording, book and page number, and date of recording.[18]

This description illustrates an old saw among archivists: one does not have to actually *see* the records being described in order to describe them! That philosophy is based on the inevitability of corporate, and especially government, records. In the federal Inventory 15, *General Records of the Department of State, 1789–1949*, there is a subgroup named *Records of the Chief Special Agent*, and in that subgroup a series CORRESPONDENCE WITH SPECIAL AGENTS. 1918–21. 10 in. (series entry 353, p. 90). The archivist's rationale is that if one knows what the *function* of the office of the chief special agent is, then one can safely say that the correspondence with special agents will relate to that function. Indeed, the entry reads:

Correspondence . . . with special agents of the Department, regarding their commissions, accounts, reports and investigative activities.[19]

This oversimplified (but true) premise does not, however, apply to personal papers, since individuals do not have a prescribed function that can be gleaned from their correspondence, diaries, and other writings. The papers of Felix Frankfurter at the Harvard Law School Library contain a series with the following description:

> Personal Miscellany: Biographical, Bibliographical, 1914–1965. 3 MS boxes and 12 folders.
>
> The bulk of this series consists of congratulatory correspondence and other items relating to Frankfurter's nomination to the Supreme Court of the United States by President Franklin D. Roosevelt, and to the subsequent confirmation by the U.S. Senate (38 folders). Other items in this series include social matters and reprints of speeches and writings of Frankfurter and others.[20]

Series Arrangement Statement

The statement of arrangement in the series is important, because it provides instruction to the researcher about how to approach the material. The statement is directly derived from the arrangement process undertaken by the curator or staff, or the filing scheme of the records. All that is required is that the register series entry indicate what order the papers are in to facilitate access. Arrangement may be a simple chronological order, a complex decimal notation system, or anything in between. Looking again at the Shufeldt papers register, we find a mixed arrangement:

> **18–29 Subject File, 1861–1883 and undated. 12 containers.**
>
> Correspondence, reports, memoranda, manuscripts, maps, printed matter, newspaper clippings, drafts of writings, bills and receipts, and miscellaneous items, pertaining to Cuba, the Tehuantepec Survey Expedition, and the world cruise. The material concerning Cuba and the Tehuantepec Survey Expedition is chronologically arranged while that concerning the world cruise of the USS Ticonderoga is arranged according to the area covered by the cruise.[21]

These series entries from typical manuscript registers also show that indexing is possible but problematic. Some series have subject citations that can be indexed, but others do not. Again, turning to Shufeldt:

> Copies of correspondence and reports sent by Shufeldt as Commander of various ships. A few of the volumes are indexed. (*op. cit.*)

And elsewhere:

> Diaries, notebooks, log abstracts, log-books, navigational data, journals, and other assorted writings, chronologically arranged. (*op. cit.*)

There is obviously not much there to index. Curators who anticipate indexing, either manually or by computer, could insist that subjects be included in descriptions whenever possible, but the complexity of doing so and the time investment often overwhelm such good intentions.

The order or arrangement of the material in the series is the curator's way of assisting the researcher without creating item indexes to everything. To paraphrase an old saying, let the arrangement fit the material. This will be discussed in the section on organization in chapter 7, so that when it comes to description the curator merely has to reflect that arrangement in the finding aid.

Folder Lists

There is no art, and little skill, in preparing folder lists. The job is essentially mechanical, deriving the information that they carry from the folders themselves. If any curatorial effort is required relating to folders, it is the preparation of the folders themselves, and not the transcription of that information into the register.

In corporate offices, records are kept in folders that are labeled for efficiency and convenience, the better to locate them in a filing cabinet drawer. If an unlabeled folder is discovered the situation is soon corrected. If not, there is chaos in the office. Archivists, therefore, can expect to find labeled folders in rational order.

In personal papers there are two conditions that mitigate against a series of neatly labeled and ordered folders. Unless the creator of the collection is a well-organized, methodical individual, or has secretarial help, it is rare that a label and a new folder can be found at the same time, or, if both are present, that there is any inclination to place one in the typewriter, annotate it, and affix it to the other. What one finds are: recycled labeled folders with old label information scratched out and new information crudely penciled in; an unlabeled folder with the folder title entered on the body of the folder in pen or pencil; a folder with no notation as to its contents; variously annotated folders whose annotations do not match the contents; or loose papers, unfoldered. It is in the processing (arranging) stage, therefore, that folders are formalized, corrected, created, and otherwise organized and structured. The descriptive process merely presents this information in tabular form, lined up sequentially after the series description.

The Shufeldt papers register at the Library of Congress has the following entries illustrative of folder headings:

SUBJECT FILE, 1861–1863 AND UNDATED (Continued)
    Tehuantepec (Mexico) Survey Expedition, 1861–73
[Folder] 21   Bills, receipts, and inventories
                   Maps
                   Miscellany
                   Newspaper clippings
                   Printed matter
    World Cruise (USS Ticonderoga), 1879–83 and undated
[Folder] 22   West Africa
                   Angola
                   South Africa
                   Congo
                   etc.[22]

How precise an institution makes the register relating to folder information is a question of cost. The theory is that either the repository or the researcher must bear the cost of precision, and the compromise is to provide the entry information and let the researcher take it from there.

Item Lists

Listing of individual items within folders is almost never done in registers today. It is an extremely rare occurrence in large twentieth-century collections, except those that contain the rarest material of high intrinsic value.

One reason why a curator would list individual items might be in the case of a widely diverse assemblage of materials of high research or intrinsic value. Let us imagine a collection of an extremely popular figure in the field of nuclear physics who has attained his eighty-fifth birthday and has received congratulatory messages from world leaders in the sciences and government. The curator might well want to list the contents of each folder and bring out the fact that these letters are from Fermi, Szilard, Oppenheimer, Bohr, Truman, Churchill, Groves, Harriman, etc. A collection of items of such high signature value, in fact, might force the curator to list each document in the folders as a security measure and a check against possible future misplacement. But the incidence of such "potent" collections is small, and it is quite sufficient in most cases merely to state that the folder contains twenty-five letters in the general correspondence series.

A peculiar example of item listing, but within the context of the series description, shows up in the Inventory of the Records of the Department of State. The Decimal File series [no. 205] uses just 15 lines [in the original printed text] to describe over 13,000 feet of records, while series 630, "Miscellaneous Manuscripts. ca. 1756–1918. 1 ft.," in the same inventory used 66 lines to describe one foot of material in the following manner (only the first nine lines used for illustration).

> Most of the following original and copies of documents were presented to the Department of State: blank warrant of Governor Robert Dinwiddie of Virginia for the arrest of mutinous or seditious militiamen, 1756; agreement signed by Louis de Kerlérec, governor of Louisiana, appointing Okana-Stoté, Chief of the Cherokee, as a captain in the service of the French, 1761; photostat of a petition from indian traders of Pittsburgh to George Crogthan, protesting against unlawful trade with the Indians, 1767, etc.[23]

This prompts the observation, familiar to many curators, that the smaller the series or file, the more detail it takes to describe it, on the basis that the information cannot easily be generalized with any meaning.

The inventory and register, therefore, proceed from the general to the specific, and how specific they become is determined by the curator, based on the needs of the researcher and, to some extent, on the needs of the repository. But it should be stressed that the printed or published register is a dying format at large institutions, and its demise will probably follow at smaller institutions over the next decade. It is dying because it is too structured, too frozen in form, and not easily searchable. It is being replaced by automated structures and will soon be supplanted by them, but, as stated earlier, the burden of thousands of manually produced registers still rests on the curators and researchers, and the conversion of these paper structures to electronic form is one of the major challenges facing manuscript curators at the turn of the century.

INDEXES, CALENDARS, AND OTHER FORMATS

Indexes

Oddly enough, the availability of new technologies or techniques of computer-aided description is accompanied by a return to some old formats that were all but abandoned a few decades ago. When the Library of Congress confronted the computer and its immediate predecessor, the manual unit-record sorting equipment, in the 1950s and decided to use them to assist in controlling its manuscript collections, the first application was a massive item index to the papers of the twenty-three presidential collections that it holds. Item indexing began to go out of fashion around the era of World War II with the advent of larger and larger collections of personal papers, and the infusion into manuscript processing of some of the newly emerging archival practices. The burdensome amount of manual labor, writing or typing filing cards, perhaps six to each document (one each to be filed under collection name, to, from, date, place, subject), and then filing them in proper order in an ever-growing card file, naturally led to larger and larger backlogs of items to be indexed, which was actually a disservice to the prospective user. When manuscript curators began to consider themselves archivists rather than librarians, the item concept of description fell into disfavor and the professional literature concentrated on mass description at the collection, series or folder level.[24] The appearance of the manuscript register at the Library of Congress in the early 1950s temporarily sealed the fate of item indexing in most major repositories.

But then in the late 1950s the Library of Congress received a major grant to produce a microfilm copy of all of the presidential papers that it held, numbering twenty-three collections from Washington to Coolidge.[25] The inadequacies of the existing indexes to the papers led the Library of Congress to consider indexing the microfilm after putting the papers in order for filming.

Punch-card, unit record equipment was being used in the library for payroll and other purposes, and its application to the presidential papers problem was investigated. The theory was that each item (some 1.2 million) would have to be indexed only once on a punched card that could contain the five or so elements of information that would be included in each. The machine, a simple card sorter, could then sort the cards into the index terms, and another machine, the printer, would read the sorted cards and print out the results mechanically.

Without dwelling on the process, which has been described in the literature,[26] it is fair to say that the project was more complex and difficult than anticipated and took twenty years to complete, with as many as ten staff members assigned to it at times. Unfortunately, multiple sorts were not made. The documents were sorted and printed in only one order—alphabetically—and the cards were disposed of, preventing any later manipulation of the data.

At the National Archives a similar reversion to antiquated descriptive methods occurred when the computer was employed as an early descriptive aid. For the bicentennial of the Declaration of Independence, the National Archives received a grant from the Ford Foundation to index the Papers of the Continental Congress (PCC), which were already on microfilm. A different software program was used than at the Library of Congress, full-processing computers instead of unit record equipment were employed from the beginning, and the index was produced in much less time, largely because it consisted of only 50,000 documents. The index, printed in five large volumes, is displayed in two structures, one alphabetical, the other chronological, but the alphabetical contains in one listing the names of addressees, authors, signatories (to petitions), limited subject terms, names of ships, geographical references, etc.

At the completion of the projects, both institutions indicated that if item indexing were ever employed again, it would have to be on material of such high research value that it would be worthwhile, or on material that lent itself to item controls, such as motion picture film, videotapes, reels of sound recordings, and similar media. Not only was the process very expensive, even with the aid of computers, but there was doubt about the value of the product for most researchers. The presidential papers project required reordering the documents before filming or indexing them. That reorganization into a small number of series, with each series having an appropriate arrangement imposed on it, could be self-indexing if the researcher knew of the series and their internal organization. The PCC project at the National Archives was faced with a different problem. The papers existed in bound volumes in an organization whose rationale was not apparent, and earlier had been microfilmed in the order in which they had been bound. There was no opportunity to rearrange them physically, so the National Archives rearranged them intellectually, keyed to the disorganized physical order. The project was justified by the seminal nature of the papers for a study of the development of the federal system and the progress of the Revolutionary War. Using the theory stated earlier, the curator must make a decision about where the institution draws the line on investing in processing the papers, and where the researcher must make an investment in order to accomplish specific research.

Calendars

Another form of item indexing, but even more detailed and labor intensive, is the calendar. As the word implies, a calendar is a description of documents in chronological order. Thus, it is but a form of item index and can be accomplished by including a date field in an automated index entry, and then sorting and listing on that field. The traditional calendar had a brief two- or three-line narrative description of each document. I say "had" because calendars in the classic sense are so rarely produced anymore that it is difficult to find one as an example. The example shown here is from a Library of Congress publication of 1904.[27] However, a new "complete" calendar of the James Monroe papers is being produced as this is being written. This "comprehensive" calendar of the papers of James Monroe is assembling information on Monroe documents globally for display on an Internet connection.[28]

Institutional Guides

One advantage of a published institutional guide is that it provides an opportunity for an essay on the repository's holdings, strengths and weaknesses, as well as instructions on the use of materials, how to apply for research access, what special materials might be available, and how the collections relate to other research materials at the institution or in the area. Disadvantages are that they consume considerable staff time to produce, the editorial and

LIBRARY OF CONGRESS

Manuscripts Division of

PAPERS

OF

JAMES MONROE

LISTED IN CHRONOLOGICAL ORDER
FROM THE ORIGINAL MANUSCRIPTS
IN THE LIBRARY OF CONGRESS

COMPILED UNDER THE DIRECTION OF

WORTHINGTON CHAUNCEY FORD

CHIEF, DIVISION OF MANUSCRIPTS

WASHINGTON
GOVERNMENT PRINTING OFFICE
1904

November	3.	Edward Livingston. Answer to question proposed by Jared Ingersoll, William Rawle, Joseph Borden McKean, and Peter Stephen Du Ponceau.
	27.	James Madison to Charles Pinckney.
December	6.	James Pendleton to Monroe.

1803.

January	3.	John Randolph, jr., to Monroe.
	7.	Monroe to Thomas Jefferson.
	10.	Thomas Jefferson to Monroe.
	13.	" "
	18.	Robert R. Livingston to Talleyrand-Perigord.
	29.	Edmond Charles Genet to Monroe.
February	23.	United States, Senate. Resolutions respecting the navigation of the Mississippi River.
	26.	Stevens Thomson Mason to Monroe.
	26.	United States, Senate. A bill directing a detachment from the militia of the United States, and for erecting certain arsenals.
	26.	United States. An act, etc., making further provision for the expenses attending the intercourse between the United States and foreign nations.
March	1.	Wilson Cary Nicholas to Monroe.
	2.	James Madison to Robert R. Livingston and Monroe.
	4.	John Pintard to Monroe.
Ventôse	9. 19.	Talleyrand-Perigord to Robert R. Livingston.
	16.	Robert R. Livingston to Talleyrand-Perigord.
Germinal	21. 1.	Talleyrand-Perigord to Robert R. Livingston.
	—.	John Pintard. Notes on the Mississippi River, East and West Florida.

publishing processes are expensive, and the volumes are frozen in time, quickly becoming out-of-date. Researchers must always note not only the publication date of a guide, but more importantly the "cut-off" or "close-out" date, when the assemblage of entries ceased in order to prepare for the publication. They are gradually being replaced by frequently updated information on the repository's World Wide Web (WWW) page.

Special Guides and Lists

Although an alphabetized collection guide might be helpful to the staff in answering questions about the existence, size and location of individual collections, researchers would be better served by a guide organized in a structure more related to their research. All repositories have material that can be described in combinations or cumulations centered on a subject, topic or chronological period. Thus, there can be guides to literary collections, African-American collections, women's collections, the city, political figures, the Revolution, Civil War, or Indian agents. A single collection may appear in more than one guide, such as the papers of an African-American woman active in the affairs of the city. If basic descriptions of each collection are uniform in style and structure, the individual entries can be mixed and matched in various guides related to subjects, providing a great number of combinations aimed at specific audiences. As we will see later, the key to such combinations is a comprehensive database, uniformly structured, and provided with accurate indexing terms.

But the concept of printed guides is rapidly becoming antiquated. Most "guides" or comprehensive collection analyses are, at a minimum, produced in electronic form through word processing and, ideally, in a Standard Generalized Markup Language (SGML) format for mounting on the World Wide Web, which will be discussed in chapter 6. If the contents are coded in Machine-Readable Cataloging (MARC), SGML or Hypertext Markup Language (HTML), the data elements are separately identified in retrievable fields or units. The ability to search these fields in combination with others, or to perform Boolean selective searches, leaves the choices up to the user, not the archivist. A search for Connecticut clergymen can be launched by combining a search in the geographical field and the occupation/profession field of the records in a selected file.

This kind of "key word" searching is extremely simple in most of today's systems, because it relies only on explicit reference terms in the search field (e.g., Connecticut and Clergymen, usually truncated as clergy* to retrieve any form beginning with clergy). It is not as easy to search conceptual terms, such as "New England," unless they have been defined by the creator of the database. Even less probable is the ability to search such concepts as "mystical revelation," "religious intolerance," or "discrimination."

The scholar who enters a repository or an off-site data link expecting to find an item index to every person mentioned in any of the material there may find such a file at certain institutions (the Western Historical Manuscripts Collection, University of Missouri-Columbia, is one), and many institutions produce greatly detailed guides with extensive indexes to significant parts of the collection, but it remains true that in many cases today's researchers will be confronted with guides or registers that take the approach of providing a general description only in the series entry, and folder headings below that.

Summary

The descriptive process has one primary goal: to provide easier access to the collections. At present it is not as structured as traditional library description, wherein information has been defined and delimited, and each item received is somehow fitted into its proper place in that predefined universe through a classification system. Manuscript collections are too diverse in their content to be confined to such limits. Archivists have even a different perspective: their universe is that of the corporate body—government, business, or other organization. They already have purview over everything created by that corporate body, and their practice is not to collect but to dispose of what is not needed. The three branches of information science, therefore, have three different approaches to their material: the librarian classifies; the manuscript curator describes; and the archivist explains.

Researchers will encounter most of the formats described in the preceding pages, in that they will find repositories with card catalogs, finding aids, special lists, institutional guides, and most of the other forms mentioned. All of that is beginning to change, however, as the computer invades the manuscript repository and the library/information community. More and more, it is possible to access collection information via computer terminal, both at the repository and from afar. Institutions are mounting on various "gophers" and "webs" collection and repository information from the most general instructions to prospective researchers to the specific item lists of some of their holdings. The structure and implications of this revolution will be discussed in chapter 6.

If a curator has gone to all the trouble discussed in this chapter to acquire, select, arrange and describe the repository's collections, the final step in the process should be to report them to a national catalog or enter them in an automated national database. But published collection catalogs lag from one to two years behind reporting by the repository, and many researchers do not have ready access to the national automated databases. A more direct method for attracting the attention of those who are prospective users of the collections is to catch them in their study by putting notice of availability in the journals that researchers read. Most professional journals carry some news of recent archives and manuscript acquisitions or openings, but unfortunately, that practice is declining and it is becoming more and more difficult to remain aware of recent acquisitions in the nation's thousands of document repositories. The notices most often get to the journals through quarterly lists sent to them by repository staff, but the same staffs are often frustrated by the absence of their submissions in the publication, or the heavy editing imposed to reduce the list to the editors' concept of "importance."

Two other related forms of notice are common. If the institution publishes a journal or newsletter of its own, it can guarantee the appearance of recent acquisition notices, and researchers interested in the repository's area of collecting will subscribe. The effort of gathering the quarterly reports, editing them and putting them in shape for publication can then lead to reprinting them in a cumulated list for the institution's annual report, perhaps accompanied by a narrative description of some of the more significant acquisitions. The Library of Congress formerly published recent acquisitions in its *Quarterly Journal*, spotlighting different parts of the collection each quarter. This resulted in one issue per year highlighting the recent acquisitions of the Manuscript Division and two or three other custodial units. The library has now turned to issuing an annual *Library of Congress Acquisitions. Manuscript Division*,[29] which contains fuller descriptions than the earlier form, but, unfortunately, it is produced with a two-year lag.

With the production of this wide spectrum of publications about the collections, the manuscript curator has fulfilled a professional obligation of making available to researchers the important unique documents in the repository. We have no comprehensive studies to inform us of the effectiveness or ineffectiveness of indexes, finding aids, catalogs or other guides. User studies in the manuscript field falter for a number of reasons, but most of them are untrustworthy because of smallness of sample, inability to obtain cooperation from the researcher, fears of charges of invasion of privacy if registration slips for use of collections are gathered and analyzed, and the imprecise nature of original research and the resulting imprecision of establishing cause and effect between items looked at and conclusions reached. Automated finding aids, which carry metadata about frequency of access and material searched may help in the future, but research methodologies vary to such a great extent that scientific samples would be difficult to prove. Yet curators have a sense of what is being used and for what purposes; thus the best information about use and popularity of collections and finding aids may have to rely on anecdotal evidence. Curators are trying to produce good road maps to the past that will ultimately be used by researchers who are known to travel their routes largely by dead reckoning.

NOTES

1. Hugh Taylor, "Transformation in the Archives: Technological Adjustment or Paradigm Shift?" Tom Nesmith, ed., ibid., 230.

2. William Least Heat-Moon, *Blue Highways* (Boston: Little, Brown, 1982).

3. Dan Meyer, archivist, Department of Special Collections, Regenstein Library, University of Chicago, to author via E-mail, February 6, 1995.

4. T. R. Schellenberg, *The Management of Archives* (New York: Columbia University Press, 1965), 85.

5. National Archives and Record Service, *Staff Information Circular* 15 (July 1950): 21.

6. A brief discussion of the politics surrounding this issue in the National Archives may be found in Donald R. McCoy, *The National Archives, America's Ministry of Documents* (Chapel Hill: University of North Carolina Press, 1978), 78–80.

7. Edward G. Campbell, "Functional Classification of Archival Material," *The Library Quarterly* 11 (1941): 431–441; Schellenberg, *Management of Archives*, chap. 7; National Archives and Records Administration, *Life Cycle Systems Data Elements Manual* ("Data Elements 800") (Washington, D.C., NARA, August 4, 1988), Appendices 2a, 2b, 2c.

8. Richard C. Berner, "Arrangement and Description: Some Historical Observations," *American Archivist* 41 (April 1978): 169–181; Richard C. Berner and Uli Haller, "Principles of Archival Inventory Construction," *American Archivist* 47 (April 1984): 134–155; Katharine E. Brand, "Developments in the Handling of Recent Manuscripts in the Library of

Congress," *American Archivist* 16 (April 1953): 99–104; ibid., "The Place of the Register in the Manuscript Division of the Library of Congress," *American Archivist* 18 (January 1955): 59–67; Frank G. Burke, ed., *Inventories and Registers: A Handbook of Techniques and Examples* (Chicago: Society of American Archivists, 1976); Bruce W. Dearstyne, *The Archival Enterprise* (Chicago: American Library Association, 1993), chap. 7; Kenneth W. Duckett, *Modern Manuscripts* (Nashville: American Association for State and Local History, 1975), chap. 5; David B. Gracy, II, *Archives and Manuscripts. Arrangement and Description* (Chicago: SAA, 1977); Lucile Kane, *A Guide to the Care and Administration of Manuscripts* (Nashville: AASLH, 1966), chap. 6; Edward E. Hill, *The Preparation of Inventories*, Staff Information paper No. 14 (Washington: National Archives and Records Service, 1982); Fredric Miller, *Arranging and Describing Archives and Manuscripts* (SAA, 1990), chap. 5; Edward Papenfuse, "Finding Aids and the Historian: the Need for National Priorities and a Standard Approach," *American Historical Association Newsletter* 10 (May 1972): 15–19; Schellenberg, *The Management of Archives*, chaps. 7, 15, 16, 19, 20.

9. Katharine E. Brand, ibid., 99–104.

10. See chapter 4.

11. Richard H. Lytle, "Intellectual Access to Archives: I. Provenance and Content Indexing Methods of Subject Retrieval," *American Archivist* 43 (winter 1980): 64–75; "II. Report of an Experiment Comparing Provenance and Content Indexing Methods of Subject Retrieval," *American Archivist* 43 (spring 1980): 191–208.

12. Unfortunately, the word "provenance" has two different meanings between archivists and manuscript curators. For the former it means the original order that the archival materials are found in; for the latter it means the derivation (ownership) of the collection when it was acquired. Another term used differently by the two fields is "appraisal." To the archivist it implies an evaluation of records to determine retention or disposal; for the manuscript curator it implies evaluation of the papers for monetary purposes, as when claiming a tax deduction.

13. Library of Congress. Manuscript Division, Preface to *W. Averell Harriman. A Register of His Papers in the Library of Congress* (Washington: Library of Congress, 1991), vii.

14. Richard C. Berner, *Archival Theory and Practice in the United States. A Historical Analysis*, 9.

15. Frank G. Burke, "The Application of Automated Techniques in the Management and Control of Source Materials," *American Archivist* 30 (spring 1967): 255–278.

16. Cf., the Ker Collection register at the University of North Carolina Manuscripts Department and Southern Historical Collection.

17. U.S. Library of Congress. Manuscript Division, *Robert Wilson Shufeldt. A Register of His Papers in the Library of Congress* (Naval Historical Foundation Collection. Washington: Library of Congress, 1969), 4.

18. California State Archives. Office of the Secretary of State. *Records of the Secretary of State*. California State Archives Inventory No. 6. Compiled by W. N. Davis, Jr. (Sacramento, Calif.: 1978, rev. 1980), 14.

19. National Archives and Records Administration, *Inventory of the General Records of the Department of State, 1789–1949*. Inventory 15 [Microfiche Edition] (Washington, D.C.: NARA, 1992), series entry 353, p. 90.

20. *Felix Frankfurter: An Inventory of His Papers in the Harvard Law School Library*. Compiled by Erika S. Chadbourn (Cambridge, Mass.: Manuscript Division. Harvard Law School Library, 1982), xi.

21. Shufeldt, 6.

22. Shufeldt, 10.

23. *Inventory to the General Records of the Department of State*, No. 15, series entry 630, 181–182.

24. See endnote 8.

25. The bulk of the John Adams, John Quincy Adams, Rutherford B. Hayes, and Warren G. Harding presidential collections went to other repositories.

26. Fred Shelley, "The Presidential Papers Program of the Library of Congress," *American Archivist* 25 (January/October 1962): 429–433; Russell M. Smith, "Item Indexing by Automated Processes," *American Archivist* 30 (April 1967): 295–302; Marion M. Torcia, "Two Experiments in Automated Indexing: The Presidential Papers and the Papers of the Continental Congress," *American Archivist* 39 (October 1976): 437–446.

27. *Papers of James Monroe: listed in chronological order from the original manuscripts in the Library of Congress* (Washington, D.C.: GPO, 1904).

28. The calendar is sponsored by the College of William and Mary and supported by the James Monroe Consortium, consisting of Ash Lawn-Highland in Charlottesville, Virginia, the James Monroe Museum in Fredericksburg, Virginia, and the Commonwealth Center for the Study of American Culture at the College of William and Mary.

29. (Washington, D.C.: Library of Congress, annual.)

· 6 ·

Tradition Confronts Technology

[WARNING: This chapter will self-destruct in 1999. After that date use for historical consumption only.]

In this age of automation, as the computer assumes the ascendancy more and more in our daily lives, the manuscript researcher cannot ignore the technology around us. Blinking cursors on variously hued screens beckon with promises of untold amounts of information lurking in the electronic circuitry, awaiting a call through the depression of a few keys or the click of a mouse. In many ways, the world has opened before us with the arrival of the ubiquitous electronic Aladdin's lamps. The promises of yesteryear have not only been fulfilled, but have been exceeded as the storage, transfer and retrieval of information accelerates and reaches deeper and deeper into the sources so long gathering dust on shelves or hidden from view during library off-hours. Researchers can ignore the advances in technology applied to documentary sources, but they do so at their own peril, because changes are occurring so fast that the old tried-and-true techniques are becoming less and less viable. In the library proper the familiar card catalog of holdings already has all but disappeared. On the other hand, researchers who embrace the new technology to the exclusion of traditional processes do so at their peril, as I will attempt to point out in this chapter.

What options are open to the manuscript researcher? The first is the use of an automated form that might not strike the user as a product of the computer because it looks like any other printed list, index, catalog or other finding aid. Products that come about because of simple word processing can be discounted because they are merely document storage, retrieval and formatting devices with only limited manipulability of the contents. If, however, the researcher is looking at the Library of Congress master record of manuscript collections, the indexes to the presidential papers at the Library of Congress, the index to the Papers of the Continental Congress at the National Archives, the *Directory of Archives and Manuscript Repositories in the United States,* or similar lists and indexes produced locally at institutions, the product is that of an automated system of some kind.

These products are off-line, in that one cannot interact with the computer directly; and they are batch-processed, in that the computer prints the entire product at one time, and if any corrections are made to the database it most likely will have to be completely printed again to present the modified text. This process is a halfway step between a publishing system and an on-line access computer system, and is losing its effectiveness as the interactive on-line systems move into the mainstream in reference libraries.

The second option open to the manuscript researcher is mediated searching, in which the search is actually done by an information professional, such as a manuscript reference specialist, using a computerized system and responding to the request of the researcher. The intermediary and the researcher may be separated and communicating by mail or telephone, or they may be together, with the researcher asking questions and the reference specialist manipulating the computer program in order to search for answers.

Mediated reference searches most often are done on-line, where queries are presented to the system and responses received. Mediated searching is most likely to occur when the information base is accessible only through a technical system which is unfamiliar to the researcher, who may be unwilling to expend the time and energy to learn it. These do not have to be national information utilities, like the Research Libraries Information Network (RLIN) or On-line Computer Library Center (OCLC), but could be common reference systems used at a number of repositories for bibliographic purposes, such as the program Pro-Cite or popular archival programs used by professionals such as MicroMARC/ AMC, InMagic, Minaret, GenCat, or a number of others.

Local systems generally contain only limited interinstitutional information, and require knowledge of special codes and search routines that one would not expect of most researchers. Indeed, archivists claim that some of these programs are powerful engines, but their complexity requires considerable training or practice. The sophisticated databases are essentially working systems for the archivist and librarian to provide information needed to administer a large collection. Reference service from them may be only a secondary consideration.

Whenever dealing with an intermediary to locate archives or manuscript material, a researcher can expect a session of question negotiation, where the librarian/curator queries the patron based on knowledge of how the reference tool is structured and what kind of request it will respond to most efficiently. Query negotiation can be as simple as a request for any data about Roy Knabenshue or as complicated as inquiring about any papers of pioneer Chicago balloonists. In the name search the main point is to spell the name correctly and understand how to request it in the system; in the subject search the sticking point may be the word "balloonist." Is balloonist found under "aviation" or should one use "aeronautics"? If not under either, could it be located under "sports?" Is it possible that the key words are "lighter than air"? [The Library of Congress Subject Headings put balloonist under "Airships;" an alternative is under "Fairs."] A trained intermediary may be able to apply the correct terminology, depending on what rules are employed in the computer database.

If the reference question is on a highly technical subject the intermediary may have recourse to an on-line thesaurus that applies to the database. Not all thesauri are created equal, and success or failure may depend on the one applied to the specific database. A dedicated reference person may stick with the researcher and try many approaches, but the press of other duties may terminate the search before the researcher feels fully satisfied that all options have been exhausted; he or she then departs with a sense of frustration. If the system were not mediated, but direct, the researcher might have the time and the inclination to browse, find clues, detour onto different paths, benefit from serendipity, and perhaps come away finding the wanted reference or, conversely, assured that the system does not contain the desired information. In that process the researcher becomes familiar with the system as well as with the search protocols. Unfortunately, that knowledge does not assure familiarity with other systems that will require searching, thus detouring the researcher from the main purpose of the task—to do research, not to learn multiple computerized systems.

In all, a mediated search is only a partial learning experience for the researcher. Perhaps it results in a heightened realization of the possibilities for inquiry that can be applied in the future, but that does not guarantee better understanding than before of the program, its shortcuts and its quirks. Yet mediation has to be accepted in many institutions that have their own dedicated systems. Even if the system being queried is one of the large reference utilities, such as RLIN or OCLC, or a regional system, such as the Western Library Network (WLN), or Illinet, an Illinois-based network, there is only a slight chance, at this writing, that a search will be successful. This is partly because of the limited archives institutional participation in such systems, but also because of the methods that archivists and curators are employing to enter data into the systems. Since the descriptive methods for personal papers are quite different from those used for archival records, precision as to names, events, geographic locations, and even subjects is much more pronounced in a manuscript register than in an archival inventory. The "provenance" approach to archival records requires different question negotiation from the "content indexing" approach to manuscripts.

Thus, an intermediary approach is limited in many of the ways that the use of printed finding aids is limited. Intermediaries are site-specific and time-specific. If a researcher has questions off-hours, on holidays, or when the research facility is closed, the questions must be held until the facility is open and a reference staff member is present. With that information in mind, we can turn to the third option available to researchers using the new technology: direct researcher access to the computer.

The ideal search method is to have one's own terminal, linked to the research institution's computer, and the ability to use the reference system that holds the data. Intermediation is replaced by self-service, which provides on-line, off-site searching that is not time-specific, since the search can be made anytime that the linked computer is in service, which is commonly twenty-four hours daily.

Other conditions that then have to be considered relate to the availability of the reference utility. Does the computer link allow access to RLIN, OCLC, and regional systems? Since RLIN is a product of the Research Libraries Group, many if not most non-research libraries—e.g., county public library systems—do not "belong" or "subscribe" to RLIN, and thus access to it is not available through those libraries. Nonparticipation can be especially important for the manuscript researcher since RLIN is the largest carrier of records in the Archives Manuscripts Control format, even if not the largest archival database.

The other national utility is OCLC, and most libraries that have utility services subscribe to OCLC, but its coverage of archives and manuscripts is less than that of RLIN.

Let us say that the researcher is at a major research library, in a university that subscribes to both utilities. Access to them, however, is controlled by passwords, since there is a site license contract or a per-search charge levied by the utilities for any searches through their systems. Not all students, faculty or staff will have passwords, and those that do may not know it. Some institutions use the bar code or other library card numbers as personal identification numbers, or PINs, for users, combined with a name identifier.

If the researcher determines that the university system provides access to the reference utilities, and successfully enters the computer system, he or she is then confronted by either a command-driven query navigation or menu-driven process.

Command systems normally provide the user with a screen that is blank except for a blinking cursor. Faced with a blinking cursor, the researcher may sit for long minutes contemplating what to do next. When first entering the system an observant user might have noticed introductory material that provided some basic commands, such as "Help" and "Exit." Typing "Help" or "?" on the blank screen may then bring up a paragraph, or a list, or some codes that can be used to move the process along from the point where the user became stuck. Sometimes the "Help" screen is of little help at all, since it relates its message in the jargon of the library profession or of the computer service center. One system in common use confronts the researcher at the first screen with an instruction to choose one of the following before proceeding: LAW, PAC, EXIT. LAW and EXIT seem clear enough, but has everyone already learned that PAC means Public Access Catalog, which is the computerized equivalent to the old card catalog? In some institutions it is referred to as the OPAC, meaning the On-line Public Access Catalog. It is at this point that the user reaches for the system manual, or reads the instruction sheet prominently displayed near the terminal. Anyone doing research in these systems for the first time should take a familiarization "tour" of the system, either from a printed manual or an on-line "Introduction," "Tour," or that enigmatic "FAQ," or "Frequently Asked Questions." Although each process takes some of the researcher's time, it is probably less of an expenditure than trying to muddle one's way through the system untutored.

Menu-driven systems are easier to navigate, in that they at least provide the user with some choices, and do not leave everything up to one's imagination in order to progress through the program.

But let us assume that the researcher has mastered the general system and knows how to navigate into the OPAC, E-mail, and that ubiquitous "Other Systems" heading. In most researcher-oriented systems all of these commands will be displayed in a menu, from which the user has choices. Choosing "Other Systems" may then bring up another menu that reads:

OTHER CATALOGS AND DATABASES[1]

   39. BIB File (Eureka)
135. Books in Print (BIP)
   35. British Library Document Supply
   36. Company Profiles
   37. Ctr for Research Libraries (CRL)
   39. ESTC: English Short Title Catalogue (Eureka)
   43. Federal Domestic Assistance Catalog
   41. GPO (FirstSearch)
   64. NPS-National Register
136. Reed's Publisher's Directory
   44. U.S. Government Publications
   41. WorldCat (FirstSearch)

A researcher confronting such a screen would benefit from knowing that Eureka is the general search system for RLIN, while FirstSearch is the general search system for OCLC. It can be assumed, therefore, that there would be greater chance of finding a manuscript listing in Eureka than in FirstSearch. Selecting either one brings up new menus and instructions. In OCLC's FirstSearch there is a choice of topic areas relating to Education and Humanities, Government and Business, Medicine, or a List of All Databases. Selecting "WorldCat: Books and other materials in libraries worldwide" brings up a menu that instructs the user in search procedures:

SEARCH	DESCRIPTION	EXAMPLES
Subject	Type the label SU: and a word(s). (subject headings and titles)	su:criticism su:freedom of speech
Author	Type the label AU: and the author name or any part of the name.	au:hemingway au:saul bellow
Title	Type the label TI: and the title or any word(s) in the title.	ti:estuary ti:love in the asylum
HINTS:	Other ways to search . . . type H <database name> LABELS. Include plural (s and es) or possessive . . . type + at end of word. Return to Database Selection Screen . . . just press Enter.	
ACTIONS:	Help Limit Database Wordlist BYE Reset	

Opening up Eureka in RLIN presents a completely different landscape:

WELCOME TO EUREKA
Current file: Bibliographic File (BIB)

You can begin a search at any time. Type:
BROWSE To scan lists of author, title, or subject headings.
FIND   To search by word or heading.
CHOOSE To choose a different file for searching.
Type HELP at any time for help.

The Bibliographic file (BIB) contains information about more than 22 million books, periodicals, recordings, scores, archival collections, and other kinds of material held in major research institutions

See next screen for a list of files you can CHOOSE

Press Enter for more information, or start a search with FIND or BROWSE.

                                              OPTIONS

COMMAND:

This screen seems "friendlier" than does the OCLC instruction screen, except that one may wonder what the term OP-

TIONS is doing there. But if one types FIND at the COMMAND prompt, another screen appears:

EUREKA	File: BIB	Find

[No search]

PARTIAL COMMAND: Find

Type an index, or type CANCEL.

Exact Indexes	AU	Authors (person/ organization)	au	white, t?
	SU	Subjects	su	venice italy—hist?
	TI	Titles	ti	room of one's own?
Word Indexes	AUW	Authors (person/ organization)	auw	xerox
	SUW	Subjects	suw	ecology vermont
	TIW	Titles	tiw	own room
	CO	Codes—ISBN, CODEN, and others	co	bugyah

For help with continuing your search, type the index alone.

Although some of the instructional material seems clear, there are codes and phrases that can be puzzling. What is the distinction between looking for venice italy—hist and for ecology vermont? What are ISBN, CODEN and bugyah, and what could they do for me? Why does RLIN separate name indexes from word indexes, while OCLC does not? Finer nuances become evident when one actually attempts searches in both databases. The OCLC search for author (au:hemingway) will not succeed if the colon is not included and if there are any spaces before or after it. The RLIN search does not require the colon and permits spacing. Of perhaps more importance to the researcher is the fact that neither of these search engines provides searching in the specific database formats present in the systems. RLIN has an archival and mixed collections format (MARC/AMC—formally known as Archives and Manuscripts Control, and still referred to by that name in many publications) that can be accessed in the basic database used by librarians and archivists for entering data, but at this writing there is no way (explicitly indicated) to search FirstSearch or Eureka in just the AMC records portion of the database. There is a screen in RLIN that purportedly lists separate databases that are accessible, but there are only four of them (BIB, Records for books, serials, sound recordings, etc.; AVE, Avery Index to Architectural Periodicals; HST, History of Science and Technology; and IIN, Inside Information). Changes, however, are planned, and an archives-only search will probably be available in the future.

It might be informative when searching for Hemingway to have a list of everything in the database that relates to him (2,572 entries on March 31, 1995), but not if the only information sought was the location of his literary archives. OCLC provides a series of screens listing 52 permutations of the database, but archives and manuscripts are not among them.

In March 1997 the international publisher Chadwyck-Healey, Inc., introduced *ArchivesUSA*. Unlike OCLC and RLIN, which began as library cataloging tools and only later developed their research and reference components, Chadwyck-Healey built on its previous products in the print, microfiche, and CD-ROM media reference tools. *ArchivesUSA* employs the concept and design of *DAMRUS* for up-to-date repository information, joins it with the complete *NUCMC* file from 1959 to 1993 in the printed version and electronic versions after 1993, and adds to them the information from the *NIDS-US* index that is already on CD-ROM. Chadwyck-Healey had already produced a five-volume printed index to *NUCMC*, 1959–1985, which it enhanced by indexing all *NUCMC* material since that period.

ArchivesUSA is available through the World Wide Web (at WWW.Chadwyck.com), for which the company offers site licenses to subscribers. A subscription also includes a CD-ROM version, which may be purchased separately by individuals of the subscribing institution. Both versions are maintained with an annual update of the contents.

As a specific database for archival material, *ArchivesUSA* has research advantages over other existing systems. First, it includes all seventy-two thousand plus *NUCMC* entries, dating to 1959, whereas most other data bases contain *NUCMC* entries only since 1985. Second, ArchivesUSA includes summary statements of repository holdings for 4,400 institutions, together with repository addresses, phone and FAX numbers, E-mail and website addresses (where they exist), hours of service, and a statement of materials solicited. Finally, the database includes the *NIDS-US* index to some 42,000 collections in 300 + repositories, many of which are not in *NUCMC*.

In addition to sheer numbers of manuscript collections that may be accessed in the database, *ArchivesUSA* includes archival information relating to government records at all levels that were excluded from *NUCMC* because they are maintained by the governments or institutions that created them. Thus, the National Archives, the state archives, and many university-agency-held archives are now available on-line or through the CD-ROM.

The search protocols of *ArchivesUSA* are presented on the screen as forms to be filled out by the researcher. The structure of the form changes with the selection of different search options. Thus, in order to search just for repository information the form appears as:

Repository form

A search at the collection level is accomplished through the collection form. Each search brings forth information presented in a *DAMRUS*, *NUCMC*, or *NIDS* format, with accompanying indexes from *NUCMC* and *NIDS*. This comprehensiveness provides the researcher with the opportunity to search at the reposi-

Collection form

Copyright © 1977 Chadwyck-Healey Inc. Reprinted by permission of Chadwyck-Healey Inc.

tory, collection, or finding aid level, and to move up or down between them. Searches can be combined, the results compiled, and selected lists created for downloading. Searches may also be made from any of the search fields, thus providing a list of all repositories in a state or a city, all repositories that have a common collecting area (e.g., labor), or all collections that contain selected keywords or phrases. Every search field offers a view of its keywords or authority list with the depression of a key or click of the mouse.

Because *ArchivesUSA* contains Web site addresses, it is possible to click on it and be connected directly to the submitting repository. This is not possible in the CD-ROM version.

The researcher attempting to use on-line search services is confronted with a series of impediments: (1) does the researcher's institution provide access to the national databases, including RLIN, OCLC, and *ArchivesUSA?* (2) Can the researcher access these directly, or is it necessary to go through an intermediary? (3) How complex are the databases, and therefore how much time and effort should go into mastering them? (4) What are the prospects for retrieval? Although, for instance, the Edith Dolan Riley Collection at the University of Washington is represented in *NUCMC*, it is in neither RLIN nor OCLC. But, because *Archives-USA* contains the totality of *NUCMC*, the Riley entry will be found there. The same is true with many government archives because *DAMRUS* and *NIDS* included them.

If these conditions are not favorable for researcher direct access to the information utilities, is the researcher denied the convenience of electronic access to manuscript and archival resources? We can turn now to a growing system that has potential great benefits but also some hazards—the Internet.

The Milton S. Eisenhower Library at Johns Hopkins University converted all of its manuscript finding aids that were created and maintained in word processing files to a standardized format (ASCII) and then loaded them into a gopher-compatible database server, which was then linked to the Hopkins computing facility and assigned an Internet address. Gopher servers consist of software which connects a single institution's computer to others on the Internet, assembles files of a specified type, and presents menu options to the user. Although a researcher may think that because the Johns Hopkins gopher has been accessed it is the source of the information being received, the reality is quite different. If one connects to Hopkins and sees a menu listing a choice of forty-two or more other institutions, it means only that by selecting one— such as the University of North Carolina (UNC)-Chapel Hill—the Hopkins gopher is then disconnecting itself and linking the user directly to UNC. The gopher is much like a switchboard, and after the connection is made the responsibility for what happens is that of UNC, not Johns Hopkins.

The archivist of the Ferdinand Hamburger Archives at Johns Hopkins indicated in late 1993 that 155 Hopkins archival inventories and 203 manuscript registers were converted and entered into the system for network access. At last check, there were 42 other institutions on the gopher with over 2,500 inventories and registers.[2] Some institutions have even entered digitized graphics in the system, accessible to those who have a computer with a graphics card, special software, and enough random access memory (RAM) to accommodate the files. The Internet has been enhanced by various search software, such as "Yahoo" and "AltaVista," that perform different functions in searching for titles or names in all of the collections in all of the institutions that are linked to the Web. Such tools permit the researcher to bypass the gopher process of going first to Hopkins and then picking off the repositories one at a time, but it is not surprising that the Web, Standard Generalized Markup Language (SGML), and Hypertext Markup Language (HTML) are replacing or supplementing gopher searching. Work on an engine named Mosaic led its developers to produce the Netscape Navigator, or just "Netscape," a second-generation Mosaic-like program that gives researchers the ability to link information sources by using a mouse that provides "point and click" capabilities. It is this and a continuing series of breakthroughs that have led to a phenomenal growth of Web users and given archivists the opportunity to build on the automation progress that they have been struggling with since the 1960s.

The advantages of the Web over entering collection information in RLIN or OCLC, according to one Hopkins staff member, are:

> no high membership costs, no expensive dedicated network line access or maintenance costs, no necessary adherence to MARC/AMC, greater local control over everything from hardware and software choice to choice of presentation format (i.e., finding aids, full-text, or images), and potentially more powerful searching capability.[3]

The concept of the gopher menu item "Manuscript and Archives Repositories—at Johns Hopkins" is misleading, since other institutions' holdings are also entered (the listing came about because Johns Hopkins originated the system and was the first to be available through it). But gopher searches do not change the fact that finding aids in a manual, analog format must be searched vertically or page by page, one at a time, in order to locate series or folder headings pertinent to a search. An early plan at the Library of Congress was to try to enter the series descriptions *and* folder lists into a computerized system, which would then allow horizontal searches through all of the finding aids, resulting in a list of "hits" and an indication of which finding aid each "hit" was from. On the assumption that a researcher using a collection in person would be guided into the material by the actual words on the folder labels, the self-indexing aspect of the system could be justified. The Hopkins plan is based on the same theory: enter all registers and inventories verbatim into the system, and then provide for a full-text, keyword index to each one, or to all of them.

There are obvious pitfalls with free-text indexing and free-text searching of folder labels, but in many ways free-text searching is superior to structured searching because the folder label terminology was applied either by the creator of the collection or by the processor in the repository that received the collection. That terminology does not conform to Library of Congress Subject Headings, the Art and Architecture Thesaurus, or any other standard vocabulary. To make each folder heading conform would be impossible under the best of circumstances because of the labor involved in reentering all of those folder labels. *NIDS*, with its 34,800 microfiche, containing some 2,436,000 inventory and register pages, with perhaps twenty-five to fifty folders listed on each, presents a daunting workload for conversion. The specificity of terms used in folder labels also makes them inappropriate for the Library of Congress Subject Headings, and hit-and-miss for the Art and Architecture Thesaurus. Trial and error is the common practice of researchers in documentary sources. (The National Archives does not call its main reading room a "Reading Room" or "Research Room." Common parlance is that it is the "Search Room," because that is what mostly goes on there.)

Was this early gopher project, then, the beginning of the ultimate system? It appeared to have prospects, but was far from perfect. The difficulty with the information in the finding aids gopher is the same as the problems with Eureka and FirstSearch, only compounded. When the researcher worked through Hopkins to get to UNC it was necessary to use UNC procedures in order to perform a search. The first problem is that the UNC material is not just that of the manuscript and archive holdings, but contains other elements of its information system, and the researcher is therefore confronted with another menu that must be navigated to get to manuscripts. Once there, the search protocols, or the codes and keystrokes that must be used in order to activate a search, are peculiar to UNC and do not relate to any search processes used in other repositories. It might, therefore, require activation of a UNC "Help" screen in order to figure out how to use the system. At that point the researcher has first had to enter the Internet, then find a menu item that will lead to the Hopkins site, then choose a menu item that will open up the collections at UNC, then determine how to get into the manuscript file, then understand the query codes. The UNC index can provide considerable support to the researcher's inquiry, depending on the indexing terms used in that collection. There is no guarantee that the manuscript collection will follow the same subject heading rules as the book collections do. A search that I initiated in the UNC-Chapel Hill Southern Historical Collection for anything on "barnstorm*"[a] led me to two collection finding aids, A. P. Watt and Company and Mary Susan Ker, but not to the location of the subject within them. When I accessed the A. P. Watt and Company entry to look at the "barnstorming" entry, I was presented with a collection of a British literary agent consisting of 213,000 items + 33 volumes, 1888–1962, that was described in 240 screens. Since there is no internal indexing, I would have had to scan them until I found the reference.

I then shifted to Ker for a search, but was suddenly confronted with the message "Sorry—too busy now," even though I was conducting my search on a Sunday morning. However, I kept trying, and soon was granted access to the Mary Susan Ker Collection, 1852–1910, containing 6,400 (*sic*) items in 12.5 ft. of shelf space. It seemed intriguing to find a reference to "barnstorming" in a collection of the daughter of a cotton planter whose correspondence was mostly with family members in the Mississippi Valley in Louisiana and Mississippi. The Scope and Content Note belied the dates in the collection title line, since there was a subseries of diaries dated 1886–1923 (Ker's death), and another subseries dated 1902–1958, where I suspected any reference to "barnstorming" might be found. I began a screen-by-screen search of the collection, which also is not internally indexed, but when I had gone through twenty-seven screens and noted (by the program information at the bottom of the screen) that I was only 20 percent through the search and would have to page through a very long

---

[a] In most computer searching the use of the asterisk (*) denotes any combination of letters following those explicitly employed. Thus "barnstorm*" would search for barnstorming or barnstormers.

register before locating a reference to "barnstorming," I gave up (in another attempt later I found it near the end).

An *ArchivesUSA* search (CD-ROM version) on "barnstorm★" resulted in retrieval, within less than one minute, of seven collections from North Dakota, Ohio, Texas (3), Washington, and Wyoming. Ker was not one of the collections retrieved, so I searched for :"Ker" by collection name, globally, and retrieved three collections from the University of North Carolina, one of which was the papers of Mary Susan Ker. It was both a *NIDS* and a *NUCMC* entry, MS61–159, which placed it twenty-four years before *NUCMC* records were created electronically and sent to the cataloging utilities. The index terms accompanying the entry did not list any form of "barnstorming."

When I shifted my search to RLIN and attempted to find "barnstorming," using the term both truncated and complete, led me only to a sound recording by Joe Walsh titled "Barnstorm." I then shifted to "aviation," and was presented with 9,544 entries. The only way that I thought of limiting that search was to try "aviation barnstorming," which produced no results, as I anticipated, since "barnstorming" alone had drawn a blank.

Still in RLIN I tried Mary Susan Ker as an author, which produced a reference to a microfilm titled "Southern Women and Their Families in the 19th Century: Papers and Diaries." The Ker collection was only one part of this, but it was listed as the Mary Susan Ker Papers, 1785–1923, which are different dates than those given in the collection's gopher entry, but the same as in the *ArchivesUSA* entry. There was no reference to the collection itself, except in this microfilm edition. The subjects listed for the entry, in Library of Congress Subject Heading format, made no mention of barnstorming. At that point I was suddenly ejected from RLIN with a curt note that I had been on the circuit too long, and I found myself back at my home base.

What one comes away with after these sessions is a sense that on-line computer searching for manuscripts at this point is a very inexact art (please see disclaimer at the head of this chapter). Not many institutions have entered their manuscript holdings in the RLIN and OCLC national utilities. When they have, some have done so in one or the other and some are in both. Although the Library of Congress has entered its *NUCMC* data in the utilities, it has done so only since 1988, which leaves almost thirty years of *NUCMC* unavailable through that source. *ArchivesUSA* has picked up the slack for archival collections, and expanded the coverage to many institutions not covered elsewhere.

The gopher system also is not the best approach to the searches that researchers want to conduct. They are for the most part mere surrogates for the original finding aids, structured in a very formalized but not standardized style and accessible mainly through page-by-page searching. The individual institution entries, such as those that can be accessed through the Hopkins gateway, are not accessible through interinstitutional indexes, and within a single institution the indexing is erratic. Once a researcher does find a collection that appears to be promising in content, the search must be undertaken through page-by-page scanning, which is easier in a paper document than it is on a screen. However, my search for Ker materials would not be possible if I had to go to Chapel Hill to do it, or ask the university to send me copies of all of its finding aids.

Much more advanced than gophers are those systems that use hypertext structures to conduct electronic searches. Hypertext can be thought of as a series of layers of information that can be approached through opening up lower layers by activating a word or phrase in a higher layer. In a fully implemented hypertext system if one were reading a text on the screen that dealt with classical musicians and came across "Beethoven," it would be possible to key on that word (via keyboard or mouse) and activate another screen that would provide a biographical sketch of the composer. In that sketch there might be a list of works, and on the term "symphony" a keying could open up a list of the nine symphonies, indicating the key and opus number of each. Keying on the ninth (D Minor, Op. 125) could bring up information summarizing each of the movements, and a reference to Friedrich Schiller's poem, the *Ode to Joy*, as a text for the choral fourth movement. Keying on "Schiller" would then take the researcher into a wholly different subject, with similar possibilities for exposition.

The hypertext structure can be applied to a wide variety of texts, and, indeed, in recent electronic variations might even provide the music for the Beethoven selection. It is on this hypertext structure that some sources on the World Wide Web operate; it therefore has considerably more potential for exploration than the gopher structures.

A manuscript search in hypertext could hypothetically bring up a list of repositories that have manuscript collections in the system, key on University of North Carolina at Chapel Hill, and from the menu of options provided, key on Southern Historical Collection, which would produce a list of the collections. Upon entering the term "aviation" the system presents a list of collections containing that term, from which the researcher can key on Ker, with perhaps a highlighted aviation term from the general introduction, or the scope and content note. Further keying leads to each of the sections in the Ker collection where an aviation topic is mentioned, providing a choice of accessing the term if it appears in the scope note, a series listing, or a folder title. Selecting any one of these will present the actual text of the reference, one of which might be in a series description for a branch of the family, which would then lead to a specific box and folder where "barnstorming" is discussed in relation to an adventurous family member.

This "peeling off" of the layers takes the researcher deeper and deeper into the contents of the material, and provides an option for disengaging from the search should the clues lead off into unwanted byways. Serious development of such a system, long sought after by archivists, began when the University of California (UC) at Berkeley library created a prototype standard for encoding archive and library finding aids in the form of a Standard Generalized Markup Language Document Type Definition (SGML DTD). The work was supported by a Department of Education grant, followed subsequently with grants from the Commission on Preservation and Access and the Bentley Library Research Fellowship Program. As work continued on the project the Council on Library Resources and the Library of Congress National Digital Library lent further support, with the library promising to provide maintenance on the DTD standard, renamed the Encoded Archival Description, or EAD, after full endorsement by archivists. As this is written, an experimental Web site has been mounted and is available for access on the Internet.[4]

The options provided are for an HTML search or a SGML search. If HTML is selected the screen provides an option to: Browse the *Electronic Finding Aid Collection*. Selecting that option then produces a *List of Finding Aid Collections by Institution*, which (as of this writing) includes seven institutions: UC Berkeley, UC-San Diego, UC-Los Angeles, Duke University, Library of Congress, State Historical Society of Wisconsin, and Arizona State University. At that point the researcher can immediately enter a search object, or first select from the institutions in order to target the search. The former permits searching the same object over all eight institutions. The latter would restrict the search to the institution selected.

There is a detailed "Help" program available at the click of the mouse to explain the search mechanisms, with examples of proximity searching, truncation, and other options. What the researcher soon discovers is that this search engine is standardized at all levels, so that the same search formats can be employed across all institutions or at a single institution across all finding aids or in just a single finding aid. In that respect the Berkeley project has accomplished something that no one else has to date— interinstitutional (and, indeed, intra-institutional) descriptive standards.

I conducted a test of the system by entering in the SEARCH box the phrase "labor within 3 words of union★." This is one option for proximity searching combined with truncation, which would retrieve "labor union," "labor unions," "labor unionization," "unionizing labor," etc. Searches are not case-specific, so that capitalization need not be adhered to.

The result of that inquiry produced eighteen "hits," indicating that there were eleven hits at UC-Berkeley and seven at Duke. A click of the mouse on Berkeley resulted in the names of three finding aids: Cross (Ira B) California Labor Newspapers, 1; Nicaragua Information Center Papers, 2; Trefethen (Eugene E), Jr Papers, 8. A click on Trefethen brought up information that the CONTAINER LISTING alone contained eight references to "labor within 3 words of union★." Then a click on CONTAINER LISTING brought me to the specific box where the phrase "labor union" appeared (Box 26, 2 references; Box 50, 2 references) and so on.

Thus, the Berkeley approach seems to be paying off for the researcher. The system at this writing has a number of negative attributes that must be recognized, although all are potentially solvable. First, the experiment is just that, an experiment, carried out within a limited time frame that is determined by the funding provided as testing money. Finding continuing support after the tests may prove difficult in today's funding market, with government-granting agencies downsizing or disappearing altogether, and no indication that the private sector wishes to extend itself beyond testing these systems.

Second, even with a fast (28.8 bps) modem and a system capable of quick data transfer, I sometimes waited three minutes for the next choice to appear after clicking on an option. The fact that Internet protocols do not deliver whole databases at one time, but only those specifically requested, means that every time another part of the database (in this case the Berkeley finding aids) is called for, the Internet must go back to Berkeley and retrieve it—it is not lurking in my own system awaiting a call.

Third, at this stage there are very few finding aids in the system, which is understandable for an experiment. Berkeley itself has entered 83 finding aids, but the Library of Congress has only 39 (out of 10,000 collections), The State Historical Society of Wisconsin has 14 in the system, etc. With funding uncertain, there is a question of how many institutions will undertake the SGML marking-up process on their own finding aids.

Fourth, the search mechanism is essentially a keyword search looking for explicit terms, modified by the truncation and proximity searching possibilities. But if a term is not specifically mentioned it will not be picked out by the search engine. For instance, a search for "labor union*" will not pick out a specific reference to AFL/CIO if the more generalized term "labor" or "union" is not present. Conceptual searches, as mentioned at the end of the previous chapter, present a problem. In other words, there is no classified or structured index under which lesser or parallel terms are subsumed. In order to counter this problem to some extent, the Berkeley project has included a section on helps for searching.

In spite of these shortcomings at the present time, the hypertext systems that are being applied to finding aids, with the Berkeley project in the lead, appear to be the wave of the future. What is needed, perhaps, is for some union between an institution that will convert finding aids into SGML format, and the thousands of finding aids that are already on microfiche and indexed in the *NIDS/ArchivesUSA* project. At this writing, *NIDS* contains 782 finding aids from the Library of Congress Manuscript Division alone. Adding the thousands of finding aids now accessible through Hopkins would bring together a significant research resource on the Internet.

Is the World Wide Web the answer, then? Will it replace Eureka, FirstSearch, and gopher structures? That is almost a certainty, but the problems of automating manuscript and archival finding aids are not confined to electronic access.

A typical manuscript collection, described in a register, may have ten or fifteen series. In a *NUCMC* type description it is possible to enumerate ten to fifteen series in the "Scope and Content Note," providing to researchers a good idea of the type of material contained in the collections. Archivists contemplating automation have considered the series to be *the* information source for records, and have treated the series entries as separate entities, comparable to a *NUCMC* entry. This makes some sense from a format consideration, since a series can be described in just five data elements: title, dates, extent or size, narrative description, and organization or arrangement. Archival series descriptions, however, are not so much concerned with subjects as they are with form of the material. One could search through dozens of series listings in archival inventories without finding a single subject that would appear in an index.

It is not possible to provide an in-depth description of an *archival* record group in ten or fifteen lines of text. Nor is it possible to provide a meaningful description by responding to ten or eleven rather simple questions. Most importantly, it is not possible to provide an index to a record group, as one can to a manuscript collection, because there are few index terms in an archival description, at least not at the series level. If one tackles the problem at the record group level it is possible, from the "Introduction" to an inventory, to find subjects or topics mentioned broadly as being accessible "somewhere" in the records, but that can hardly be good enough for the researcher who is not working at the records site.

A prime example is that richest of all research series in federal records—the central file of the Department of State, which appears as:

DECIMAL FILE. 1910–44. 13,620 ft.
    Correspondence of the Department of State with its diplomatic and consular officers, other Government agencies, foreign governments, Congress, the President, and the public, dealing with practically all activities of the Department except those relating to appointments, passports, publications, accounts, and a few other subjects. This correspondence composes the central file of the Department from 1910 and is arranged according to the decimal subject classification adopted in that year. This system provides for nine major subject classes, as outlined above. The decimal file is divided into three time periods, 1910–29, 1930–39, and 1940–44; the classification scheme, however, is continued without changes through these periods. Lists of the papers in this file and card indexes to them

are also divided into these three time periods and are described
in entries 198–200. For a list of parts of the decimal file, 1910–
29, that have been microfilmed, see appendix IX.[5]

It is notable that there are no indexable terms in that description
of *two miles* of records, except for those that are listed as *not* being
present—appointments, passports, publications and accounts!
Compare this with an entry for a manuscript collection in
NUCMC, which lists the series (without explicitly identifying
them as such) and then gives some hints of names and subjects. As
an example, the Papers of George F. Addes (1910–   ) in the Archives of Labor History and Urban Affairs, Wayne State University,[6] are described as:

> Labor union official. UAW-CIO financial reports, minutes,
> local union correspondence and appeal cases, key plant file of
> the UAW Research Dept., Addes' general files, and a tran-
> scribed oral history interview in which Addes describes his ex-
> periences. Subjects include the 1946 General Motors strike,
> health insurance programs, and appeals. Correspondents in-
> clude H. W. Anderson, Herbert Brownell, Jr., John M. Coffee,
> Frank E. Hook, Harry F. Kelly, C. M. LaFollette, Roy Reuther,
> Walter P. Reuther, and Roy W. Woodruff.

The series, which have expanded descriptions in the register,
are: UAW-CIO financial reports, minutes, local union correspondence and appeal cases, key plant file of the UAW Research Dept.,
personal general files, and oral history interview. Together they
constitute 66 feet of documents, which would fill approximately
200 manuscript containers.

Each of the subject terms used in this Addes note is indexed
in *NUCMC*, as are individuals Anderson, Brownell, Coffee, Hook,
Kelly, LaFollette, the two Reuthers, and Woodruff, with the reference back to the entry number for the Addes collection, and the
full context is seen there by the researcher.

The essential difference between automating access to archives, as opposed to manuscripts, therefore, is that manuscript
collections are much more amenable to the process because of their
smaller size and, oddly, lack of predictable order. Since the contents
of manuscript collections do not represent organizational function,
are not mandated by statute, regulations or manuals, and present
idiosyncratic materials representing life experiences or creative

outpourings, they cannot easily be described in generalities. Description at personal levels generally provides terms that are meaningful in an index, be they personal names, topics, events, themes, titles of works, or even forms, such as "poetry."

Summary

With most information about repository holdings now being produced in electronic text format (word processing) or in print that can be scanned into electronic text, the Web or CD-ROM entries become a mere by-product of a routine institutional procedure, demanding no special skills beyond what staff can already perform. Converting traditionally structured text into SGML and hypertext formats is not a natural by-product of the archivist's work, but can be accomplished by knowledgeable staff with some training, such as is being tested at Berkeley. With most university faculty members and students being provided with access to computer networks, and to the Internet, the manuscript and archives tools are becoming available to all, without special training or the knowledge of complex procedures.

In addition to searching for specific records or manuscript collections in these various systems, the researcher now has available a vast array of information *about* repositories, their procedures for research, their facilities, hours of service, and even their ability to respond to researcher questions via E-mail. The entire general *Guide to the National Archives*, 1995 edition, is on-line through the National Archives Web site, as are many of its other information resources. Quick answers to general information questions are available at the touch of a few keys—detailed research answers to specific questions are a bit more difficult to arrive at.

However, anyone who attempts research into archival or manuscript collections through these various systems will find that the searches themselves can be time-consuming and demanding. The researcher must have some tutorial in using each system if there is to be any success, and the systems are not standardized.

All of the systems are limited in content as well as in access mechanisms. Users must first determine if they can get Internet access, then know what databases are available to them, then know whether passwords are required for entry, as in the commercial utilities of RLIN and OCLC, or the *ArchivesUSA* database. Once in, the protocols of each system must be understood, as well as the limitations on coverage of institutions, or of an institution's holdings. A 1993 study concluded that:

> we have come to view bibliographic network and online catalog descriptions as an expensive and complex form of "see reference." Although these online systems can indicate that archival materials relating to an inquiry exist, they are not really able to communicate the quality or quantity of information available in primary sources.[7]

It is fair to say at this writing that none of the automated systems except *ArchivesUSA* compares in coverage with the currently available printed sources, such as *NUCMC* or *DAMRUS*, or provides comprehensive indexed access to complete finding aids as *NIDS* does. There are certainly more entries in *ArchivesUSA* with its more than 4,000 institutions, 72,000 collections, and indexes to 52,000 finding aids than in any of the others, but none of the systems—electronic, printed, or microfiche—contains the actual documents in the collections, with a few minor and experimental exceptions. These conditions will change, and there is more leaning towards standards in the archival profession now than at any time in the past,[8] which is being driven by the realization that automation demands structure. These changes can only be of benefit to researchers, who, until now, have been the forgotten or ignored players in the archival automation game.

Notes

1. This is an exact representation of a screen from the University of Maryland's VICTOR program. The entries are in alphabetical, not numeric, order.

2. An actual count in April 1994 of the entries for the then extant 16 institutions came to 2,663, but there are some duplicate entries and a number of brief notes indicating that a register is available but has not yet been converted to an electronic format.

3. Alan Braddock, "A Gopher in the Repository." Unpublished paper written for a Manuscripts Administration course at the University of Maryland, dated November 30, 1993; and "Teaching an Old Gopher New Tricks, or How to Improve Internet Access to Archives and Manuscripts Information." Typescript, dated fall 1994. I am indebted to Mr. Braddock, at that time an interlibrary loan librarian at the Eisenhower

Library, Johns Hopkins University, for much that follows about the finding aids Gopher.

4. Through "http://sunsite.berkeley.edu/FindingAids/".

5. National Archives and Records Administration, *Inventory of the General Records of the Department of State, 1789–1949*, No. 15, series entry 205, 53.

6. *NUCMC*, MS71–619.

7. Robert P. Spindler and Richard Pearce-Moses, "Does AMC Mean 'Archives Made Confusing'? Patron Understanding of USMARC AMC Catalog Records," *American Archivist* 56 (spring 1993), 340–341.

8. Bureau of Canadian Archivists, *Toward Descriptive Standards. Report and Recommendations of the Canadian Working Group on Archival Descriptive Standards* (Ottawa: The Bureau, December 1985); *Rules for Archival Description* (Ottawa: The Bureau, 1992); Michael Cook and Margaret Procter, *Manual of Archival Description* (Aldershot, Hants, England: Gower, 2d ed., 1989); Steven L. Hensen, *Archives, Personal Papers, and Manuscripts: A Cataloging Manual for Archival Repositories, Historical Societies, and Manuscript Libraries* (Chicago: Society of American Archivists, 2d ed., 1989); Nancy Sahli, *MARC for Archives and Manuscripts: The AMC Format* (Chicago: Society of American Archivists, 1985–); Stephen M. Spivak and Keith A. Winsell, *A Sourcebook of Standards Information: Education, Access, and Development* (Boston: G. K. Hall and Co., 1991), especially part 5, "Information Exchange and the Utility of Standards," which includes articles by several members of the archival profession; Karen M. Spicher, "Finding Aid Gophers and Archival Access." Unpublished student paper, University of Maryland at College Park, January 23, 1995, 17 pp.; Victoria Irons Walch, *Standards for Archival Description: A Handbook* (Iowa City: Society of American Archivists, 1994).

· 7 ·

Organizing a Life

We should not bequeath puzzles to posterity.

Maynard Brichford[1]

Manuscripts are not collected as artifacts. Institutions collect in order to serve a research public, whether that is as narrow as one faculty or as broad as all comers. The task or process of building a research collection obviously does not stop with gathering in someone's papers, but has to proceed to the imposition of some rationality and order over what may very well be chaos. Once the collection is safely in the repository, logged in and shelved where it can easily be located, it must be put in some queue for processing and preparation for research use. Although curators regularly bemoan the size of their backlog, it is a natural phenomenon in an institution where many large collections can be accessioned in a week's time but each may take months to process. If backlogs grow too large, the institution must reexamine its collecting policy and its human and financial resources, as well as its ability to store the material.

Collections in backlog are not necessarily handled on a first-in first-out basis. There may be many reasons for processing collections ahead of others that have been in backlog longer. There may be some difficulties with a deed of gift that could stall further action on a collection until the legal matters are resolved. There may be a significant research demand for a recently arrived collection that would push it ahead of those likely to be less in demand. The curator may hold back a collection in a special field awaiting the availability of a processing staff member who specializes in that field and who is meanwhile completing other work. There may be a flurry of activity to process many small collections, regardless of their term in backlog, in order to get them out of the way and to give a processor a change of pace from dealing with a series of large collections. Some collections may be considered early because of their physical condition and the need to get much of the material to the preservation laboratory, or because they are needed to provide material for an important exhibit. As with much else in manuscript repositories, there is no standard rule for clearing out the backlog: the curator measures the situation and applies local imperatives.

When it is time, and a collection reaches the front of the line for processing, the curator of a sizeable institution must make some decisions. Is it archival material or a collection of personal papers that is the next in line to be worked on? If it is large, what level of processing should there be? Who is the best staff member (if there is a choice) to deal with the material from the standpoint of familiarity with the topic, agency or individual?

Once the assignment is made, and assuming that the collection is large and complex, it is not unreasonable to expect that the staff assigned to process the material may disappear for a week while searching out biographies, period histories, and special coverage of the times, the place or the society of the subject whose papers are being processed. The purpose is to gain familiarity with names of important players, colleagues, and rivals, and to understand locations, events, issues and conflicts. All of this background is necessary because personal papers deal with manifest events, and not the background to them. When a letter contains reference to the name of a third party or an issue, the author is assuming background knowledge on the part of the recipient, and does not go into great explanations. "I talked with Arnett about the situation in Illinois and he agreed that Baker would be a good person to help us out." Who are Arnett and Baker and what is the situation in Illinois? The processor should know, or be able to find out, aided by the date of the letter and other evidence.

This is not to imply that the processor reads every word of every letter and pieces together all of the information relating to the life of the subject. But the processor should be able to classify documents into different groupings, by subject, topic, period of career life, etc., and determine whether they represent personal, professional, business or other relationships. A familiarity with the life, times, associates and activities of the subject will assist the processor in placing documents in logical groupings for research purposes.

With the conclusion of basic research on the subject's life and times, the processor lays out a plan for organizing the material, and, if appropriate, discusses the plan with superiors in the same unit (e.g., Special Collections). The plan may be tentative, depending on how thoroughly the collection has already been analyzed, but, with all preliminaries agreed upon, the processor can begin processing the papers. This consists of four essential steps: analysis, selection, organization and description.

ANALYSIS

Analysis really begins with the first viewing of the material, but continues until the last document is foldered and boxed. It merely implies that the processor, knowing the plan for preparing the collection, analyzes the material to see if and how it fits into that plan, asking questions of appropriateness or importance. Analysis can also concentrate on physical condition, with a view to tagging deteriorating materials for preservation action. Analysis will also alert the processor to the fact that a collection may not be what it was originally thought to be. A collection of personal papers may turn out to contain a considerable amount of archival material if the subject was a member of a corporate body and kept files or records that are really records of the corporate body. Conversely, an archival collection (or record group) being processed may contain a considerable amount of personal papers of one or more corporate officers. These discoveries will perhaps lead to a revision of the original processing plan, and the construction of groupings that reflect the true configuration of the material.

Analysis obviously continues throughout the processing stage, not stopping with selection, organization and description that follow. The interesting phenomenon that occurs during the initial analysis after serious processing has begun is the development of the processor's intimacy with and attitude toward the subject. It is much like finding a long-neglected box of someone's letters on the top shelf of a closet, and systematically sifting through and browsing, with pauses to read closely some of the more interesting ones. The person begins to emerge from beneath the text, and one picks up verbal habits, attitudinal insights, biases, areas of excited interest, emotions, and, with any luck, a bit of the person's psyche. Perhaps being a reader/intruder is awkward, looking in on this long-departed person's revelation of viewpoints and commentaries on events of the day, not knowing what follows tomorrow. The reader wonders how the writer could not have known that the action contemplated would be disastrous, or that the relationship that seemed to be flowering in the words of the author would either fade into inconsequentiality, end tragically, or go on to be acclaimed by others.

These impressions do not apply only to letters of people with sentimental involvement; they can occur also with politicians or military figures, who can be just as passionate about their careers as any young lovers are about each other. General George Patton, writing to his wife Bea, "bitching" about the fools that he had to suffer, both military and political;[2] Abigail Adams, complaining to far-away John about the epidemics hitting Braintree, and how she was continually changing the linens of the little ones who were so ill;[3] a Black woman, recently freed from slavery, pleading to the District of Columbia Freedmen's Bureau that her husband be released from the penitentiary for "assisting three colored women, & four children, to escape from slavery."[4] It is in this analysis process that the processor gets to know the people whose papers may represent the only legacy that they bequeath to posterity, to make us all aware of the constancy of the human condition.

That being the case, how does an institution avoid retaining every scrap that reveals some human activity, sentiment, decision, bias or dream? The social historian and biographer would say, "Keep everything!" But decisions must be made, and hewing to a retention or disposal plan is imperative if space, budgets, and, indeed, the comfort of the future researcher are to be considered as relevant. In sum, in most collections there must be some selection of what to keep and what to throw away.

Selection

Although the idea of "selection" relating to manuscript materials is anathema to most researchers, it is a legitimate activity, especially if it is sanctioned by the deed of gift, supported by prearranged selection criteria, and safeguarded with selection review procedures. Some of the decisions are easy: the processor selects for disposal such items as multiple copies, insignificant documents, and extraneous printed matter. Multiple copies may be carbons of letters that are no different from the retained copy, reproduced minutes, agendas, reports, drafts, and similar documents. Insignificant items are easier to dispose of in recent collections than in older ones. It is inconceivable that an insignificant note by Thomas Jefferson would be disposed of, if it were in his hand and especially if it bore his signature. On the other hand, an insignificant note by a twentieth-century U.S. senator to a secretary transmitting information about a routine appointment with a constituent might not be treated so piously. The same may apply for transmittal memoranda, and items found in the file relating to routine constituent appointments. The processor and curator must ask the question: "Who would use this, and why?" In purely personal papers there are always routine bills, canceled checks, undecipherable cryptic notes, household documents, newspaper or magazine clippings that were of momentary interest, and all of the literary or graphic detritus that clutter up desk drawers the world over.

Large institutions generally have policies based on age. With time, quantity of material reflecting an age becomes less voluminous, and more important for an understanding of the age. The "natural sifting" has taken place, through personal disposal, neglect, fires, and wartime recycling campaigns. The Library of Congress and the National Archives (among others) have established dates before which all material will be retained, regardless of form or content. As the decades go by, these dates creep forward, maintaining a rolling lag-time of somewhere around one hundred years.

Extraneous printed material comes in many forms in collections of personal papers, and sometimes in great quantity. The author of a journal article may receive ten or twenty reprints from the publisher. After sending a number to colleagues and to those who are supposed to be impressed, the author still has ten in the file, but the collection need retain but one or two as a record of the author's output. The subject of the collection, if professionally active, may also receive a considerable number of published articles from friends, colleagues, and others who want to inform the recipient of their work. Although some of these may be said to provide a clue to the readings that influenced the subject, especially if they have margin notes or other annotations, most are probably only peripherally related to the work of the subject, may have been read in an offhand way (perhaps the work of a former student, now off in another field), but are not significant for an understanding of the subject's own work. Again, the question of relevance and importance is posed in anticipation of disposing of the printed material. Some items require little agonizing, since many collections contain an accumulation of those odds and ends that burden all of us, but that most of us have enough sense to throw away shortly, if not immediately, after receipt. I refer, of course, to notices of Sears Roebuck tire sales, flyers announcing new scholarly publications, solicitations for funds for this or that cause, or political newsletters from a plethora of local, state and federal politicians. Since it is certain that these materials will be found elsewhere, and that anyone doing research on Sears advertising techniques or the history of the History Book Club will not be looking at this collection for such material, it can all be set aside for disposal.

A study by Richard W. Hite and Daniel J. Linke, describing experimental procedures for "selecting out," or "weeding" manuscript collections at the Western Reserve Historical Society provides some pointers, and some figures on the result of the process.[5] It is not surprising that congressional constituent mail ranked high on the disposal scale, and genealogical or family papers ranked low. From such studies one can project certain "standards" that curators might consider when looking for ways to reduce bulk without impeding understanding of the subject collected.

But, as with every other aspect of manuscript collecting, there can be "guidelines" but no across-the-board standards. In many repositories the general guidelines are to consider for disposal such routine things as household papers (unless this is a family history collection, perhaps), bills and receipts, Christmas cards, social invitations, hostess seating charts, movie theater stubs, concert programs, etc., etc. But curators look at who the subject is, and why that person's papers were taken in the first place. The processor at the Library of Congress assigned to work on the papers of Evalyn Walsh McLean would have read interesting biographical material on Mrs. McLean from obituary notices, newspaper accounts, biographical sketches in the popular print media, and, indeed, even fictionalized literature. Her story is great Americana—born to poor Irish parents, the daughter of a picaresque father who headed for the Colorado gold fields to make his fame and fortune and was exonerated by striking it rich in a mine that he had won in a card game. The family moved to Washington, D.C., where the turn-of-century wealth found an appropriate stage to strut on. Evalyn Walsh met Ed McLean, spoiled, hedonistic son of a newspaper magnate who owned the *Washington Post*, among other holdings, married him, and they indulged themselves in their personal pleasures: Evalyn bought jewelry, including the infamous Hope Diamond. Then they built a house on a hill in upper northwest Washington, which they called "Friendship." Evalyn and Ed used the house to entertain the political, royal, and generally public elites of the western world. (An apartment development, "McLean Gardens," now occupies that portion of upper northwest Washington known as "Friendship Heights.") Ultimately things fell apart. Evalyn tried to have Ed committed to an institution based on his mental condition, aggravated by alcohol; she became somehow involved in the Lindbergh kidnapping case, continued to throw controversial parties during World War II when her money was all but depleted, and yet gave over properties to the Red Cross, entertained the troops at Friendship, and maintained in the public's eye her image as the prototype Washington hostess. After her death in 1947 documentaries as well as fictionalized movies and biographical television programs were based on her life.[6]

Knowing all of that, what would the processor of the Evalyn Walsh McLean collection find valuable enough to keep? Among other things there were household receipts for purchases made— such as $6,000 for floral displays for *one* party; there is the bill-of-sale for some jewelry, including the Hope Diamond bought from Galt & Sons, jewelers, for $150,000 (the same Galt family as the contemporary Edith Bolling Galt Wilson, wife of the president). There were also Christmas cards—from the royalty of Europe and the great oil states of the Middle East, as well as from senators, FBI Director J. Edgar Hoover, the president, cabinet members, members of the diplomatic corps, heads of state and major industrialists of the era. There were dinner seating charts, indicating that "Friendship" was the place where world figures who may have found it awkward to associate in public saw opportunities for dinner chitchat and postdinner cigar-smoking conversations that may have eased (or perhaps hardened) international tensions, all out of sight of the press corps, or perhaps, in those more polite days, immune to attribution or even identification in the next day's *Post*. One such chart, typical of many in the collection, indicates the following seating:[7]

Mrs. McLean

British Ambassador	Finnish Minister
Mrs. Reed	Mrs. Stettinius
Australian Minister	Sir Earl Poge
Mrs. Miles	Miss Elsa Maxwell
William Herdson	Senator Taft

Mrs. Hoff

Where then, are the standards for disposal of household receipts, seating charts, and Christmas cards? Evalyn Walsh McLean provides a case in point for the imposition of "guidelines" but not "standards" in the selection of material for disposal. The interposition of the curator's institutional judgment remains an important consideration in what researchers will know about the great as well as the obscure.

The deed of gift, of course, may have included a section relating to the disposal of unwanted material, and may, in fact, have indicated that the donor (not completely trusting the professional capability or social understanding of the institution) requests that all discarded material be returned for inspection and further disposition.

The question always arises about what to do with irrelevant but intrinsically valuable material. Older collections may contain a considerable number of original, stamped envelopes in which the recipient's letters arrived. These may have philatelic value, but no other, and it might be possible to transfer the philatelic material to that part of the institution most interested in philately. If the collection has been in the institution for a number of years, the donor is deceased, and all other reasonable avenues of recourse have been investigated unsuccessfully, the institution may feel it appropriate to sell the unwanted or inappropriate part of the collection and use the revenue for manuscript-related activities (not for capital expenditures). Practicality, legality, and even frugality may be the keywords here. As with the process of analysis, selection proceeds throughout the arrangement or organization of the collection.

Organization

Organization, or arrangement, is a process routinely performed in personal papers, but less frequently in archival records. Since corporate bodies are assumed to have mechanisms for controlling their records—with filing manuals, secretarial staff, and even records management controls—it is assumed that the archival imperative of respecting original order will prevail. Arrangement of archives could be imposed on the records of small organizations that did not have very good procedures for handling their records, or in the case of larger organizations where disorder in the records is apparent. Sometimes disorder stems from the inadequacy of physical facilities, in which case the organization may be forced to break files and send them to storage more often than either it, or the future archivist, desires. The archivist or curator then decides whether this breaking of files is a natural and "organic" action of the corporation or if it is merely an expediency which could be corrected once all of the files are reunited at the archives. The key remains: are these corporate files or personal papers to which one is going to apply an arrangement scheme?

Personal papers more often require the interposition of the curatorial staff, which generally does not follow a professional standard, but instead organizes papers to reflect the subject's life and to facilitate researcher access.

This freedom to organize a collection of personal papers, rather than accepting the order in which they are received, is one of the major distinctions between the options available to manuscript curators and archivists working with corporate records. Archivists are concerned with decision processes, action, channels of communication, chains of command, evidence of structure, hierarchies and continuity over corporate time. To make any sense, the records of an organization should reflect its official mission, function, processes and structure, and the archivist will be wise to verify that the records are in the order prescribed for them by the organization itself, and then essentially leave them alone, or at the most correct inconsistencies or unintentional disorder.

The manuscript curator is not dealing with a structured, documented order of things. The personal life of an individual may be orderly, but there is no document that describes that, and certainly no imperative that the individual was obliged to follow some scheme or plan in the creation and maintenance of personal files. Any order that exists is probably circumstantial, and may even have been expedient for the work habits of the creator—that is, things might have been placed where they are because of the space available, the configuration of the working area, the number of residential or office moves engaged in during a career, or the availability of a large desk, filing cabinets, bookshelves, and other functional furniture. Chances are, the organization of the subject's files will not relate to the functions and activities of the subject's life. The manuscript curator, therefore, is free to construct a practical scheme that is presumed to be beneficial to the researcher or end user of the collection. In the scheme of things, the librarian handling a published biography of an individual has little choice but to place it in its proper location within the librarians' universal classification of knowledge, which results in a Library of Congress classification designation, and various local options beyond that, depending on local cataloging rules, size of the library's collection, and other technical considerations. For the records manager or archivist the Calhoun letter to Knox quoted in chapter 1 could go in only one place in the State Department, and its place tells us something about Calhoun, his position, the structure of the Foreign Service, the structure of the State Department, and a variety of other, noncontent matters.

The Calhoun letter to Harriet Monroe had no such preordained destination. She could have kept it any place that pleased her. When examining the entire corpus of a donor's personal papers, the manuscript curator has to make some sense out of all of the material, and structure the collection accordingly. The task of doing that requires analysis of the contents of the documents, development of a structure of organization, judgment as to the destination of each document in that structure, and ultimately a statement that describes what was done and where things can be found.

There are few if any manuals describing this process in enough detail to permit the neophyte archivist to apply a rule.[8] Indeed, the rule-based process of librarianship does not exist in manuscript processing.

The need to organize a manuscript collection imposes a burden on the manuscript archivist that can consume hundreds of staff hours, with many implications. In the realm of expertness, the processor becomes an expert in the life and activities of the subject of the collection. Indeed, there may be no other person who has perused and organized the literary remains as thoroughly. The knowledge gained can be invaluable if it is reflected in the final description of the collection. The availability of the processing archivist in future months and years can be a source of understanding of the collection for future researchers, even though the reference service on the collection may be done by another staff member. Since few people summarize their daily existence in diaries the way that corporate organizations summarize theirs in reports, there is little access to resources documenting the relationships, thoughts and actions of an individual. Manuscript finding aids are the curator's attempts to provide those resources.

In the realm of productivity, a processing team that is engaged with a large collection over a number of months cannot at the same time work on reducing the backlog of incoming materials. A librarian may temporarily "mark and park" a volume until it can be definitively cataloged; an archivist may find it possible to maintain the filing scheme of newly arrived record series and prepare some kind of preliminary inventory (the National Archives used to call such documents a "title inventory") that would still provide access to the record series; but an unorganized manuscript collection cannot easily be summarized and evaluated.

The simplest arrangement for personal papers, and one carried out in all too many collections in the past, is chronological. After all, it is argued, the author of all these papers lived a chronological life, therefore the papers should reflect that. True, in a simple existence of an individual who kept simple files, perhaps correspondence with a spouse or parent, other family member or friend. But in today's collections of papers of busy, professional, public and complex individuals it soon becomes clear that each life was lived on a number of planes, and the records left behind will reflect that complexity. There is the personal, family-and-friends side of existence, which, however, can become complex if the family and circle of friends are large and complex. Then there is the professional life, itself on many levels, involving underlings, peers, superiors, and peripheral influences, such as editors, publishers, business associates, deans, cabinet members, and many others.

In addition there is the material of professional life: notes, drafts, proofs, books, laboratory notes, scientific expedition diaries, data, data and more data, photographs, motion pictures, publications, criticisms, reviews, awards, and prizes. To put all of this material in one chronology would be to confuse and perhaps deceive the researcher. The curator must realize that not everyone who consults X's papers is interested in X, but some are probably looking for A, B, or Y. The researcher then asks, "What do you have in the papers of X relating to Y?" The answer must necessarily be: "The papers of X are in chronological order. Tell us when Y might have written to X and we will produce the documents, if they exist."

The alternative, of course, is to prepare a document-by-document index to the papers, and rearrange the index by subject, name, and other indicators. In today's computerized repository the process of rearranging and searching the database is relatively easy. One can alphabetize a file on a specific data element (author of document), perform a word search, or perform a search of a string of words. The difficulty, however, is that all of that information must first be in the computer before it can be rearranged, searched or scanned. That implies item listing every document, in considerable detail. A decade ago the National Archives prepared a computer-generated item index to 50,000 documents in the Papers of the Confederation, Continental and Convention Congresses. As collections go, 50,000 items represent a relatively small one. Yet it took five years and thousands of staff hours to create and verify the information, even before the computer could process the data.[9] Perhaps today's optical character recognition equipment could easily scan existing finding aids and indexes and convert them to a machine-readable database that could be searched, but that still implies the intellectual and physical process of describing the manuscripts in great detail in the finding aid. Documents cite dates in a variety of nonstandard formats, or even by the names of saints; locations often are the names of great houses or estates, rather than cities or towns; personal names are cited with multiple variations, or undifferentiated from namesakes. The intellectual process of analysis and transcription or interpretation cannot be avoided, and it is that process that makes item indexing prohibitively expensive.

The alternative is an arrangement pattern that has aspects of self-indexing about it, and that may be different for each type of material dealt with, such as correspondence, reports, speeches, etc.

It is here that the curator addresses the archival concept of "series," whether called that or not. A series is a gathering of materials that have some similar attributes, either intellectually, physically, or by format. The determination of a series is relatively simple and yet causes more confusion for the student or nonarchivist than any other archival concept, with the possible exception of the subgroup.[10]

Almost every archival text provides a definition of a series. Data element dictionaries and terminology manuals belabor the definition of series. Many archivists have added their own twists to the definition.[11]

A typical collection of personal papers may have a correspondence series, a diaries series, a speeches and writings series, a photo series, and a newspaper clippings series. Each, it can be seen, has characteristics that bring it together with others of its kind. Series may be large or small, but they stand alone and ideally are not mixed, since they require different means of arrangement and description. Thus, if one has ten filing drawers of correspondence and one photo album, there would be two series.

Series, however can also be subdivided, in a process that seems to have little standardization from repository to repository. There can, for instance, be a correspondence series, subdivided into business correspondence, professional correspondence, and personal correspondence subseries. Other institutions would not create subseries but classify each as a series in its own right. Perhaps more common practice across institutions would be a writings series that contains subseries for each kind of writing: short stories, plays, magazine articles, poetry, etc. A photos series might be subdivided by medium, into 35 mm. slides, master negatives, mounted prints, and proofsheets subseries. Applications of the principle vary, but largely by virtue of the very nature of the material and the application of common sense, most repositories ultimately produce series and subseries that look very much like those produced in other institutions. I propose, perhaps irreverently, that for corporate records a series is equivalent to what is listed on a file drawer label in the office, where file drawers are labeled with such rubrics as "Contracts," "Quarterly Reports," "Correspondence," "Performance Reviews," "Position Descriptions," etc. In short, series are what are established by the clerical staff to make sense out of the location of materials of different characteristics or purposes. Therefore, they come to the archivist already defined, and the archivist merely acknowledges and respects that order. If the archivist believes that the designations are confusing or unscientific, there arises the dilemma of leaving them as they were found or violating the tradition (for it is nothing more) of respecting original order. Manuscript curators are not bound by such guidelines, and most often must create the series structure *ex post facto* to satisfy the need to overcome chaos and guide the researcher.

Before processing, the curator determines what level of control is going to be established. It may be that all correspondence is going to be arranged by author, and that all authors with the same initial letter will be grouped in separate folders for filing, but no further order will be imposed. It will be the responsibility of the researcher to look in the "C" folder for any Calhoun letters, and if the folder is stuffed, perhaps there will be two, three, or more "C" folders.

Or, the curator may decide to arrange all of the correspondence in the folders so that it is at least in alphabetical order, thus making it easier to find Calhoun in the "C" folders, but still requiring a search by the user for Calhoun letters from December 1911 or from March 4, 1912.

Finally, the curator may decide on an item arrangement, so that all letters from the same person will be grouped together and then put in chronological order. This is the ultimate arrangement and provides the researcher with an easy path to the Calhoun letter of March 4, 1912. It is possible, of course, that the researcher is interested in all letters received by the subject on March 4, 1912, in which case the alphabetical arrangement will be of no help. The curator, therefore, has to analyze the collection and anticipate research use. In a large collection containing considerable correspondence with prominent people and organizations, a biographer may want all of it in straight chronological order, but how many biographers of this one person will there be? One? If, then, the major use is going to be studies of the correspondents, or of the subjects (which can often be assumed from the name of the correspondent) in the collection, future researchers will be served by finding material arranged in accordance with some scheme other than chronological.

It is not unprofessional at all to pose the question: "What seems natural?" "How would I do it in my own files? How would a researcher most likely approach these documents?" The answers would probably result in a variety of arrangements suited to each type, form, or series of papers.

If there is a great amount of correspondence between two people, and only those two people, such as a writer with an agent, a politician with a promoter, or a husband with a wife, the only logical arrangement of that correspondence is chronological. There is also no other reasonable way to arrange a multivolume diary or journal, although the diaries might have been subdivided by chronological span to coincide with great events in the life of the subject, such as college, the war years, world travel, etc.

On the other hand, if the subject carried out considerable correspondence with a number of correspondents on a range of topics, it seems reasonable to arrange that series alphabetically by correspondent and then, if the institution decides to process deeper, chronologically under each. There may even be reason to use more than one arrangement for correspondence if it is initially divided into important correspondents and routine correspondents. In the papers of a political figure, for instance, an alphabetical arrangement of the correspondence with other key political figures would expedite research, but a straight chronological arrangement of routine constituent mail, where the individuals are unknown, would also seem logical. Indeed, the routine constituent correspondence may first be arranged by issue, or topic, and then chronologically, although one would expect that a political figure would have already organized the office files according to a filing scheme, relieving the curator of the burden of trying to devise one.

For an author or poet, researchers might find it helpful to have the series of writings alphabetical by title or first line, although some may argue that a chronological arrangement of literary works better reflects the author's development. It is assumed, however, that if the author has had any success at all there is a bibliography of his or her works that provides the chronological structure, and that researchers using the file will probably approach it by title of a work rather than by date of publication. To state that the primary consideration is the ultimate ease of access by a researcher is too much of a simplification of a complex topic. The curator has no prescient idea of who the future researcher will be or what the thrust of the research will be. A person studying stylistic development of a poet would probably want a chronological order of all poems; someone analyzing the impact of the poet's works on the public would probably want the published works separated from the unpublished; and someone analyzing the poet's use of imagery in certain known works would probably like to approach them by title.

Forecasting the needs of researchers using a large correspondence file can be even more difficult. As an example, the correspondence of Stephen A. Douglas (in the University of Chicago) runs to 23 feet (ca. 16,000 items) of material, just for the years 1835 to 1861, and just including letters *to* Douglas. It is arranged chronologically from beginning to end, with no subseries. That arrangement apparently worked well for George Fort Milton, a researcher who produced a major editorial work on Douglas.[12] Subsequent researchers, however, were not so much interested in "the little giant" as they were in those with whom he corresponded. A request to the library for any correspondence between Douglas and William Seward could not be responded to easily. Using the Milton book as a sort of "finding aid," the researcher could look in the book's index for citations to Seward letters, and then ask to see them, but there is no guarantee that Milton cited every Seward letter in the Douglas collection. An item index would seem to be the only solution, but it is one that few repositories can afford when confronted with collections of thousands of documents each.

Curators may employ a subject arrangement most logically in a collection with many case files or special studies that may not have resulted in single written works. A journalist or investigative reporter may spend years building files on drugs, gun running, fraud in government, atomic energy, etc. There seems no other logical way than to arrange these files or this material alphabetically by subject or topic.

A novelist's papers may be arranged alphabetically by work, with subdivisions under the title of the work to encompass manuscripts and preliminary materials, editorial correspondence, publishing contracts and associated correspondence, reviews, fan mail, etc., so that the future researcher will be able to study all aspects of *The Sun Also Rises* or *Humboldt's Gift* in a unified file. Whether this is more desirable than having all publishers' correspondence together, regardless of which book is being discussed, is a choice that the curator must make, perhaps in consultation with prospective users (English Department faculty, for instance) or even with the subject, who may be available for consultation, but who may shrug and imply that such decisions are those of the professional archivist.

Confronted with the problem of arranging photographs in a collection of personal papers, the curator decides on the research value of the photos themselves. Are these family pictures taken at outings, summer vacations, graduations, weddings and other ceremonies or gatherings? Or are they studies of things in which the subject is interested: butterflies, steam locomotives, buildings and urban scenes, the young or the elderly? If the former (snapshots) the golden rule is to do nothing to disturb original order, which can often be ascertained from numbered strip negatives, if they are available. It is only original order, which is chronological, that facilitates identification of locations and individuals, where there are doubts. The picture of a child playing in the surf of an otherwise unidentified beach is largely unidentifiable out of context. But in relation to other photos from the same roll, the lighthouse in the background, the composition of the rest of the family and friends, even the make and model of the car in the parking lot, or the family dog can positively date the photograph and put it in its proper setting. The photographs of the serious amateur, out to document a subject, will, if the amateur is conscientious, be arranged and identified. If they are jumbled the curator decides how much work the staff should do to make up for the deficiencies of the creator of the collection. In all of these decisions, the curator must continually weigh the distribution of costs between the institution and the researcher. Processing collections is labor intensive, as is research. Institutions often compromise on how much they will spend in labor and how much they are willing to have the researcher spend. Many curators will say that they go just so far in organizing the collections, and let the researcher assume the responsibility from that point on. For instance, the curator may opt to stop the arrangement process after placing all documents for each month in folders marked with the month, but not to arrange the documents chronologically any further. The burden for finding specific documents in any specific month is then up to the researcher. There must, however, also be a consideration for security, since the better the control that is gained over a collection, the easier it is to determine if anything is missing.

All of these decisions confront the curator in each collection processed, and the solutions may be different in each, based on the simple premise that no two people are alike, nor are the life patterns that they establish. It is that assumption that makes it even more important for the processor to know the subject, that is, people and issues, being dealt with in a collection. That knowledge will be the basis for the organization of the material.

If it is important for the curator to think of the researcher in the context of investment of time, which is money, it is also important to keep in mind the fact that it is for the researcher that all of this work is being done in the first place. But the researcher may not be some unknown scholar who someday will come into the repository; for the most part, the researcher will be the staff of the institution, responding to reference questions in the reading room, or coming in by mail, phone, FAX, or E-mail.

What all of this implies is that researchers should find the arrangement of collections natural and simple. Arrangement should flow from and be dictated by the material itself. Complex structures of arrangement wherein the incoming correspondence is arranged in one way and the outgoing in another, where material is given decimal classification numbers to match some broader scheme external to the collection, or where subjects are defined and applied in order to make the material fit in with the book collections in the library catalog, are unnatural manipulations that only complicate an already complex body of material. The role of the curator is to simplify the arrangement of material in order to aid the researcher, not to complicate the arrangement in order to fulfill some external, theoretical mandate. A practical arrangement is one that is almost completely self-indexing, thus avoiding the necessity for extensive descriptive finding aids. A simple description of the order of the materials should be all that a researcher needs to navigate through a complex collection.

But there is an option available to the archivist and curator that is not at the disposal of the librarian. The former can explain the whole process, what was found, what was done with it, and how to get into the collection, through the descriptive tool—or the finding aid. As one archivist so cogently put it: "We should not bequeath puzzles to posterity!"[13]

NOTES

1. Maynard Brichford, *Archives and Manuscripts: Appraisal and Accessioning* (Chicago: Society of American Archivists, 1977), 8.

2. George S. Patton, Jr., to Beatrice Patton, "Family Correspondence," Box 35. The Papers of George S. Patton, Jr. Library of Congress Manuscript Division.

3. Abigail Adams to John Adams, September 17, 1775, *Adams Family Correspondence*, ed. L. H. Butterfield, vol. 1, *December 1761–May 1776* (Cambridge, Mass.: Belknap Press of Harvard University Press, 1963), 278.

4. *Freedom: A Documentary History of Emancipation, 1861–1867*, ed. Ira Berlin (Cambridge, Mass.: Cambridge University Press, 1985), 1: 346, #143.

5. Hite and Linke, "A Statistical Summary of Appraisal . . .": 23–29.

6. A recent sketch of Evalyn Walsh McLean's role in Washington society during World War II appears in David Brinkley, *Washington Goes to War* (New York: Alfred A. Knopf, 1988), 156–164. See also Ralph G. Martin, *Cissy. The Extraordinary Life of Eleanor Medill Patterson* (New York: Simon & Schuster, 1979).

7. The Evalyn Walsh McLean Collection, Box 112, "E.W. McLean Miscellany," folder "Seating Charts." Manuscript Division, Library of Congress.

8. Fredric Miller, *Arranging and Describing Archives and Manuscripts* (SAA, 1990).

9. John P. Butler, comp., *Index. The Papers of the Continental Congress, 1774–1789*, 5 vols. (n.p., no pub., "Published 1978." "For sale by the Superintendent of Documents, U.S. Government Printing Office, Washington, D.C.").

10. See Berner, *Archival Theory and Practice in the United States*, chap. 4, for an elaborate explication of this entire question.

11. See, among others: Lewis Bellardo and Lynn Lady Bellardo, *A Glossary for Archivists*, 32; Maygene Daniels, in Maygene F. Daniels and Timothy Walch, *A Modern Archives Reader: Basic Readings on Archival Theory and Practice* (Washington, D.C.: National Archives Trust Fund Board, 1984), 342; Kenneth W. Duckett, *Modern Manuscripts* (Nashville: American Association for State and Local History, 1975), 344; Frank B. Evans, Donald F. Harrison, and Edwin A. Thompson, "A Basic Glossary for Archivists, Manuscript Curators, and Records Managers," *American Archivist* 37 (July 1974), 415–433 and reprinted separately by the Society of American Archivists; Oliver Wendell Holmes, "Archival Arrangement—Five Different Operations at Five Different Levels," *American Archivist* 27 (January 1964), 30; Fredric Miller, *Arranging and Describing Archives and Manuscripts*, 7.

12. George Fort Milton, *The Eve of Conflict: Stephen A. Douglas and the Needless War* (Boston/New York: Houghton Mifflin Company, 1934).

13. Brichford, *op cit.*

· 8 ·

GOOD DEEDS DO NOT GO UNREWARDED

Because of the implications of eternity, it is an awesome act
when a public repository formally takes unto itself a collection
of manuscripts. . . . The projected shadows of posterities look
down upon the scene; sometimes they seem so hatefully to
glower, at others to be shaken with unpleasant laughter.

David Mearns[1]

There is little reason for researchers to be concerned with the
technical services function of the library that they use. Where
a book was bought and how much it cost, what cataloging process
and stack layout resulted in the volume being where it is, and
related matters are irrelevant, as long as the work is easy to find
and retrieve in open stacks.

The administrative files and processes behind a manuscript
collection, however, can have important consequences for researchers, and the more they know and understand, the clearer will
be their options in making effective use of a collection. The terms
of receipt and use of a group of personal papers often reflect the
act of bringing in and caring for the work of a life, and it has
human implications. Indeed, as Mearns suggests, it is a solemn
commitment to undertake the task of becoming the final resting
place for the literary remains of the famous as well as the inarticulate. An institution taking this step to immortalize the chosen ones
has also assumed the solemn responsibility of caring for its new
charges, and presenting them to all comers, regardless of their intentions to treat or mistreat the lives, honor or sacred trust of those
perpetuated. The document box becomes more than a literary
crypt, and the label on it more than a memorial inscription. How
long is forever? one might ask; but there is not a curator alive
who will venture to guess. Should the papers of the once eminent

politician be tossed away when he or she no longer appears in the historical anthologies? Should the poets be disposed of when the hoi polloi no longer read their poems? Of course not, one would say without hesitation. It is among the lives and works of the forgotten and the unknown that research jewels are found, glistening below layers of old, forgotten causes, like diamonds in the hold of a derelict galleon.

But, if everything is assiduously collected, in accordance with an institution's intellectually constructed acquisition program, and pursued through the efforts of scholars, administrators, colleagues and the assistance of AT&T, MCI, Federal Express, Atlas Van Lines, and other means of information and transport, the researcher should be fully aware of what contract was entered into, and what the long-term requirements are to uphold the oaths of the party of the second part; in short, what the institutional commitment was.

That commitment is related to the acquisition policy, but choosing the specific collection to be brought in and protected is perhaps analogous to selecting furnishings for one's home. The consideration of the perfect collection was partly based not only on space, but also on how the pieces fit in with the general "decor" (the collecting theme, in this case), upkeep costs and preservation requirements. Although a collection of General William Tecumseh Sherman's papers that are in very bad physical condition may not be rejected on that account, curators are aware that the accessioning of the collection commits the institution to do something about that condition. Bringing in the corporate records of a major railroad company may so overextend the staff of an institution that other projects will suffer and outside help might be needed. Funding agencies are loath to support bad decisions, and will question why a repository accepted such a mass of material if it did not have the resources to process it properly.

A relatively new problem confronting archivists stems from the advance of technology. Accessioning a collection of critical demographic records that are on computer tape may be saving valuable information from destruction, but is the repository prepared to undertake rewinding, cleaning, documenting, and running the data set that was probably created on obsolete technology? An acquisition policy implies the ability to administer any materials acquired under it. This is especially problematic in the collecting of scientific, mathematical, medical, or other materials now primarily created and maintained on computer. An institution will probably find it better to change its acquisition policy and leave the highly technical collections to those repositories capable of dealing with them, unless there is the prospect of improving its own capability in this area.

Many implications flow from the type of material that is collected. Computer tapes require different treatment with different equipment than do photographs; maps, charts and posters pose storage and maintenance problems; archives of the disaffected, such as the radical groups of the 1960s, demand preservation considerations beyond what is normally expected for traditional correspondence files because of a general lack of structure, cohesion and care of the records; and mixed media collections, such as the recent deposit of the Louis Armstrong collection at Queens College, New York, require dealing with old 78-rpm shellacked disks, 33-rpm LPs of vinyl, forty-year-old reel-to-reel recording tapes, thousands of photographs, correspondence, scrapbooks rife with unstable materials, and five trumpets used by the performer, one of which is gold-plated.

Even within traditional collecting fields, however, there are special conditions that curators face. As an example, a university collecting contemporary literary collections is confronted with more than manuscripts and correspondence. Depending on how thorough the author is, how far back the material dates, and, indeed, what the form of literature is that he or she is engaged in, there can be a great quantity of supplementary materials that have to be analyzed and evaluated for retention. It could be assumed that for every work there is perhaps a sketch, or, more formally, an outline of what is intended. Perhaps there are also some vignettes that later are woven into the finished work.

Depending on the type of literary work and the thoroughness of the author, there may be a considerable number of note cards that constitute a bibliography. This bulk could be extended by research notes, sometimes organized and straightforward, sometimes ranging between scribblings on the backs of envelopes and neatly typed notes on 5x8 cards with topical headings. Catherine Drinker Bowen commented on the poor form of an interviewer who takes notes during an interview: "Private persons are scared by it and even veterans of public life sometimes retreat at the sight."[2] When John Gunther deposited his papers at the University of Chicago, consisting of the research materials for his major "Inside" books (*Inside Europe, Inside Latin America, Inside U.S.A.*, etc.), much of the research material consisted of his "sniblets." These pesky items came about because he traditionally went into interviews with party leaders, lowly politicians, heads of state, and others, without a notepad. He would sit and chat amiably for a few minutes, thus relaxing the interviewee into a talkative mood. When the subject began discoursing on what Gunther came to hear, he would casually ask for a piece of paper in order to jot down that "important point." Back at his hotel Gunther would then snip the sheets of paper from the interview into subject areas of the discussion—politics, finances, international relations, etc., to be in accord with the chapters of the planned book, and the sniblets were filed accordingly. In most cases the only way to reassemble the interview is to match up the sniblets by type and hue of paper, which usually carried a letterhead identifier for the interviewee or the hotel where Gunther was staying. Sometimes he would bring along hotel stationery, or wait until he returned to the hotel and then quickly jot down on the hotel stationery the points he wished to remember.[3] How should the curator present these pieces to researchers? Try to reassemble them, even if only intellectually? Leave them in their folder, pregnant with information, but unidentified as to source, and let the researcher figure it out? Toss them out as being indecipherable gibberish? One could say: if you take Gunther, you accept his work method and all that entails, and to the researcher: if you study Gunther, you put up with his idiosyncrasies.

Literary collections often include drafts of a work. Some authors draft in longhand and then have it transcribed by a typist. Others draft on a typewriter or a word processor, making corrections and retyping. The word processor complicates matters, because drafts can be revised in the system and not printed until the author is satisfied, whereas formerly one could follow the changes from draft to draft (when they were kept). The question then becomes one of considering the floppy disk or other electronic medium as part of the file.

Continuing the creative process, the author probably produced a final, clean draft that was sent to the publisher, and, after a number of reviews and comments, perhaps a revised final draft that the publisher accepted and sent to the printer. The printer then set type and returned galleys—or unformatted pages—for the author to proofread against the original manuscript (all of this, of course, prior to the advent of computerized composition at the printer's).

Quite often there were three galleys, with one for the author to proof, a second for another party to proof, and a third to contain the combined, compiled corrections that were sent back to the printer for corrections.

The next product was probably the page proof, containing all of the corrections recommended, and formatted to show chapter breaks, paragraph headings, footnotes if there are any, places where illustrations, charts, printer's devices, or other nontextual material would be located, page numbers, etc. If the book were complex and the editor or author demanded it, the printer could also return a set of "blue lines" or a copy stricken from the final plate showing the work as it would appear in the bound copy, with illustrations, notes, title page, and all of the paraphernalia. Blue line copies provided the final chance to verify that the captions fit the photographs or charts, that the illustrative material had not been printed in reverse, and for all last-minute verification.

All of this material for just one published work can create considerable bulk, and therefore the researcher has to be aware of the implications of dealing with literary figures. Of course there are degrees of importance. The papers of a university professor of English who was author or coauthor of some minor poetry and textbooks might receive quite different treatment from the papers of a Saul Bellow or William Saroyan. In the case of the professor, the collecting institution may see no rationale for preserving all of the stages of publication, and the curator always asks the question: who is going to study this material and for what purpose? In the case of a textbook author, all answers may lead to the decision to keep very little. In the case of Bellow or Saroyan, however, the answer may indicate that everything should be kept because future researchers will be interested in the progress of literary thought as the author moves from outline to final product, the influence of editors on structure and style, the development of language and its most effective use, imagery and its source, and a variety of other topics which only the full scope of the literary remains can reveal, and with which an entire academic discipline concerns itself.

But what if there were considerable quantities of notes, multiple drafts and redrafts, editor's comments from the publisher, a lively correspondence about the developing work between the publisher and the author and perhaps some literary friends, two complete sets of galleys and a page proof? And what if the author were prolific and produced ten or fifteen major works, a variety of minor ones, plus some unfinished efforts, articles, reviews and literary commentary? Add to this the associated materials consisting of publishers' contracts, reviews, arrangements for book-and-author parties, letters of appreciation, praise or criticism, offers from Hollywood, literary prize correspondence, and just plain fan mail. One can then begin to see the institutional space and labor implications. The Mearns caution about a phenomenon consorting with a quandary (chap. 4 p. 74) rings in the curator's ears. In February 1995 the Library of Congress Manuscript Division acquired "58 cartons and one large rolled map" from the papers of novelist Herman Wouk. The 58 cartons contained

> chiefly typewritten drafts with holograph annotations, proofs, galleys, and research material for Wouk's novels, *The Winds of War* (1971), *War and Remembrance* (1978), and *Inside, Outside* (1985). Also includes books, photographs, and a map of Germany under Adolf Hitler.[4]

This collection represents only three of Wouk's nine published novels, and then there are the plays (*The Caine Mutiny Court Martial*, for one) and movie versions of his writings. A biographer of Wouk may therefore experience a personal confrontation with the phenomenon and the quandary.

If bulk is the curse of success in the literary field, it is also true in politics. The papers of recent political figures, with secretaries, word processors, auto pens, and large constituencies, can grow to enormous proportions and easily be larger than the collections of all nineteenth-century presidents combined. The papers of Ronald Reagan number some forty million documents; those of Lyndon Johnson numbered around thirty million. Yet the twenty-three presidents represented in the Presidential Papers collections at the Library of Congress provide a *total* of only 1.2 million documents from 1789 to 1928. That was not their total output, of course, but it represents what survived in the main body of their materials.

These "collections" of "personal" and "official" papers are not considered to be federal records, and until the Reagan administration they came to the government through the negotiation of a deed of gift. The Presidential Records Act, passed in 1978, became effective with the next elected president, whoever that should be, and thus Reagan was the first president to have no choice in the matter of where his "official" papers should go. But there is no such law pertaining to judges or legislators, and in some states the papers of the governor (or, more correctly, the records of the governor's office) are also not covered.

The Presidential libraries are notable, however, for the thousands of collections of "personal papers" of other people who were in some way associated with the president. There are family papers, papers of people who served in the military with the man who became president, political colleagues from Washington and the president's home state, neighbors and early business associates, staff from the president's earlier career as state governor, member of the House of Representatives, senator or vice president. In a *Guide to Manuscript Collections in the Presidential Libraries*,[5] which encompasses only the seven presidents from Hoover through Carter (sans Nixon), there are over four thousand "collections" of papers and oral histories. Each of these has been voluntarily conveyed to the government through a formal document of some sort, mostly the deed of gift.

Presidential libraries, historical societies, universities, and even specialized institutions, like those dedicated to recent figures such as Everett Dirksen, Carl Albert, Hubert Humphrey, Howard Metzenbaum, George Mitchell and Mark Hatfield, thus confront the masses of material accumulated by twentieth-century politicians. A commitment to collect and retain such papers implies a commitment to provide the space and services needed by them. The Hite and Linke study cited in chapter 7 analyzed the disposable nature of constituent materials.

The more traditional collections that one thinks of when speaking of modern manuscripts are those medium-sized assemblages of personal papers of people who were significant— otherwise they might not be worth collecting—but in local affairs, in families (always important to members) or within a profession or field of study, such as a physician, physicist, or head of an influential garden club. As with other subjects, the researcher must be prepared to deal with a wide variety of material types, including letters, two-way correspondence, a diary at the personal level or a journal listing significant professional events.

Researchers using manuscripts can today expect photographs, either unassembled and scattered throughout the collection or neatly mounted in albums and labeled. It is not unreasonable to anticipate audio tapes, whether reel-to-reel or cassette. In some cases there may even be recording media similar to Dictabelts, which require that they be played on a specific type of device. Beginning in the 1980s one can expect to find home-produced videotapes, in Beta or VHS format (or other formats if European), and, depending on who is the subject of the collection, perhaps some commercial-size (3/4-inch or larger) videotapes of appearances on talk shows or other news or entertainment programs.

There may well be scrapbooks, containing photographs, menus, invitations, programs, newspaper and magazine clippings, and all of the things usually found in scrapbooks (i.e., scraps!). The researcher may consider it a mixed blessing to find that a collection contains a number of folders, or even drawers, of newspaper clippings, unarranged, jumbled together, representing notices in newspapers of various activities, and if the subject was of such a stature as to have a clipping service, the clippings will be replicated as wire service copy finds its way into national, regional or local newsprint.

Then there may also be a few anomalies, such as collections within collections. Some people make a hobby or a business of collecting the papers of others, either because of professional or familial ties, or for fun or profit. Imbedded within a collection of a twentieth-century figure, therefore, may be a significant collection of the papers and works of a Revolutionary War figure. Or, more commonly, the papers of one corporate leader may contain assemblages of papers of associates. The papers of a federal judge may contain the papers of a clerk with whom he or she was associated; the papers of a legislator may contain the papers of an aide. The papers of William Russell, at the Historic New Orleans Collection, contain little about Russell himself, but some sixteen thousand items relating to New Orleans jazz, its managers, performers, and fans. That is where one would find material on Bunk Johnson, Kid Ory, Jelly Roll Morton, and even Scott Joplin or the elusive Buddy Bolden. At the Library of Congress the great Peter Force Collection contains little about Force, but considerable material on Revolutionary and Federal period personalities. The Papers of Felix Frankfurter, at the Library of Congress, contain two document boxes of papers of Associate Justice William Henry Moody, which, for some reason, came with the Frankfurter collection. They remain there, even though the Papers of Associate Justice Moody are *also* in the Manuscript Division![6] There is a similar case in the Robert Wilson Shufeldt collection at the Library of Congress, where there is a series in two containers devoted to explorations in Africa of Shufeldt's youngest son, Mason.[7]

Many collections do not relate to external events but provide inner reflections of a person through a diary or confiding letters. The importance of such inner reflections may not be a consideration in the case of the textbook author, but if the writings of a literary or political figure stem from these inner musings it is of value to future researchers. Similarly, the writings of an individual, collected over many years, can indicate intellectual development.

THE RESEARCHER AND THE DEED OF GIFT

The architect Mies van der Rohe once noted that it is more important to try to follow reason than grand ideas when designing a building. One could say the same about any kinds of controls that the curator wishes to place on the repository's collections. There are basically only a few questions that have to be answered about each collection from a control standpoint (as opposed to intellectual understanding). The institution certainly wants to keep track of what holdings it has, where they came from, their legal status as to ownership, where they are in the stacks, how big they are, and what physical condition they are in. These may seem like bare minimum information requirements, but they constitute the most often requested information from administrators and staff, and some are of interest to the researcher. Even before receipt of the material in the repository some of these information elements will be in the collection case file. Certainly, the name of the collection, the source, and the conditions of ownership should be in the file. A simple locator file for the backlog (newly received, unprocessed collections) can contain the other elements of location, size and condition.

Primary among the case file controls, and containing stipulations that affect the researcher, is the deed of gift—the contract that provides for the transfer of the material, legally transfers ownership of the collection, or a part of it, to the repository, and states terms under which the transfer is made. If there are complicated codicils about copying, use, restrictions or housing the collection, the curator usually consults with counsel before signing the deed, or even has a higher officer of the institution sign, because in almost all cases the gift is to the institution, not to the Department of Special Collections or other organizational entity. The formal deed of gift for manuscript collections is a relatively recent phenomenon, however, and one cannot expect to find them for most of the collections accessioned prior to World War II. Our legalistically conscious society has prompted their recent rise in popularity, and in some cases has saved the curator's reputation, mostly in cases relating to access.[8]

Prospective donors do not always wish to sign a deed of gift immediately, for a variety of reasons. The transfer of documents to a repository may be hurried because of circumstances such as a sudden death, an unexpected relocation of the donor, requiring the deposit of materials rather than moving them to the new home or corporate headquarters, or because of an emergency such as fire or flood. Donors may also wish to stretch out their donations to a repository for tax purposes. A large collection, valued for a considerable deduction by an appraiser, may be divided into a number of segments by the donor, with the entire collection deposited at the repository, and each segment in turn being deeded to the repository over a number of tax years. In either case, whether the donation is sudden because of circumstances or methodical for tax purposes, the curator seeks to have the deposit accompanied by an agreement that is legally defensible, stating the terms of the deposit, describing the material deposited, how long it may be before the status is changed to a gift, what responsibilities the repository and the depositor bear, and who is responsible for certain costs associated with the collection. The case of the Martin Luther King papers, Boston University, the King Center in Atlanta, and Mrs. King illustrates the complications that can arise from a faulty, imprecise, ambiguous or missing deed of gift, and that can leave the researcher confronted with a collection where one might not expect to find it, or terms for use that can affect research.

Before his assassination in 1968 Martin Luther King, Jr., deposited a pre-1961 segment of his personal papers in Boston University, from which he had received his doctorate in theology in 1955. After his assassination it was revealed that the civil rights leader had left no will. The deposit in Boston University was documented only by a letter of intent dated July 16, 1964, but was never formalized in a deed. Subsequently, Mrs. Coretta Scott King, the widow and executor of Dr. King's estate, sued Boston University for transfer of the papers to the King Center in Atlanta. In 1993 a jury verdict denied the request, based on Dr. King's letter of intent, and the papers remained at Boston after the Massachusetts Supreme Court upheld the decision in 1995.[9] Perhaps much of the court activity would have been avoided if Dr. King had signed a deed of gift, for even with a letter of intent the widow was able to carry the case to the courts.[10]

The deed of gift is just one form of document that falls under the general laws of charitable donations, including gifts, which cite the three parts of a transaction that define a gift: an offer, an acceptance, and the delivery of the material. These laws are based largely on English precedent, especially the Statute of Charitable Uses of Elizabeth (43 Eliz., ch. 4 [1601]).[11] In the United States the term "charity" is expanded to imply any institution or organization that is established to benefit an undetermined number of people.[12] Thus, the courts have determined that museums, historical societies, educational institutions, etc., are considered to be charitable, and have historically looked sympathetically on them and the objects they receive, and "will take somewhat unusual and stringent measures to enforce and protect [a gift]."[13] If any of these actions—the offer, the acceptance, or the delivery—is missing, the courts have often declared that no gift was made. There have been cases where a prospective donor announced an intent to give, made the intent public, and packed the material for shipment, but died before the transfer was completed, left no will relating to the material, and had signed no deed of gift. The courts determined that there had been no "gift."[14]

Considering the importance of a deed to possible future claims against an institution, it is not surprising that it should be safely guarded and retained. In many institutions such retention is in the files of the legal office, but even in such cases the manuscript curator should retain a copy in the collection case file for easy accessibility in the event that some verification of its terms is needed, or a researcher inquires about those terms.

Just as in the case of a deed, a deposit agreement should be in the collection case file for future reference. The same holds true for evidence of the purchase of material, which normally consists of a bill of sale, stating as much as possible, either on its face or in an attachment, what was bought, from whom and for what amount, and the date of the transaction.[15]

These three document types are contracts that show legal ownership or disposition. Except in the case of a bill of sale, they should contain any stipulations of the donor concerning use, copyright, copying, or other limitations. Their presence in the repository's files is important in the event of misunderstandings, false claims of ownership, or litigation relating to the possession of these (sometimes) valuable materials.

The deed, in fact, contains a number of elements important to researchers other than change of ownership. It can provide in detail one of the peculiarities of manuscript donations—controlled post-donation use by the donor.

Donors of manuscript collections can, and often do, insert statements in the deed of gift of their papers restricting access or use, and some even insist that only they provide the authority for researchers to use them. Edith Bolling Galt Wilson, the second Mrs. Woodrow Wilson, controlled access to the president's papers from the time of their deposit in the Library of Congress in 1940 until her death in 1961. Every time a researcher wished to use the Wilson papers a permission slip was sent to Mrs. Wilson's house on S Street in Washington, for approval by her or her secretary. It is not known that approval was ever denied, but the seeking of it was enforced.

If we consider the issues raised in chapter 1, for example, at the time the Calhoun letter in the State Department files was transferred to the National Archives there was a fifty-year rule of access in effect. Except under special dispensation from the restriction on access classification, researchers could not see the Calhoun letter until at least 1962. During those fifty years any biographer of Yuan Shih-Kai or historian of the overthrow of the Manchus would have been denied the insights of Calhoun relating to those topics.

A biographer or historian who had sought out the letters in the Monroe papers would find that they could have been used as early as 1936, and prior to that time they could have been consulted at Harriet Monroe's office, if she granted such access.

This distinction about how access is granted is a critical difference between government (and corporate) records and personal papers.[16] In the former there are laws or regulations that affect whole classes of documents, and only rarely touch individual items. In the case of the State Department the diplomatic files were closed in their totality, regardless of the specific sensitivity of each letter, report or other document. Subsequent to 1962, when the files containing the Calhoun letter opened, the Freedom of Information Act of 1976 has permitted researchers to request access on an individual basis, but there are nine reasons why the State Department might not grant access even after such a request (see chapter 11). In general, also, the closing of State Department records has been reduced to thirty years. All of these terms are stated in statute or by presidential Executive Order, and are not administered at the discretion of the State Department or its officers.

Under what conditions would one be permitted to transfer title in personal papers to an institution and yet continue to control that material? The simple answer is: under conditions agreed upon in the contractual arrangement between donor and donee, and that contractual arrangement is the deed of gift. Because of circumstances of perceived ownership of presidential papers prior to 1978, Mrs. Wilson was able to control access to high-level government documents created by or received in the White House. The wife of Secretary of State Knox could not do the same for his State Department files.

Any restrictions on access to the Calhoun material in the Monroe papers are the result of an agreement between the University of Chicago and the donor. The donor of personal papers may negotiate any use limitations that are acceptable to the receiving institution. The entire collection may be closed for a term of years; specific documents or files may be closed; or any material may be subject to access approval by the donor on a case-by-case basis. The terms may be changed, either in agreement between the donor and institution, or, in rare circumstances, by court order. If Harriet Monroe or her estate saw no reason to deny the Calhoun letters to researchers they could be open for access on their first day in the repository.

A recent classic case of the implication of access restrictions was one in which a hue and cry went up because the donor decided *not* to restrict his collection. It was the case of the gift of papers of Supreme Court Associate Justice Thurgood Marshall to the Manuscript Division of the Library of Congress. For many years the library has been assembling a magnificent collection of the papers of the justices, and now holds the collections of justices Story, Thurgood Marshall, Harlan, Holmes, Black, Frankfurter, Brennan, O'Connor, and many others. As noted earlier, the papers of Supreme Court justices are not classed as federal records subject to the Federal Records Act, but are available for disposal by the individual justices. When Thurgood Marshall deposited his papers in the Library of Congress over the last years of his term, he stipulated in the deed of gift that they should be open to researchers without restriction upon his death. When he died in 1992 the library implemented the terms of the gift and opened the papers, much to the chagrin of other members of the court—most notably Chief Justice William H. Rehnquist, on the grounds that internal operations of the Supreme Court were too recently and explicitly documented in the collection. The members of the Supreme Court tried to get Librarian James Billington to reverse the decision, and seemed to threaten some sort of action or retaliation if he did not.[17] This stand was even supported by some journalists.[18] Billington stood his ground, reminding the justices, politely, that they should be aware of the sanctity of contracts legally negotiated, and if the library abrogated the deed there would be no assurance to future givers that it would honor their deeds, which might call for *limitation* on use of sensitive material in their papers.[19] A veiled threat by some members of the Court to remove papers already donated, or at least to discourage court members from donating papers in the future, was ineffective, and there appeared to be no diminution in the ongoing deposit of their collections to the library.

Billington argued correctly that if members wanted their papers restricted for a period of time, the library would be willing to negotiate the terms of the restriction. Just as the library would honor such contractual restrictions, it would also honor contractual nonrestrictions, as in the Marshall case.

It is interesting to note that a few months after this incident (which blew over, in the library's favor), the Court was again embroiled in a dispute with a scholar who received taped copies of oral arguments made before the Court in some landmark cases that are contained on a series of taped sound recordings of the public proceedings of the Court, and deposited in the National Archives. The researcher then issued cassettes of the oral arguments, accompanied by background, explanation, and elaboration on the importance of the case—a wonderful teaching tool; in fact, the target audience for the tapes was the classroom teacher.[20]

The argument of the Court here was that the Court itself had put restrictions on the use of the oral tapes, even though they did permit access to them for scholarly research purposes. In 1986 the Court made it a stipulation for depositing the tapes in the National Archives (the Court is not covered under the Federal Records Acts and has no legal imperative to deposit materials in the National Archives) that the contents would not be reproduced for "commercial purposes." The researcher signed the agreement that the Court insisted the National Archives have each user of the tapes sign, but then went ahead and reproduced the tapes anyway, on the basis that these were public statements made in a public forum, and therefore in the public domain. The Court threatened action, and, indeed, instructed the National Archives not to serve future

Court tapes to the particular researcher without the express consent of the Marshal of the Court. Again the Court had to back down, and ultimately informed the National Archives that continued restrictions on use of the tapes "no longer serve the purposes of the Court," and there the affair ended.[21]

What these incidents exhibit is the introverted view that the Court has of its business, even when it is public business. It would be a fair bet that the majority of archivists in the country would agree that the Court did not have a leg to stand on. If nothing else, most archivists and manuscript curators are acutely aware of the obligations of contracts legally entered into, and the distinctions between public and private property. The Marshall case and the case of the tapes of the oral arguments exemplify the bases on which access to public and private materials is obtained.

If there are lessons for the curator in these two examples, it is that the research institution must keep track of what restrictions apply, either by law or by legal agreement, and then be certain to administer the access limitations accordingly.

Why do institutions permit such outside control, for which they assume the burden of administration? Simply to make sure that they get the collection. When the chief justice hinted that if the Thurgood Marshall papers were kept open by the Library of Congress he would suggest that other justices be induced to give their papers elsewhere, he missed the point completely, as Librarian Billington reminded him. Other justices gave their papers to the library because they knew that under the library's procedures they *could* control access to them through the terms of the gift. Billington's stand on Marshall was an announcement that the library would honor its commitments no matter what the terms of limitation were. That is not to say the library would accept a collection slated to be closed for one hundred years. It would not honor *any* restrictions, but would honor any restrictions *to which it agreed in the deed of gift*. Without that commitment it is certain that many sensitive collections would go elsewhere, or worse, be destroyed. The deed, therefore, can be a powerful document that can have an impact on researchers interested in the study of recent historical events.[22]

When Jacqueline Kennedy Onassis died in 1994, her thirty-six-page will settled much of her estate, and included reference to her personal papers, which were bequeathed to her two children, John Kennedy, Jr., and Caroline Kennedy Schlossberg. In the be-quest is the statement that the heirs should "take whatever action warranted to prevent the display, publication or distribution in whole or in part of these papers, letters and writings."[23] Since there is no time stipulation in reference to the material, it is assumed that this will keep her personal papers from ever becoming public.

This complexity, and the relationship between personal papers and government records as to access times, can be illustrated also in the case of the Kissinger telephone logs. When Henry Kissinger left his position as secretary of state in 1977 he took with him the telephone logs that he had kept during his four years in that position, and "donated" them to the Library of Congress for deposit in the Manuscript Division. The terms of the donation, in the deed of gift, restricted all access not approved by Kissinger to twenty-five years or five years after his death, whichever is later.[24] The National Archives cried foul, and claimed that such documents created in the course of his official duties were official records of the department and should rightfully become part of the archives of the agency, deposited in the National Archives.

The counterclaim was based on the fact that as federal documents the phone logs would be subject to access through the Freedom of Information Act (FOIA), whereas in the Library of Congress they were under the control of the donor. A ruling by the attorney general noted that the Federal Records Act did not give the archivist of the United States the authority to determine what documents are records, but that authority lay with the head of each agency. Under that ruling, the secretary of state declared that the phone logs were not official records, and they remain in the Manuscript Division under Kissinger's control. This is yet more evidence of the power of the deed of gift.[25]

The deed of gift may contain other provisions that have an impact on the researcher. In it the donor declares the status of the intellectual property held in the letters, writings and other materials in the donated collection, or copyright (see chapter 11). In a typical deed of gift the donor states what he or she wishes the disposition of copyright to be, and may open up the whole research process by dedicating the copyright to the public, putting the material in the public domain. However, such dedication would apply only to the material in the collection in which copyright resides in the donor, since the donor has no dispensing power for other holders of copyright. In short, Harriet Monroe could (under the 1978 act) dedicate to the public all the rights in *her* letters and writings, but she could not assign any rights in Calhoun's. In the deed, therefore, a researcher may be granted free access to the material in the collection, but only limited, if any, reproduction rights.

The deed of gift can also contain provisions for disposal of irrelevant, unimportant, or specified materials. In it the donor and the institution can agree on the disposition of ephemera, such as inconsequential notes, commercial materials, multiple copies of documents, etc. It is in the language of this part of the deed where one may later determine why certain material cannot be located that one would expect to find there.

When contracts such as deeds and deposit agreements, with their codicils, amendments, and time-sensitive obligations, go into the case file they change its nature and utility. Unlike the file a library might keep on its book purchases, or even that a special collections department might keep on its rare book donations or purchases, the manuscript case file becomes truly a significant administrative tool, documenting the receipt, processing, description and even use of the collection for the rest of its life in the repository. Therefore, in addition to the original correspondence with the prospective donor, the case file grows to include the preliminary description of the collection that was made at the site where it was kept by the donor, the shipping list when it was transferred to the repository, the deed or other document showing transfer and changed ownership, and any subsequent descriptions of the collection as developed by the repository. Some repositories try to keep in the case file any correspondence about the collection, including reference mail. Although such a procedure could provide considerable future assistance in responding to difficult questions about a collection if the questions had previously been answered by another staff member in another era, keeping *all* correspondence relating to an active collection could soon create its own space and management problems.

The researcher may never see a case file or a deed of gift, even though most institutions would not be averse to making them available for perusal. But when the staff member informs the researcher of restrictions—either on access or copying—it is a safe bet to say that it is the deed of gift that is the source. The researcher should be aware, however, that terms of deeds can change over time. When I was doing research recently in a repository and came across a document that I wished to quote from, I checked the copyright statement in the finding aid and found that copyright in the collection was controlled by the donor or the estate of the subject. Since the statement dated to the early 1960s I asked the staff to check the case file for any changes, and was pleased to find that there was a document in it that stated that copyright was now dedicated to the public, as of six months before. I then felt free to copy the material that I needed, with the appropriate attribution of source.

If the curator is thorough in drafting the terms of a deed of gift, with considerable assistance from the legal staff, it will ease the burden of future staff members when decisions have to be made, and it will provide the researcher with a rationale when there are questions of arbitrariness in the way collections are restricted. It is certainly true, therefore, that for staff and researcher alike, good deeds do not go unrewarded.

NOTES

1. David C. Mearns, "Historical Manuscripts, Including Personal Papers," 313.

2. Garraty, 209.

3. See, for instance, the University of Chicago. Department of Special Collections. Manuscripts. The Papers of John Gunther, Box 18, for many examples of notes kept on cut-up strips of stationery from the Gran Hotel Bolivar, Lima, Peru, 1940. Some conveniently have the name of the interviewee scribbled in a corner of the "sniblet."

4. Library of Congress. Manuscript Division. Accession record 21138, February 9, 1995.

5. Dennis Burton, *Guide to Manuscript Collections in the Presidential Libraries.*

6. U.S. Library of Congress. Manuscript Division, *Felix Frankfurter. A Register of His Papers in the Library of Congress* (Washington: Library of Congress, 1971), 70, containers 254–255.

7. *Robert Wilson Shufeldt. A Register of His Papers*, 6.

8. Raymond H. Geselbracht, "The origins of Restrictions on Access to Personal Papers at the Library of Congress and the National Archives," *American Archivist* 49 (spring 1986): 142–162.

9. "Boston University Wins Dispute over King Papers," *The Washington Post*, May 7, 1993, A2; "Coretta King Loses Battle on Papers," ibid., April 13, 1995, A7.

10. For a discussion of the implications of not having appropriate documentation for institutional holdings, however, see Ronald Becker, "On

Deposit: A Handshake and a Lawsuit," *American Archivist* 56 (spring 1993): 320–328.

11. The Statute of Elizabeth (Charitable Uses Act), 1601, 43 Eliz., chapter 4, lists the following charities: "Relief of aged impotent and poore people, some for Maintenance of the sicke and maymed Souldiers and Marriners, Schooles of Learninge, Free Schooles and Schollers in Universities, some for Repaire of Bridges Portes Havens Causwaies Churches Seabankes and Highewaies, some for Educacion and perfermente of Orphans, some for or towardes Reliefe Stocke or maintenance of howses of Correccion, some for Mariages of poore Maides, some for Supportacion Ayde and Helpe of younge tradesmen Handicraftsmen and persons decayed, and others for releife or redemption of Prisoners or Captives, and for aide or ease of any poore Inhabitantes concerninge payemente of Fifteenes, setting out of Souldiers and other Taxes; Whiche Landes Tenements Rents Annuities Profitts Hereditaments Goodes Chattells Money and Stockes of money nevertheles have not byn imployed accordinge to the charitable intente of the givers and founders thereof. . . ."

12. 15 Am Jur 2nd Charities ss 3.

13. Am Jur 2nd Charities ss 5.

14. *Hebrew University Association v. George D. Nye et al., Executors* (Estate of Ethel S. Yahuda), 169 A.2d 641.

15. There is a good elaboration on these points in Gary Peterson and Trudy Huskamp Peterson, *Archives and Manuscripts: Law*, 24–38.

16. Geselbracht, 142–162. As might be suspected, the literature on the question of access is extensive; some of the articles appearing just since 1980 include: Roland M. Baumann, "The Administration of Access to Confidential Records in State Archives: Common Practices and the Need for a Model Law," *American Archivist* 49 (fall 1986): 349–370; Joan Hoff-Wilson, "Access to Restricted Collections: The Responsibility of Professional Historical Organizations," *American Archivist* 44 (fall 1983): 441–448; Alice Robbins, "State Archives and Issues of Personal Privacy: Policies and Practices," *American Archivist* 49 (spring 1986): 163–176; Anne Van Camp, "Access Policies for Corporate Archives," *American Archivist* 45 (summer 1982): 296–298.

17. "Chief Justice Castigates Library," *The Washington Post*, 26 May 1993, A1.

18. Carl T. Rowan, "The Library Betrayed Justice Marshall," *The Washington Post*, May 29, 1993, A19.

19. "Librarian Rejects Restrictions," *The Washington Post*, May 27, 1993, A1, A20.

20. "Marketer of Court Tapes Risks Supreme Censure," *The Washington Post*, August 30, 1993, A6.

21. Alfred Wong, Marshal, Office of the Marshal, Supreme Court of the United States to Trudy Peterson, Acting Archivist of the United States,

November 1, 1993, and attachment: "Agreement Between the Supreme Court of the United States and the National Archives and Records Administration." Records of the Office of the Archivist, National Archives and Records Administration, Washington, D.C.

22. Raymond H. Geselbracht, ibid.

23. *The Manuscript Society News* 15, no. 3 (summer 1994): 93.

24. Provided to me by John Haynes, Manuscript Division, Library of Congress, September 1994, from the Kissinger Deed of Gift.

25. John M. Harmon, Assistant Attorney General, Office of Legal Counsel, U.S. Department of Justice, to Allie B. Latimer, General Counsel, General Services Administration, 13 January 1981, in records of the Office of General Counsel, General Services Administration, Washington, D.C.

· 9 ·

The Cultural Crypt

The past is a tenuous, shadowy reality, half misunderstood,
half forgotten. For us to live with it, it must be accessible,
physically and mentally, and it must be valued and cared for.

Shirley C. Spragge[1]

The physical layout and convenience of an institution may say much about its philosophy of accessibility and its attitude towards the public. Certainly, in the past few decades documentary research institutions have undergone changes in their physical structures, but ironically, it has occurred at the same time that there has been an opposite change in the public attitude. Researchers should be aware of how archivists think about their public image and their increased encouragement of research in their holdings, but at the same time take note of the growing threats to the security of their collections, and how these threats impact on the ease with which the researcher finds access to them.

The Library of Congress Manuscript Division moved from the main building to the annex, which opened in 1939 and is now known as the John Adams Building. It was on the third floor and occupied most of the south end, with research room, processing areas, stacks, and administrative offices all in the same suite, accessible only through a single doorway from the elevator lobby. Researchers, therefore, had to enter the building past a guard post, take an elevator or climb the stairs, and enter the division through another guarded door before reaching the research area. Getting out required passage past the two guard posts. Once inside the building, however, the visitor could go anywhere that was not physically restricted.

The National Archives Building, constructed in 1934, had two access approaches to the research room on the second floor.

One could confront a rather massive Indiana limestone facade on Pennsylvania Avenue at Eighth Street, which has as its sole opening a rather undersized (for the mass of the building), understated doorway that gave very little clue as to what was beyond it. Allegorically, it was reminiscent of the door that Alice confronted on her way to Wonderland. Once inside, the visitor found a square lobby and straight ahead, posted in a swivel chair behind a desk, was a federal protective officer, whose main task was to point and endlessly repeat for visitors the fact that there were two curved stairways or an elevator that they could take to the exhibition hall one floor up, or they could take the elevator two floors up to the Central Search Room. However, one could also approach the exhibition hall from the Constitution Avenue side of the building, and climb the thirty-nine steps to the portico. Once inside there was another federal protective officer whose main task was to keep people in line and moving out of the doorway when the hall was crowded. From the main exhibition hall one could proceed through a "circular gallery" that was originally just a hallway connecting the Constitution Avenue side with the Pennsylvania Avenue side. At the neck of this horseshoe-shaped hall was a gate that could close off the business side of the building from the tourist side. In the 1960s that gate was rarely closed, and thus visitors could access the building's offices and research rooms through it. There was no package inspection at the gate.

In the Library of Congress the researcher was also asked to deposit coats, umbrellas, and other nonessentials in a cloakroom on the ground floor, but briefcases, purses, and research-related materials were allowed in the reading room of the Manuscript Division.

In the National Archives there were no lockers or active cloakrooms, so researchers placed coats and personal items on a rack in the hallway, or entered the search room with everything that they brought into the building with them, and placed them on the floor or on a chair next to their workstation, or put them on the tabletop at which they were working.

In a class in manuscript administration that I have taught since 1975, the students join me in an exercise to design a model or ideal manuscript facility within a large university library. On the blackboard we sketch an empty shell of a structure and decide on which level we would like our facility to be, in which geographical quadrant it would best be located, the internal configuration of the reading room, placement of the stacks, the composition of a reference collection, the location of furniture, and availability of facilities such as copying machines, microfilm readers, and, recently, computer terminals. All of this is done after the students read their assignment on security, preservation, and internal workflow. I cannot recall a year when the design pattern was dramatically broken: located on a middle floor (neither the main floor nor directly under the roof) because Special Collections are special, and therefore need not be immediately accessible to all who enter the building, and security dictates that rare materials not be too close to public exits. Locating under a roof or below ground can have dire effects if the physical structure is not sound and either the roof or the basement leaks; if there are windows, locate in the northeast quadrant (least direct sunlight, and thus, also, least radiant heat); restrict public entrance to one door at which a staff member is permanently posted and which has a barrier before entry to the reading or search room; provide lockers outside of the research area for all personal belongings; and position the circulation or service desk so that all worktables are in view of the staff.

These considerations obviously stem from what the students read about security, but they also convey a certain lack of awareness of modern construction techniques for public buildings, and especially for libraries. And yet, the midwest floods of 1993, the Georgia floods of 1994, the California earthquakes of the past few years, the major fire at the National Military Personnel Records Center (part of the National Archives) in St. Louis in 1973 that burned off the top floor of the building and 400,000 cubic feet of records,[2] major thefts by Charles Merrill Mount and David Blumberg (see below), and many, many earlier incidents of like nature have produced a cautious attitude in curators, and, in the case of my students, in prospective curators.

In 1980 the Manuscript Division moved to the third Library of Congress building, the Madison Building, where it is located just inside the main Independence Avenue entrance in two large suites. To the left of the main hallway is the reading room, preceded by banks of public lockers and blocked by a security officer. Beyond the reading room are the stacks and processing areas. To the right of the hallway are the staff offices, with a receptionist inside the entryway.

The National Archives main building downtown has not changed its configuration, although it has locked the gate between the exhibition hall and the rest of the building, and replaced the single federal protective officer with contract security guards at the Pennsylvania Avenue entrance, with at least four on duty during business hours. It had an airport-type security system with personnel metal detector and briefcase/purse electronic scanner (now removed), and added banks of personal lockers in the hallway outside of the Central Search Room. However, in June 1994 it dedicated the second National Archives Building at College Park, known as Archives II. As distinct from downtown's old "mysterious door" entryway, Archives II presents a three-story-high glass façade leading to a bright and spacious lobby. The analogy now is not Alice, but "The Lady and the Tiger," because the researcher confronts three choices from the main lobby. To the left is a security desk beyond which is the entrance to the staff and administrative offices. In the center is a security barrier, with security staff and turnstiles that provide access to all research areas upon presentation of an appropriate research card. Except for these two checkpoints, access is unguarded and provides unrestricted entry to the cafeteria, which is open to the public, and to the auditorium, meeting and lecture rooms, a reception area, and an extensive room containing 367 personal lockers.

I mention these details because they illustrate two attitudes confronting the researcher: the newer facilities are modern, well designed, and convenient of access; but are under much tighter security than they were fifteen or twenty years ago. There are good historic reasons for both of these changes.

In Washington and on many of the nation's campuses, heightened security awareness for public buildings came with the Vietnam and civil rights demonstrations of the 1960s and '70s. Whereas the off-the-street patron could casually enter most buildings in the Capital or on most campuses before Vietnam, the demonstrations, riots, seizures, disruptions and even physical destruction of property, including library materials and whole card catalogs, forced the establishment to put its guard up, and to restrict access. International terrorism and demonic hijacking schemes confronting commercial aviation led to the security measures that now are standard operating practice at airports, under orders from the Federal Aviation Administration. The manufacturers of crowd control and security devices found a sympathetic market in government and academic institutions. Getting into a White House meeting through the automobile entrance is now akin to passing through

Checkpoint Charlie between the two Berlins during the Cold War. Ironically, Checkpoint Charlie is gone and all is serene at the Brandenburg Gate, but public institutions in the United States remain in a state of terrorist readiness. Incidents of the 1990s at the White House and the terrorist bombing at the World Trade Center in New York and the Alfred P. Murrah Federal Building in Oklahoma City unfortunately confirm the need for these, and perhaps stronger, security measures.

Compounding the sociopolitical reasons for heavy physical security in libraries, archives, and manuscript repositories is the escalation of major thefts of rare materials from these cultural institutions. Since World War II, with the expansion of advanced education, use of research materials, and the concomitant growth of research facilities, there has been a continuing threat to these materials through personal thefts. In 1966 the future Archivist of the United States, James B. Rhoads, detailed the problems plaguing institutions at that time. A notorious example was the "Murphy case," wherein a husband and wife team, Murphy, defrauded repositories by removing documents that were "on order" to them by prospective buyers.[3] Some twenty years later Charles Merrill Mount was suspected by Goodspeed's Bookstore in Boston of having in his possession, and offering for sale, documents that appeared to be from the major collections in Washington, at both the National Archives and the Library of Congress Manuscript Division. Mount was no sneak thief or social renegade, but a respected (if somewhat phony) scholar, researcher, author, and trusted user of the collections from which the materials presented to Goodspeed's had been purloined.[4] Part of Mount's defense was that the collections at the two federal institutions were so vast, and the internal controls so vague, that they would not be able to prove that they had ever held the suspect documents, which he claimed he had received from a Roman Catholic priest in Ireland (unfortunately, since deceased). But, through various archival processes, unknown to most researchers and overlooked by Mount, the National Archives and the Manuscript Division were able to convince the courts that they did, indeed, recently have the questioned material among their holdings, and they were also able to show a connection between the documents and Mount's use of the collections from which they were missing. Mount's jail term ended, and his death shortly thereafter spared the archival profession from keeping a wary eye out for his appearance at a research collection at some future date.[5]

The commission of Mount's crime was simplified by his status in the research community. A portrait painter of some note, and a biographer of John Singer Sargent, Mount was respected in the art circles in which he moved, posturing as he did as an Edwardian gentleman in tweeds and carrying a walking stick, despite his humble beginnings as Sherman Suchow in Brooklyn, New York. He had even donated some manuscript material to the Library of Congress, and was a common sight in the building. The institution's trust extended to providing him with a private, locked facility for his research in the library. It is strongly suspected that the thefts were made, at least sometimes, by concealment of individual documents under his jacket or vest. As a result of the Mount episode the Manuscript Division instituted a procedure that asked patrons wearing jackets to sign a release that permits the security force to request that they be removed, should there be any suspicion of concealment.

The nature of documents as research sources, and the growing threats to their security, have led repositories across the country to increase the security of physical access to them. Access to government and corporate records, as well as to personal papers, had always been subject to some bureaucratic restrictions. Corporations have traditionally restricted access to their records on the basis of protecting trade secrets, financial data, personnel practices, and other "privileged" information. Governments have denied access on the basis of confidentiality, personal privacy, protection of intelligence sources, national security, or a number of other limitations. Even since the Freedom of Information Act of 1976, the federal government has nine exemptions that may be applied to restrict access to federal records, and the act does not cover the legislative or judicial branches at all. All states have similar acts with exemptions.

Donors of personal papers to federal or other institutions can contract with the recipient institution for the imposition of access restrictions,[6] which are only the last barricade in the fortress of restrictions placed before the researcher. Initially one must gain access to the institution holding the research sources. Aside from the fact that manuscript and archives research rooms are not always open for the same hours as the library in which they are housed, one must first get into the library. That should be no problem in tax-supported institutions, although in most state, county and municipal archives the patron must sign in and provide some statement of research purpose. On campuses a researcher will generally find ready access to the library and can wander freely through the unrestricted areas, consulting the public access catalog or the on-line public access catalog, consulting the reference collection, the open stacks, microfilm, etc.

At state, county and municipal historical societies there may be ready access to the exhibition hall and bookstore, but no further penetration without justification, or proof of membership, or a fee. Much the same condition exists at state, county and municipal archives, although the genealogical research rooms may be more readily accessible with just a sign-in procedure. Thus, access to the parent institution may be minimally limited or freely open, but this varies from institution to institution.

Because of the configuration of the downtown National Archives Building and the Library of Congress, *everybody* entering must "check in." Staff does so by displaying a photo pass, National Archives researchers do so by showing a research pass, and anyone with packages, purses, briefcases or other carried items submits them for either a visual or an electronic inspection. The need to go through this procedure when one is entering the building to apply for a job at the personnel office, view the exhibitions or a film or public performance, or join a staff member for lunch is what prompted the National Archives to have the architects of Archives II separate entry requirements by function: a simple check-in for staff areas, a research card requirement for the research complex, and open access to the public rooms and cafeteria.

Once inside a research institution, it is quite a different matter getting through the second access level—to the research area where the archives and manuscript materials are served. Since the notorious thefts by Mount, the concept of the "clean" search room has predominated at many repositories, with the Manuscript Division and the National Archives leading the way, although I remember undergoing such a procedure in the Newberry Library thirty years earlier. The "clean" search room concept implies that nothing extraneous is carried into the search room or reading room by the patron, thus providing easier inspection of what comes out. It was obvious, in earlier days, that briefcases, purses, books, newspapers, and even folded topcoats were perfect places for sequestering documentary materials. Less obvious, but still a threat in the minds of the administrators, was the admission of notepads and loose papers. Even photocopied material going in might not be distinguishable from photocopied documents (a growing percentage of official and even personal documents) coming out. The solution was to provide the researcher with such research aids once inside, and have them marked as "passable" for an exit inspection.

Libraries, dealing with material that is commonly bound, boxed or otherwise packaged, have adopted the magnetized security strip fashioned inside the bindings or containers as they are processed. The strip is demagnetized when the material is cleared through the circulation desk, and passes through the magnetometer at the exit without setting off an alarm or locking the exit turnstile. This procedure is not possible with individual documents, so the inspection process has to substitute for the electronic gate.

The document researcher, whom one would expect to be in a professional position or at least be a serious researcher respectful of the sources, thus can easily feel put-upon for the triple access controls to which he or she is subjected—building access, followed by research room access, followed by document access. The courts have held that security screening is generally not considered to be an invasion of privacy if it is applied evenhandedly to all patrons, if it is concerned only with matters of security and cannot be characterized as "snooping" into nonsecurity matters, and if there is a general notice of inspection given to the patron or conspicuously posted.[7]

Once inside the reading room, inspection is replaced by surveillance. This is carried out by staff at the circulation or reference desk, and/or perhaps by a security guard, and increasingly by electronic surveillance devices. Those inverted plastic domes on the ceiling of more and more reading rooms do not house a smoke detector or sprinkler, but a scanning television camera that can be monitored by staff.

Beyond physical security, many repositories carry out what one might call intellectual security, insisting that the researcher sign a statement promising not to publish material from the collections without the institution's permission, and perhaps even the author's permission. This is one of the aspects of the case of *Salinger v. Random House*, where the researcher, biographer Ian Hamilton, used collections that contained J. D. Salinger material, signed an agreement to consult with the libraries and the author before publishing, submitted a manuscript of his book to the publisher without permission for the quotations he did use, and ultimately was forced to back down when Salinger sued, not on breach of contract, but on the author's rights to first publication under the Copyright Act (see chapter 11 for the case). From many a curator's viewpoint, the imposition of restrictions above and beyond those contained in the deed of gift should not be their role, and they prefer not to do it. That was the crux of the Thurgood Marshall/ Library of Congress/Supreme Court incident discussed earlier.

A reasonable researcher might speculate that if research institutions could mark their materials for identification in case of theft it would reduce the security requirements at the door, relieving them of the chagrin, if not the burden, of passing through the researcher's equivalent of the Berlin Wall. The complexities of document stamping, and the simplistic interpretation of it by outsiders, may never be rationalized, but stamping is, at best, a deterrent to theft and a possible aid in recovery of stolen documents, but it provides no controls for the curator.

Primarily, stamping is impractical in a large repository. The Manuscript Division at the Library of Congress in 1996 claimed some 11,000 collections containing 56 million items. A random sampling of other institutions (from the *Directory of Archives and Manuscript Repositories in the United States*) indicates that the Michigan State University Archives and Historical Collections extend to 4,573 cubic feet, the Salvation Army Archives Bureau (New York) contains 2,921 linear feet of records, the Swarthmore (Pennsylvania) College Peace Collection contains 1,400 linear feet, and the Jessie Ball duPont Library at The University of the South holds 513 linear feet of papers. Considering that one foot of foldered documents numbers about 2,500 sheets, one can grasp the enormity of stamping each one with the institution's indicia. The process is complicated by the lack of blank spaces on many documents. Stamps should not obscure original text, but if placed in clear corners of the papers they can easily be clipped off. If placed on the back of a one-sided page the ink can bleed through. Some institutions have used embossing devices for their seal, rather than ink. But the labor involved is just as onerous as with stamping. Since the location of text on each document varies, machine processes cannot be generally employed for stamping.

Stamping presumes either deterrence or ex-post facto identification, assuming that estrays turn up on the open market, as was the case with Mount. But the psychology of those who remove documents from collections does not support the profit theory of theft.

Thus, two of the reasons for theft—covetousness and sentiment—are difficult to combat, and a stamped indicia is probably little deterrent.

Stamping also does little for the institution in unearthing losses. A folder that contains twenty-four stamped documents when it is supposed to contain twenty-five will still pose the question of which one is missing. Numbering each document as it is stamped may then reveal that the fifteenth document is the lost one, but what *was* the fifteenth document? The solution, of course, is to itemize the numbered documents in a list. This means undertaking a process that most repositories forswore fifty years ago because of the burden of effort necessary. The Manuscript Division of the Library of Congress prepared an *automated* item list of its Presidential Papers series, using as many as ten staff members at times, but the index to 1.2 million documents took twenty-five years to complete. As noted earlier, the library now claims to hold forty million items. It should also be noted that during that twenty-five-year process the library's backlog of unprocessed collections grew considerably, and unprocessed collections are withheld from researcher use. In mid-1994 the library claimed to have an *unprocessed* backlog of 6,313,160 manuscripts.[8]

Some of the solutions that curators have applied to the problem of security have included mounting and binding, and filming. Government agencies often bound their loose papers into labeled volumes for ease of use before the advent of vertical files, file folders and labels, and the post-Civil War conversion of offices to modern records control.[9] Manuscript curators occasionally did the same thing, on a grander scale, with loose document collections as both a preservation and security measure.

But mounting, binding and labeling is a time-consuming and expensive process, rarely used anymore. Perhaps the last *great* document binding project was with the Presidential Papers at the Library of Congress, accomplished in the 1960s. The million-plus items were first definitively organized (mostly in chronological order), indexed with the aid of punched cards and a computer, microfilmed, deacidified, laminated in plastic, mounted on acid-free sheets, quarter-bound in volumes, had gold-stamped spine titles applied, and then each had a storage slip-case made to its dimensions. In 1960s' dollars the cost (not including indexing and microfilming) was at the time purported to be approximately $600 per volume, with approximately three thousand volumes so treated. Since then the consensus of the profession is that plastic lamination may be more destructive than beneficial to documents, and it is frowned on by preservationists.

The security process that has carried the day with curators for the past fifty years has been microfilming. The technology proved its value in the preparation of V-mail in World War II, wherein the military postal services microfilmed most mail going to troops in the various theaters of war, thus saving precious bulk on planes and ships. The microfilming process found its way into libraries and documentary collections for two purposes: distribution of the intellectual contents of unique materials, such as manuscripts and archives, and preservation of the contents of deteriorating materials of all kinds—maps, photographs, documents, serials and books. As a method for distributing unique materials that must remain in their home institution, microfilm has proven to be unsurpassed. Once a master and copy master are made from the original documents, copies can be produced on demand, avoiding stock buildup, warehousing, and "adventure capital" investments on the part of the institution. At the same time, the master copy, made of a polyester base and silver granules and stored under ideal temperature/humidity conditions, becomes a preservation copy of the original documents.

In spite of all these benefits of microfilm for facilitating use and extending the life of the information captured, researchers have generally not been pleased with having to use the medium. Use-copies, usually made on sturdy diazo film, ultimately show signs of wear from traversing the viewing heads of antediluvian microfilm projectors, causing information "dropouts" because of scratches, nicks and other abrasions. This condition, of course, is the fault of the institution, not of the microfilm. The same could be said for the quality of the filming, where there are incorrect exposures, poor focusing, lack of proper document order, and missing targets that give the reader a clue when a new file is beginning or some other change is taking place. These are the kinds of conditions that try the patience of researchers and send them growling from the research room.

It is irresponsible for institutions to treat their patrons in a manner that discourages use of their material, although much of the blame falls on budget limitations. Yet it has to be conceded that the use of surrogates is the only way to make rare material available to a broad research community and yet preserve it for future generations.

There is a current flurry of excitement over the advent of digital imaging, where documents are scanned and captured digitally instead of photochemically. The excitement comes from some of the obvious advantages of digital over chemical reproduction. Digitized information is communicable, and therefore can be available to many concurrently from a single source—the depository. Digital images can be "downloaded" or copied at the receiving end. They can sometimes be searched through full-text searching (every word) that does not require the preparation of indexes and is therefore an electronic, not an intellectual, process and digitized images can be enhanced through adjustment of the "grey scale" to bring out dim images or dark images on a dark background. In sum, digital imaging is efficient and it is fast.

Most archivists and curators agree with the claims of digital imaging proponents, and many institutions have begun to undertake conversion of the information in their documents to electronic form. But archivists are also aware that the costs are as great as for filming, if not greater. Whether documents are going under a photographic or an electronic camera, they must be organized and arranged. There must be some indication of when files are changing or information has to be supplied to label certain material. There could be a case made that physical order and structure of files are not necessary in a digitized file, because they can be imposed electronically. But that implies that the original documents, which, after all, will remain in their original state after digitization, will remain chaotic and therefore probably be rendered useless to future researchers.

An example of such thinking is illustrated by the activities of a certain clerk in the Department of State in the 1830s. He decided that the papers of the Continental and Confederation Congresses (1774–1789), archived to the State Department Library, were not in proper order. It is assumed that they were maintained by Charles Thomson, the secretary, or clerk, of the First and Second Continental Congresses, in the structure in which they were created, that is, organized according to the structure of the institution, with the distinct committees' (Finance, Foreign Affairs, Marine Committee, etc.) files together, probably in chronological order. The State Department clerk rearranged the papers so that

> they are arranged and bound chiefly by type of document, such
> as journals, committee reports, and correspondence, and there-

under chronologically or alphabetically. Therefore, groups of records related closely by content are often widely separated, while unrelated records are occasionally grouped together.[10]

This stripped the committee files of much of their substance, and made the record of their day-to-day activities impossible to reconstruct. Later in the century the documents were bound in the new order, and in the twentieth century they were microfilmed in that order. Researchers found the 219-reel set of unindexed microfilm too cumbersome to use, and many turned to the less revealing manuscript *Journals of the Continental Congress* in thirty-four volumes. In 1978, as a result of the celebration of the Bicentennial of the Declaration of Independence, and a grant from the Ford Foundation, a five-volume index to the papers was produced.[11]

For many research purposes it is most desirable to have the documents in a rational order so that it is not necessary to consult indexes. This is especially true when the documents are on multiple reels of microfilm, as the papers of the Continental Congress are, because the index may also be available only on film, and the loading and unloading of reels in order to consult an index and then go to the documents cited can be avoided only by printing out what may be a lengthy index or using more than one microfilm reader, a cumbersome if not impractical approach to research.

Electronic search capabilities may ease some of the researcher's burdens, but there are other things besides convenience that archivists consider when they contemplate digitization. First is the lack of standardization in the industry, and digitization today is where videocassette standards were a few years ago, when one had to choose between VHS or Beta systems, which were incompatible. Although VHS has won out for the home market in the United States, it is not a world standard, as one finds out when transporting demonstration videotapes to meetings abroad, where other systems are predominant. Archivists worry that digitization faces the same hurdle of standardization before they can trust systems to be able to play back their disks or tapes universally.

Archivists are also concerned about the ongoing evolution of systems, much like the developments in the computer industry, where operating systems, equipment and transportability between systems are tenuous. The fact that the 1960 census can now be read on only two machines in the world—one in Japan and the other in the Smithsonian—is a common warning that archivists give to the advocates of immediate conversion of files to digitized format. Although many files created on earlier versions of the personal computer can be played back on later versions, there is commonly a loss of some features, and (as with humans) as the generation gap widens, the ability to communicate between the generations decreases.

What these perceived difficulties cause is a certain archival conservatism, a holding back from the digitization leap, and a continued reliance on microcopies, where the technology is standard, prospective longevity of the data is all but assured, and if all else fails a magnifying glass and a photographic light table will still make it possible to read the filmed documents. Where these supportive arguments do not apply is in the use of interactive databases that are created in database management systems, or spreadsheets in digitized form. Their strength is their ability to permit relational computing and the construction of virtual documents, where a database of pure data is programmed to present the data in different structures to respond to different queries. In effect, they contain no "original document," but just a multiplicity of items of information that can be constructed into a document through commands given by the researcher. Microfilming such information freezes it in a static format, thus devaluing the system and its many possibilities.

The Internet, "gophers," Mosaic, the World Wide Web, Java and many other innovations may be changing the technological roadblocks before our very eyes, thereby proving the cynics right—that one should wait until it all works itself out. In the new systems one does not need a physical "product," such as a CD-ROM disk or other packageable device, because all that one has to do is scan or otherwise enter finding aids, documents, graphics, and even sound and motion into a "system" and make it available for on-line access. The various protocols that determine compatibility between the receiving system and the transmitter do much to eliminate the unfriendliness.

Thus, surrogates are replacing originals, and one needs only a personal computer and access to the Internet. What will that do to the problems of access discussed above? Two of the levels of limitation are eliminated, since the researcher does not have to enter a building, then enter the manuscript or archives room. The one level of access restriction that continues to apply is that imposed on some of the documents themselves. This assumes, of course, that "entering the manuscript or archives room" via computer implies that the "room" is open, that the institution has placed its collections on-line. In 1995 the National Archives had no plans to convert even the major portion of the billions of documents in its custody to digital form, although digitizing "core holdings . . . selected documents, photographs and posters" would be a reasonable expectation.[12] The rationale is bulk, and the complexity of copying so many original documents into a digitized format. This begs the question, however, since the National Archives has been engaged in copying its holdings, at the document level, since 1940,[13] but the form has been microform. One could anticipate a change in institutional policy in the not too distant future, as digitization takes hold after some of today's problems are solved. The National Archives has, indeed, signed an "agreement that pledges collaboration toward the establishment of a National Digital Library Federation" with fifteen other institutions.[14]

With the use of surrogates—film or digital—security of the documents is largely assured, because access to the originals is granted only under extraordinary circumstances. It is then possible to squirrel away the originals in optimum environmental and security conditions, to form the "master file" of documentary culture, to be exhumed only when surrogates disappear or need refreshing, or a new technology convinces the keepers that they should be reproduced once again, in the new format. Libraries and archives thus differ, in that most libraries microfilm material in order to reduce bulk, and then dispose of a perhaps badly deteriorating original, or an original that can be found elsewhere. Archives film in order to circulate their holdings, and by keeping a master, a copy master, and a use copy they actually increase bulk in the institution, although the original might be moved off-site. Oddly, "off-site" for valuable documents is not a warehouse beyond the beltway, but an environmentally secure facility that may rival the institution headquarters for upkeep costs.

Researchers may find that a repository has filmed or digitized some of its holdings, but not a majority of them. On-site consultation of a finding aid (unless one is using the *NIDS* fiche or the Internet off-site) and the help of the staff are then the only access routes to the holdings. From the curator's perspective the finding aid performs two functions. First, it is as it says, an aid to finding material within a collection. Although the existence of finding aids outside the repository is helpful to researchers planning their research strategies, there is really no substitute for discussing research problems with the repository staff. Harriet Monroe is a case in point. One would not expect a researcher engaged in studying the Chinese Revolution of 1911 to look in the Monroe papers, but the staff at Chicago should be aware of that small cache of letters hiding out in the collection, under the innocuous title, "Personal Correspondence."

Secondly, however, the curator can consider a good finding aid as an enhancer of security. Security does not imply just theft, but any action that moves a document out of its logical place in the collection. With poor finding aids that are vague or incomplete, the researcher may have to request many folders or boxes, and do internal searching in order to locate sought-after material. Handling of loose papers easily results in disorder, not just within one folder but between or among folders. In extreme cases documents can migrate to other collections through poor handling. If the finding aid is expansive and clear (without, however, item listing every document) the researcher's search area is proscribed, and extraneous files or documents need not be served, thus limiting any damage that might be done by sloppy refiling. Conversely, a poor finding aid just confirms Mount's charges that many institutions do not really know what they have, and therefore cannot tell what is missing.

An area of document security that is rarely discussed in the literature, and has little to do with the researcher, is internal theft. Stories of dishonest staff who are confronted with charges of document theft are legion, but rarely get into print unless charges are pressed and the case gets into the courts.[15] Security restrictions on staff are lax to nonexistent in many repositories. Staff have passkeys and access to otherwise restricted areas of the repository. Staff members are often alone in a small repository, or in a secluded area of a large one. Staff members know where the valuable materials are in collections. Although professional staff may take the ethics of their profession seriously and may not wish to endanger their future career possibilities through rash or illegal acts, archives and manuscript repositories traditionally rely on volunteers, student help, or "technicians" in subprofessional positions. Among them may be zealots, intrigued by materials that they come across in their daily chores that define or otherwise support their zeal for issues or causes; family history buffs who encounter obscure documents concerning a near or distant relative; and enthusiasts for fine graphic design who are intrigued by otherwise insignificant documents that have visual or artistic appeal. The rationale for the zealots, history buffs and enthusiasts usually is that the document, in and of itself, is insignificant and will not detract from anyone's future research, and, besides, it is reasoned, the material of which it is a part has not been consulted in x years, and may not be looked at again for another x years, if ever. Once the rationalization has been made, it is not difficult to remove the document from the premises without a trace. Some document thefts, especially when perpetrated by disgruntled employees, are means of "getting even," or taking revenge for wrongs real or imagined.

Oddly enough, some institutions face a counterproblem from the same zealots and history buffs, who have been known to want to "correct the records" that they consider to be a calumny or at least misleading. Their method is to surreptitiously introduce documents *into* a collection that will present *their* view of the individual, the incident, or the institution. They may try to introduce such material legitimately, but when thwarted in that attempt will often turn to subversive means. This may happen more in official records, or archives, than in personal paper collections, because it is usually the "record" that the researcher wants to "set straight." Names spelled wrong in a census, vital dates in error on various certificates, erroneous descriptions of property, and myriad other errors exist throughout the "record," and the archivist will protect them in their original form. To accede to change in one case implies acceding to change in other cases where there is a petition for change, and the "record" of the census, name forms, vital dates, and all other information would thereafter be suspect.

There undoubtedly are cases among manuscripts where documentation has been changed, the files supplemented with later commentary, and incidents elaborated on and explained by the curator in the finding aid. But, to go back to the premise stated in chapter 1, there is a great difference between archival records and personal paper collections, especially relating to the legal admissibility of the information contained in them. Even manuscript curators generally agree that it is not their task to "correct" the statements carried in the documents in their care. That is the role of historians, or, in extreme cases, the courts. History is derived from the examination of evidence, and contradictory statements by two or more historical figures are what historians thrive on in their attempt to arrive at the "truth." How various researchers will choose to interpret the documents in the collections is not, and should not be, the concern of the archivist or curator. Their job is to preserve the file intact as received and make it available to all those qualified to see it. The researcher's role is to interpret the evidence in the file in the light of other evidence found elsewhere, and, if a professional, to disseminate the conclusions to a critical public, who will either accept it or question it.

The centrality of the research room and its staff to the research process is thus implicit in the services provided to the patron. Consultation concerning the topic being researched, a review of what access restrictions might apply to the material in question, suggestions of other sources, internal and external, for further research, any known information about copyright that could affect publication of the material found, copying assistance to shorten the researcher's visit if desired, and other services of a similar scope are what the researcher should expect. Patron recognition of the rules, regulations and laws under which the curator functions will promote an understanding of any service limitations that might be encountered, although there is always the chance that staff is undertrained or that personality traits will intrude on the efficiency and courtesy of the service provided. Archivists, like every other segment of the service population, have their bad days, and the profession is not totally devoid of unpleasant individuals.

What is primary in most archivist's minds, however, is security of the collections, and the desire to assure that uncontrolled use today does not deny the documents, and the information they contain, to generations of future researchers.

In many archival institutions the administration realizes that by entering the research complex the patron is segregated from the rest of the institution and cannot wander in and out freely to do collateral research in secondary sources. Archives II was built to take this condition into consideration, and the research portion of the building, with its own checkpoint for entry, puts the patron in the "research complex." Once through the security check, researchers can move freely from textual records to photographic, cartographic, electronic, and other records, and, most importantly, to the National Archives library for access to secondary sources. The old National Archives building combined the library with the Central Search Room, where textual records were served, but the convenience did not extend to the other media research rooms.

Not every archival/manuscript facility can be so constructed, and in such institutions (including the Manuscript Division of the Library of Congress) the research room concept does not tolerate a lot of in-and-out traffic. Inspection, personal materials storage, signing in and out, and the undesirability of leaving served documents open on a desk while one leaves the room, all dictate a controlled traffic flow. Although "breaks" for various reasons are advisable when one is struggling over raw documentary materials, unnecessary departures are avoided by placing in the reading room many of the tools needed in such research. Reference works relating to the collections, such as atlases, biographical dictionaries, biographies of some of the prominent people whose papers are there, appropriate encyclopedias, *NUCMC*, the Hamer *Guide*, *DAMRUS*, and similar reference tools should be on open shelves, available to both patrons and staff. One would naturally expect to find a complete set of the repository's finding aids, perhaps a computer terminal with the institution's manuscript holdings in the database, and Internet or CD-ROM access to other manuscript/ archival databases.

Researchers should also expect to have some basic services available to them, either on-site in the room, or on order through the service desk. Photocopying machines (which may, however, be supervised by the staff to prevent damage to fragile documents), a procedure for ordering laboratory-produced photocopies in bulk, and perhaps even a process for copying computer-generated lists onto a floppy disk for use later, all ease the task of dealing with quantities of information and make it unnecessary for the researcher to leave the room for these services. The availability of a sufficient number of well-maintained microfilm machines is mandatory, especially if the researcher is forced to use microfilm in lieu of original documents, and a reader-printer that provides legible copies (not a common result, I might add) has become a necessity in reading rooms. Of course, researchers can expect to find copyright warnings at all of these copying devices. Staff should also assist the researcher in getting large copying jobs done through a laboratory, for a processing fee.

In many ways, the manuscript or archival research room should provide the patron with the ambiance of a well-endowed bank. One would expect to find a sense of the presence of security, without obtrusion and an awareness of wealth of resources, but a staff that is pleasant, courteous, and helpful, while at the same time evenhanded and businesslike in efficiently handling security questions. In many respects the bank analogy is not far off base if one considers the value of each of the documents in the stacks. A perusal of any manuscript or autograph dealer's catalogs will confirm that the stacks of most repositories are filled with dollar-equivalents. A card with Andrew Carnegie's signature, $125; a card with an inscription, signed by Gene Ahern, "memorable" for his creation of the cartoon character Major Hoople, $95; a typewritten letter, signed by Carrie Chapman Catt, with envelope and suffrage slogan, $245 (the letter is to an autograph collector!); a printed copy of General Orders No. 69, War Department, February 22, 1864, with a *printed* signature, $95; a printed clipping accompanied by a card signed by Floyd Bennett, aviator and Medal of Honor winner, $395.[16]

These are not spectacular documents, but one Lincoln document is, at this writing, being offered for $18,900,[17] and another for $25,000.[18] The primary item featured in another catalog is a fourteen-line letter signed by George Washington advertised for sale at $95,000,[19] and comparable historical figures attract similar prices. Thus there is the need for security beyond just the protection of the intellectual content of such material.

It is not unreasonable to expect that documents of such value, concerning people of such prominence, should be housed in a facility that reflects that value and prominence. Special Collections departments in an academic library, a research library or historical society, and similar repositories are often physically special. It is there that one finds oil paintings of the institution's founders, or perhaps personages represented among the manuscript holdings. It is quite often there that period antiques and fine rugs or carpets grace the room, sometimes because they were bequeathed to the institution with the book and manuscripts collection as part of an estate. The Presidential libraries often display the presidential gifts throughout the facility, and not just in the exhibition area. There often is care taken with the document containers so that their appearance is appropriate to the person whose papers they hold—no penciled-on name labels in a scrawly hand, here! And because the rooms are handsome and well maintained, and also because such rooms often have shorter hours than the rest of the library, they are perfect settings when the administration of the library, the university, or the historical society wishes to entertain with small luncheons or receptions, where guests can browse through exhibit cases or survey the titles of the rare books in their glass-front cabinets. It is the perfect place to pay homage to the philanthropic donor, or to woo those who might decide to become one. As some of my alumni have said: "It sure beats working in Government Documents, or Cataloging!"

Whether or not all of this has any effect on the recruitment of future manuscript curators is impossible to say, but it all exudes culture, and a professional could do a lot worse than living every day with the heroes and heroines, scoundrels and scalawags, tycoons and tyrants, shakers and movers and repressed geniuses of the community, the country and, indeed, the world.

NOTES

1. Shirley C. Spragge, "Old Wine in Old Bottles: Renovating an Old Building for an Archives," *The Archival Imagination. Essays in Honour of Hugh A. Taylor.* Barbara L. Craig, ed. (n.p.: Association of Canadian Archivists, 1992), 212.

2. Walter W. Stender and Evans Walker, "The National Personnel Records Center Fire: A Study in Disaster," *American Archivist* 37 (October 1974): 521–550.

3. James. B. Rhoads, "Alienation and Thievery: Archival Problems," *American Archivist* 19 (January 1966): 197–208; Donald W. Jackanicz, "Theft at the National Archives: The Murphy Case, 1962–1975," *Library and Archival Security* 10, no. 2 (1990): 23–50.

4. Theresa Galvin, "The Boston Case of Charles Merrill Mount: The Archivist's Arch Enemy," *American Archivist* 53 (summer 1990): 442–450.

5. An interesting study on the rights of convicted felons to return to the scenes of their crimes after they have been sentenced and duly served out their term in jail is covered in an (as yet) unpublished paper by Holland Goss. Holland Goss, "The Legal Issues Involved in Denying Access to Convicted Book Thieves" (unpublished typescript, University of Maryland at College Park, May 1994), 12 pp. See also Vincent A. Totka, Jr., "Preventing Patron Theft in the Archives: Legal Perspectives and Problems," *American Archivist* 56 (fall 1993): 664–672; Susan M. Allen, "Theft in Libraries or Archives," *College & Research Libraries* 51 (November 1990): 939–943; Barbara Bintliff and Al Coco, "Legal Aspects of Library Security," in *Security for Libraries* (Chicago: American Library Association, 1984), 83–107; "Book Thief Banned from Libraries," *American Libraries* (January 1994): 17; "Inside Thief Pleads No Contest," *American Libraries* 22 (January 1991): 20.

6. See chapter 8, p. 178.

7. Bintliff and Coco, ibid., 102–103.

8. Library of Congress, *The Gazette* 5, no. 29 (July 22, 1994): 11.

9. JoAnne Yates, *Control through Communication: The Rise of System in American Management* (Baltimore: Johns Hopkins University Press, 1989).

10. John P. Butler, *Index*, The Papers of the Continental Congress, 1774–1789, 1978, v.

11. Ibid.

12. Peter B. Hirtle, "The National Archives and Electronic Access," *The Record: News from the National Archives and Records Administration* 1, no. 5 (May 1995): 38.

13. *Seventh Annual Report of the Archivist of the United States* (Washington, D.C.: G.P.O., 1942), 35.

14. *Newsletter* of the Commission on Preservation and Access, 80 (June 1995), 1. The fifteen signatories, in addition to the National Archives, were Yale University, the Library of Congress, Pennsylvania State University, Harvard College, Emory University, University of Tennessee, Stanford University, Princeton University, the New York Public Library, University of California, Berkeley, University of Michigan, Cornell University, University of Southern California, Columbia University, and the Commission on Preservation and Access.

15. See, however, Phillip H. Babcock, "Insure Against Employee Theft," *History News* 36, no. 9 (September 1981): 19.

16. All from List 310, *Autograph Letters* (Battle Creek, Mich.: Julia Sweet Newman, n.d. [July 199[4?]).

17. Heritage Collector's Society, August 1994.

18. *Catalog 32*, Remember When Auctions, Inc. (Acton, Maine, spring 1994), 44.

19. *American History.* A Price List of Exceptional & Historical Manuscripts—Imprints—Photographs. Little Rock, Ark., Sale 86 (June 1995), cover.

· 10 ·

Not by Vaults and Locks . . .

> The lost cannot be recovered; but let us save what remains:
> not by vaults and locks which fence them from the public eye
> and use, in consigning them to the waste of time, but by such
> a multiplication of copies, as shall place them beyond the
> reach of accident.
>
> Thomas Jefferson to Ebenezer Hazard, February 18, 1791[1]

Document reproduction by photographic processes is, perhaps, seventy-five years old;[2] by electronic reproduction, it is perhaps fifty years old.[3] Both developed as twentieth-century technologies. The practitioners of American documentary reproduction, however, go back more than two hundred years, to the beginnings of the Massachusetts Historical Society in 1792. Jefferson anticipated the need for such an institution in the letter to Ebenezer Hazard on February 18, 1791, quoted above, and written when the reproduction of texts was less than 250 years removed from the introduction of the printing press. The scriptorium tradition of St. Columba, Cassiodorus, Alcuin of York, and others had not completely faded, in that the best way to reproduce texts for distribution, and, incidently, for preservation, was to copy them. Scribes had been replaced by typesetters, but the process achieved the same result, with the added advantage of multiple copies from one master document, without scribal drift or cumulative errors over time. As Jefferson's letter to Hazard indicates, he was concerned about the security of historical documents, many of which had been lost and continued to be lost to fires and other catastrophes, natural and man-made. During New England winters, days were short, and light was attainable only from flame. The best way to "place them beyond the reach of accident" was, as in the scriptorium of old, to make multiple copies, which could be kept in different locations.

Prior to independence, Colonial Americans confined their

production of documentary publications mainly to laws and the codes that they generated. The dissemination of copies in those instances was to extend the knowledge of the laws, and thus their impact, to the widest audience. These were publications for reference use, not historical compilations. Where such compilations were produced, they took many years to prepare and often did not easily find a publisher. Reverend Thomas Prince undertook an edition of the Increase Mather papers, but it languished for over a century before being published in 1868.[4] However, Governor Thomas Hutchinson of Massachusetts did publish "A Collection of Original Papers Relative to the History of the Colony of Massachusetts Bay" as early as 1769.[5] In the midst of the first war with Britain, Benjamin Vaughan in 1780 published *Political, Miscellaneous, and Philosophical Pieces . . . by Benjamin Franklin*, thus launching a tradition of publishing Franklin's papers that continues today.[6]

After the Treaty of Paris in 1783, the first significant documentary series, and what one author considers to be the work of "America's first historical editor," was Ebenezer Hazard's *Historical Collections: Consisting of State Papers and Other Authentic Documents; Intended as Material for an History of the United States of America*, published in Philadelphia between 1792 and 1794.[7]

The nineteenth century saw a number of documentary editions, typically published by "part-time" historians who otherwise pursued careers as lawyers, clergy, booksellers, or related professions. Descendants of the famous also undertook publication of the works of their forebears, as in the cases of William Temple Franklin who, in 1818–19, published *The Memoires of the Life and Writings of Benjamin Franklin* in six volumes;[8] Thomas Jefferson Randolph, *Memoir, Correspondence and Miscellanies from the Papers of Thomas Jefferson*, in four volumes, 1829;[9] Charles Francis Adams, *Letters of Mrs. Adams, the Wife of John Adams*, two volumes, 1840,[10] and other Adams family papers.

The "professionalization" of documentary editing as we know it today began with the founding of the American Historical Association (AHA) in 1884 and the establishment of two "commissions" (committees): the Historical Manuscripts Commission in 1895 and the Public Archives Commission in 1899. Prominent in all of these activities was John Franklin Jameson (1859–1937), the first recipient of the doctorate in history at Johns Hopkins University, one of the founders and president of the AHA, editor of the *American Historical Review* (1895–1901; 1905–1928), a member of the history department faculty at Johns Hopkins, Brown and the

University of Chicago from 1882 to 1905, director of the Bureau of Historical Research of the Carnegie Institution of Washington (1905–1927), and chief of the Manuscripts Division at the Library of Congress and first holder of the library's chair of American History (1927–1937). This "cultural politician" devoted his career to the furtherance of the goals of the AHA for the preservation, publication, and use of documents of American history. In conjunction with his successful efforts to have a National Archives established in the United States, Jameson promoted the establishment of a Historical Publications Commission that would structure the efforts of collection and publication of documents.[11]

Out of those efforts emerged the National Historical Publications Commission (NHPC), which was established concurrent with the establishment of the National Archives in 1934. The commission, consisting of varying numbers of members, planned for documentary publication by surveying the field of such publications and promoting lists of papers yet to be done. With the receipt of funding in 1964 the NHPC began support of editing the Founding Fathers papers, and expanded into other fields. With addition of an archival support or "records" program in 1974, the newly reconstituted National Historical Publications *and Records* Commission (NHPRC) expanded its field of concern with funds doubled from $2 million to $4 million annually. The establishment of the National Endowment for the Humanities in 1965 lent further support to the publication of documentary sources through micrography, digitization, and other means of modern copying which have been added to the editors' choice of presentation and perform that function today in parallel with print editions.

The salutary effect of earlier decisions to copy documents has already had benefits for the modern researcher. In a number of the modern editions of the papers of the Founding Fathers and other early Americans, editors have had to resort to earlier printed versions of documents, because the originals have disappeared. Disasters such as the floods and earthquakes of this decade, fires in county courthouses, historical societies, historic religious institutions, and federal facilities all take their toll on future research. Press runs of even so few as one thousand copies of new editorial projects assure the preservation of the texts within them, even if the original documents are lost to "the waste of time." Researchers today therefore turn to documentary editions in some cases because they represent the only remaining version of documents long lost. Today's editions contain numerous items that are from surviving copies where the original has been lost. In a number of instances the copy is from a newspaper.[12]

The reproduction of historical documents thus became a part of the scholarly enterprise, and as late as 1905 the Library of Congress was beginning scribal copying of texts relating to America that were in the European colonial archives. This "Foreign Copying Program" began with handwritten transcripts, advanced to photostatic reproduction after World War I, and to microfilm only after World War II. Thus, the purpose of the reproduction of documents remains the same as it was when scribes copied manuscript books taken from ships arriving in ancient Alexandria—the dissemination of texts beyond the venue of the original.

Meanwhile, new major editions are under way, with most of them departing from the earlier tradition of one edition, one editor. The Founding Fathers projects were sanctioned by the original legislation creating the National Historical Publications Commission in 1934, and their ongoing status and need for support have been confirmed by commission members' votes over the years, the most recent being 1992. The commission and the National Endowment for the Humanities have been providing annual grants from federally appropriated funds for projects, and assisting editors in outside fundraising efforts. *The Papers of Alexander Hamilton* completed its twenty-seven volumes under one editor, and the largest completed edition (although not of a Founding Father)—the *Papers of Woodrow Wilson* in sixty-nine volumes under the direction of a single editor (Arthur Link)—will probably never be matched.[13]

A number of additional editions are close to completion. Any time that a project has only two volumes left in order to complete the project, one can consider that it is closer to its finish than might be apparent. With volume thirteen out of fifteen of *The Papers of Henry Laurens* already published, one can be certain that volume 14 is probably at the press in manuscript and awaiting final publishing, with the ultimate volume 15 being in progress at the editorial offices. The Laurens schedule has almost consistently been one volume every two years since volume one appeared in 1968. Terminal publication can also be expected soon for *The Marcus Garvey and Universal Negro Improvement Association Papers*, which has eight out of ten volumes in print. Not far behind is *The Papers of John C. Calhoun*, which has published twenty of its projected twenty-five volumes. In the Calhoun case, volumes have been pouring out of the editorial offices, with the last four appearing over a five-year period (1986–1991).[14] The era of the contemplative editor, mulling over the minutia of the subject's life, has passed (if it ever really existed). Change has come to the editorial process as editing moves away from being an adjunct to teaching, and editors now perform their work as a primary task and use word processing to capture texts and facilitate corrections or refinements. Documentary editors have adopted the team approach to their work as other professionals have done in other disciplines.

The ongoing Founding Fathers projects have all lost their initial editors as Julian Boyd (Jefferson), Lyman Butterfield (the Adams Family), William T. Hutchinson and William M. E. Rachal (Madison), Leonard Labaree (Franklin), and Donald Jackson (George Washington) have all passed on. Subsequent editors have seen the difficulty of making much progress toward sixty- or seventy-volume projections because of funding problems, and have heeded the critics who want to use this material in their lifetimes, so the editions have adopted the series/team approach for Washington, Adams, Jefferson and Madison. The process involves an editor-in-chief to oversee individual series editors. For *The Papers of George Washington*, for instance, there are series editors for "The Diaries of George Washington" (completed in six volumes); the "Colonial Series" (nine volumes completed through 1774); the "Presidential Series" (two volumes completed through May 1789); the "Journal of the Proceedings of the President" (completed in one volume); and the "Revolutionary War Series" (four volumes completed through 1776). Editor-in-chief for the project as of 1994 is Dorothy Twohig, who has been on the editorial staff since the beginning of the project in the mid-1970s. The project anticipates a total of seventy-five volumes to completion.

While some historians question funds going to editorial projects rather than to narrative and interpretive historical research, [15] the editions go on and the editors find themselves spending an inordinate amount of their professional time raising funds to keep the process alive. The completed Hamilton and Wilson projects, as well as smaller ones such as Booker T. Washington (14 volumes), Andrew Johnson (12 volumes), Henry Clay (11 volumes), Daniel Webster (15 volumes), *The Susquehannah Company Papers* (11 volumes), and *The Writings of Will Rogers* (22 volumes), are witness to the fact that persistence (and funding) can pay off, and a report prepared in 1992 under NHPRC auspices[16] provides some evidence of the value of these editions to historical and other research. With approximately $2 million a year from the NHPRC since 1981, and an almost equal amount from the National Endowment for the Humanities during the same period, the editorial projects are considerably less funded than the major arts, bibliographic, preservation, and museum programs offered by the federal government. Indeed, the $2 million from the NEH amounted to about 1.25 percent of its 1995 grant budget, leaving 98.75 percent for other purposes. That the NHPRC share for editing is 50 percent of its budget only speaks to the mission of that program and the paucity of the total funding for it. Those funds also support documentary microfilm projects, and in some cases provide shared support to projects receiving partial funding from NEH.

One of the features of documentary editing that has given "added value" to the material is the assemblage of widely scattered materials into one comprehensive text, not only reproduced, but also analyzed, annotated, and indexed.

For the researcher, there are certain advantages to the reproduction of documentary sources in print, but they must be approached with some insight and caution. They may not turn out to be what one would expect, and thus their promise may not be delivered. But, if the limitations of the genre are recognized, its strengths can greatly facilitate scholarship.

The first reason for turning to documentary editions for research is one of convenience. Not only might it be inconvenient to visit the repository where the originals are housed, but the gathering of documents into these editions means that to get the same texts the researcher would have to visit hundreds of institutions worldwide in order to cover the major historical figures. This is particularly true for documentary editions produced in the twentieth century. One volume of the *Papers of Thomas Jefferson* or the *Papers of Marcus Garvey* may contain documents from twenty or thirty institutions, from which the editors have gathered copies prior to producing the volume. A random analysis of a few editions shows that volume eleven of the *Papers of Henry Laurens, 1776–1777,* contains documents from nineteen institutions, stretching from the Henry Huntington Library in California to the Public Record Office in London; the *Legal Papers of Andrew Jackson* derived its material from twenty-two repositories and at least one private source, from the State Historical Society of Wisconsin to the National Archives and Library of Congress; and volume eighteen of the *Papers of John C. Calhoun,* from January to June 8, 1844, includes material from nineteen repositories, literally from Maine (the State Archives) to California (University of California-Berkeley). More than two hundred libraries hold some thirty thousand documents of James Monroe.[17]

The printed volume identifies each document's source, which provides the scholar the opportunity to consult the original (or ask to have a photocopy sent), should there be any question about the editor's treatment of it. Some of the long-term large editions, such as those of Alexander Hamilton or Woodrow Wilson, have been completed and the editorial files consisting of the acquired copies have been deposited in institutional libraries, forming facsimile collections of materials that the documentary editors evaluated as critical to a full understanding of the subject. Additionally, the photocopied material often goes beyond what was actually used in the publication. The complete thirteen volumes (plus an index volume) of Booker T. Washington, for instance, consist of a selection of documents from many repositories, the bulk, however, from the one million items in the Library of Congress. The editors made their choice on the scene, selecting approximately 10 percent of the available material for possible publication. They copied 100,000 items, but then published about 6,500. When the project ended, all copies were deposited in the University of Maryland's McKeldin Library. Because documentary editors must confront the terms of copying documents, or copyright considerations, these residue photocopied collections are not in all cases adequate for research, but they do provide information about the location of repositories containing the original material. (More on the selection process below.)[18]

For many kinds of research the use of printed sources rather than the originals also simplifies the analytic process. Printed material is considerably easier to read, and therefore understand, than is struggling with difficult handwriting. While the hand of the edition's subject may be easily mastered, most collections contain letters received by the subject as well as those sent, thus creating the possibility of a need to decipher the scribbles of hundreds of correspondents. It is also certain that research into a person's collection of letters may turn up few original letters in that person's hand, since the originals have been dispatched to a recipient. Copies may or may not have been retained, and a retained copy may differ from the one transmitted. But it is the information communicated that is important, not what the author has edited down for convenience in making a retained copy, either personally or through an amanuensis. In one of the few examples of the research team approach to history, documentary editors track down as many of the transmitted copies as possible, compare them to retained copies, and publish what, in their opinion, represents the information actually communicated by the author.

This can lead to a multiplication of versions if the editor decides to publish the retained copy, for whatever reason. Let us say that Jefferson writes to Madison, and Madison responds. The editor of the series on each of the men will have reciprocal documents of exchange, that is: the Jefferson collection will contain a retained copy of the letter to Madison, and the original Madison response, while the Madison collection will have the reverse. If Madison's original letter to Jefferson is missing from Jefferson's papers, the Jefferson editors will more than likely publish Madison's retained copy of his outgoing letter, along with Jefferson's retained copy of his reply. But when all copies are extant, researchers may have an opportunity to see all four copies, either in print or in the holdings of the editorial office, or, ultimately, at the original repository. Only the copies finally selected and edited, of course, will be in print.

Edited documents also benefit from the work of the editors in clarifying anomalies in the text. The editors, who become the experts in the lives and scribal peculiarities of the subject, often provide clues from external evidence as to the meaning of a text, unclear language, symbols, abbreviations, and even missing text, filling in gaps that would take most researchers days or even weeks to track down. Although it seems reasonable to assume that the most prevalent use of the Jefferson or Wilson editions is by researchers studying Jefferson or Wilson, documentary editions are also used by researchers for abstracting information that touches on their own subject, and not for every aspect of the life and career of the individual around whom the edition is formed. When I did some work on Prince Henry of Prussia, a contemporary of Jefferson, I consulted the Julian Boyd and earlier editions for comments that Jefferson might have made about the prince. Others use the editions for a variety of reasons. A faculty member at MIT reported that she uses "virtually all of the modern editions of the 'founding fathers' papers" as the source for undergraduate students' research papers, since the texts are legible, annotated, and accessible. Her argument is that she wants the students to center on making sense of the *content* of the documents without all of the distracting paraphernalia that comes with originals.[19] Another report from the director of the Woodrow Wilson House Museum, a National Trust for Historic Preservation property, stated that the staff at the house uses the sixty-nine volumes of the *Papers of Woodrow Wilson*, edited by Arthur S. Link, "daily, in every possible way," and then mentions the training of guide staff, "assistance in mounting exhibits, answering research questions, helping us understand the Wilsons and this house."[20]

Most documentary editions include indexes to personal and geographic names, events, objects (such as ships' names), and other content items. The editorial effort to index contents is a boon to research, since most repositories do not have item indexes to their collections, and if they do the indexes do not normally analyze the contents of the correspondence; and, to return to an earlier point, no single repository contains the breadth of correspondence found in a compiled volume.

Most documentary editors annotate each document. In addition to a notation about the location and perhaps even the provenance of each document printed, the editors add clarification, elaboration, or verification of the document's contents. The amount of annotation varies considerably from edition to edition. Criticism of over-annotation quite often centers on the time, and therefore the financial resources, needed to expand the process, which implies delaying the appearance of the edited volumes. Other critics of annotation feel that the process skews the claims of editors that they are doing "definitive" and even "timeless" editions, because annotation is a form of expository research, and can become as dated as any historical work with the later appearance of new information sources and interpretations. Expansive annotation, however, is now greatly limited by funding restrictions.

Researchers may well wonder why the big documentary editions today are assembling staffs and spending money that could otherwise, they assume, be used for historical research of an analytic and interpretive nature. Editors have no difficulty pointing to the inadequacies of earlier editions and comparing those works with today's fuller, more open and better researched editions. This can be seen in successive editions of Jefferson's papers. For the year 1775, for instance, T. J. Randolph and Henry A. Washington printed three Jefferson letters; Paul Leicester Ford printed eighteen, and Boyd produced forty-nine, covering 117 pages, although some were multiple versions.[21] Similarly, the publication of Adams family letters increased with successive editions. In 1876 Charles Francis Adams printed one Abigail Adams letter for the month of July 1777, and four John Adams letters. The Butterfield volume for July 1777 includes twenty-three letters for the month, of which eighteen are husband-wife exchanges.[22]

Much of this increase can be attributed to twentieth-century communication advances over the preceding era. The ability to travel to distant repositories, to telephone curators in other institutions, the availability of photocopying at reasonable rates, and similar conditions have worked in editors' favor. These advances, linked with the progress of the historical profession after the founding of the AHA, the establishment of the Manuscript Division of the Library of Congress in 1897, the establishment of state archives beginning with Alabama in 1901, the document surveys of the Works Progress Administration's Historical Records Survey and the Survey of Federal Records in the States during the 1930s Great Depression, along with similar programs, served to expand our knowledge of and access to documents that were unaccessible to earlier editors.

Some of Jameson's early work is a precursor of later editorial trends in documentary publication. In his "Correspondence of John C. Calhoun," Jameson published some 1,200 letters of Calhoun in supplements to the *American Historical Review*.[23] In that sampling, he established the principles of bilateral publication of correspondence, and presented the documents "verbatim ac litteratim," or as close to the original as possible when converting from script to print. Julian Boyd was to adopt these principles as the basis for the publication of the *Papers of Thomas Jefferson*, which appeared first in 1950.

In addition to quantity, comparisons show small, but sometimes significant differences between the work of earlier editors and those of mid–twentieth century. In the Andrew Lipscomb edition of Jefferson's papers, published in 1903, Lipscomb quotes Jefferson's 31 July 1788 letter as stating:

> Contrary to his expectation, he received leave; but he went to Warsaw instead of America, and from thence to join the/1 ★ ★ ★ ★ I do not know these facts certainly, but recollect them, by putting several things together.

The footnote states: "Several paragraphs of this letter are in cipher. A few words here could not be deciphered." This is the only footnote for the document.

Julian Boyd's *Papers of Thomas Jefferson*, version 13 (1956), treats the same sentence as follows:

> Contrary to his expectation he received leave: but went to *Warsaw* instead of *America* and from thence to join the *Russian army/* 4. I do not know these facts certainly, but *collect* them by putting several things together.

Boyd footnotes the filled-in text with "Preceding two words not in text *en clair*" indicating that he arrived at them either by deciphering the code or from external evidence. He also rereads Lipscomb's "but recollect them" as "but collect them." There is, perhaps, a nuance between "collect" and "recollect," but the first implies lack of original knowledge and the second implies presence of original knowledge.

A few lines later in the letter, Lipscomb transcribes a section as:

> When he was ambassador to London, with ten thousand guineas a year, the marriage was avowed, and he relinquished his cross of Malta, from which he derived a handsome revenue for life, and which was very open to advancement. Not long ago she died.

Boyd makes three corrections in that section alone, viz:

> When he was *named ambassador to London* with 10000 *guineas a year, the marriage* was avowed, and he relinquished his *cross of Malta* from which he derived a handsome revenue, for life, and very open to advancement. *She staid* here, and not long after *died.* [emphasis in original]

Again, the nuances in the different interpretations provide a different thrust to the meaning of the document. Boyd uses five footnotes to explain or elaborate on passages in this letter.

Although there were earlier examples of restoring accuracy to texts, in the main Boyd's Jefferson has become the model for precise transcription of the original documents, errors and all. Rather than sanitize misspellings, poor punctuation, local dialects, and other natural occurrences in personal writing, Boyd and his followers elected to leave the original text unchanged. This practice was in the tradition of the medieval scribes, who were not allowed to correct errors in the manuscripts that they were copying.[24]

Other examples of improved editions can be provided from the Adams family papers. In an 1876 edition of Charles Francis Adams' *Familiar Letters of John Adams and His Wife Abigail Adams, During the Revolution* [25] the editor transcribes a letter from Abigail to John as follows:

> Braintree, Sunday, 16 September, 1775
>
> I set myself down to write with a heart depressed with the melancholy scenes around me. My letter will be only a bill of mortality; though thanks be to that Being who restraineth the pestilence, that it has not yet proved mortal to any of our family, though we live in daily expectation that Patty will not continue many hours. I had no idea of the distemper producing such a state as hers, till now. Two of the children, John and Charles, I have sent out of the house, finding it difficult to keep them out of the chamber. Nabby continues well. Tommy is better, but entirely stripped of the hardy, robust countenance, as well as of a.l [*sic*] the flesh he had, save what remains for to keep his bones together. Jonathan is the only one who remains in the family who has not had a turn of the disorder. Mrs. Randall has lost her daughter. Mrs. Bracket, hers. Mr. Thomas Thayer, his wife. Two persons belonging to Boston have died this week in this parish. I know of eight this week who have been buried in this town.

The Butterfield edition of the *Adams Family Correspondence,* volume 1, December 1761–May 1776,[26] contains twenty corrections to this text. Although most of them are minor capitalization or spelling modifications, two complete sentences are restored, indicating that the 1875 edition practiced exclusion because of the general Victorian sensitivity to the text. Indeed, Charles F. Adams stated that he omitted some of Abigail's letters from an earlier edition in 1840 because of their personal nature and grave tone.[27] Butterfield adds the text in brackets at the appropriate places:

> . . . tho we live in daily Expectation that Patty will not continue many hours. [A general putrefaction seems to have taken place, and we can not bear the House only as we are constantly cleansing it with hot vinegar.]

And:

> I had no idea of the Distemper producing such a state as hers till
> now. [Yet we take all possible care by shifting her bed every
> day.]

Later in the same letter Butterfield transcribes the name as
Mrs. Randle, rather then C. F. Adams' Mrs. Randall. In the date
line at top, Butterfield corrects the date from C. F. Adams' "Braintree, Sunday, 16 September, 1775" to "Braintree Sepbr. 16 [*i.e.*,
17] Sunday 1775."

From the researcher's viewpoint the more critical issue is not
the minor language variations, although they can lead to misunder-
standing of motives, actions, and other details, but the total absence
of portions of the correspondence. Charles Francis Adams, editor
of family letters of John and Abigail, is considered to be an excellent editor, but still he was influenced by how he wanted the family—his family—to be viewed by future readers. He did not like
nicknames or other than perfect English usage. Thus, wherever the
pet name "Nabby" was used for Abby, he tended to cast it in the
proper form. In the example above, however, he does not correct
it. Abigail's speech and spelling contained many localisms, which
C. F. Adams smoothed out. He also eliminated trivia and private
matters from the correspondence and, as seen above, avoided references to illness and, in other cases, to pregnancy. The rather unsa-
vory (for the period) three-year courtship between Nabby and
Royall Tyler was completely suppressed, even though it runs
through the letters of the time. For the period 1761 to 1785 C. F.
Adams published ninety-two documents, whereas for the same period the modern Adams Family project has published 428.[28]

In addition to these internal lacunae, nineteenth-century collections of published letters most often presented only the letters
of the principal—that is, the outgoing correspondence. (William
Temple Franklin's collection of Benjamin Franklin's correspondence is an exception.) This seems odd today, since the incoming
correspondence makes up most collections, while the outgoing
must be hunted down or pieced together from retained copies.
However, there continue to be editions consisting of letters sent,
without the incoming documents. Traditions vary on how to have
the volume make sense when there is no internal reference to the
incoming queries, statements, challenges, or issues. Editors have

handled that in a variety of ways over the years. Editors of the papers of Ulysses S. Grant, Frederick Law Olmsted, Dwight D. Eisenhower, Adlai E. Stevenson and many others concentrate on the outgoing letters. For the twentieth-century figures the reasons given usually are bulk and copyright, since the editors feel it to be an overbearing burden to get permissions from the writers or their heirs, whereas they undoubtedly have permission from the Eisenhower or Stevenson heirs. Their official government correspondence, of course, is not under copyright.

The lack of incoming letters, however, is not a total denial of the information contained in them. Modern editors often use headnotes, which are introductory either to a single letter or to a group of letters on a common topic. Occasionally they will use footnotes to explain what it is that the author is responding to. Some editors divide the correspondence into topics, and group appropriate letters under that rubric, which is quite often chronological since the principals devote periods of their career to specific projects. Sometimes the grouping is by historical events. In volume 4 of *The Papers of Frederick Law Olmsted*, subtitled "Defending the Union," Jane Turner Censer, the editor, groups the 145 Olmsted outgoing letters and writings under chapters with titles such as: "Organizing the U.S. Sanitary Commission" (four letters); "The Union Defeat at Bull Run" (nine letters and a document); "Reforming the Medical Bureau" (nineteen letters, one published article); "Planning for Freedom: The Port Royal Experiment" (fourteen letters), etc. Each section has a brief, one-page introduction, with other details carried in the footnotes.[29]

The editors of *The Papers of Andrew Johnson*, volume 8, covering only four months, May–August 1865, include mostly received letters among the 816 documents published. Indeed, there are only sixty-four Johnson letters in the volume, which covers the crucial period in his career, immediately after his elevation to the presidency as a consequence of Lincoln's assassination. The material is in a straight chronology, with the barest of editorial interference, and no introductory sections, except for the introduction to the volume.[30]

The Johnson volume points up the question that editors must ask themselves when coming into that period of their subject's lives: are they documenting the man or the presidency? When Arthur Link, editor of *The Papers of Woodrow Wilson*, reached the Wilson presidency, he commented in print that he was restricting himself to the papers of Wilson the man (see chapter 2). Any researcher using these volumes is wise to read the preface and/or introduction to each volume, as well as the editor's introduction to the series. This is good advice in any documentary volume, for reasons beyond the inclusion or exclusion of individual letters.

Earlier I mentioned the indexing of the *Papers of the Continental Congress* and spoke about the terrible order they were in as a result of reorganization in the nineteenth century. These papers were never published, although there has been a 34-volume set of the *Journals of the Continental Congress* available in libraries since its publication, completed in 1937.[31] These are quite different sources, with the *Journals*, as evidenced by the title, constituting the day-to-day accounting of what went on in Congress *assembled*, and noted by the clerk. The papers, on the other hand, are the materials of the committees, consisting of correspondence, draft legislation, and similar documents.

The Papers of John Jay, edited by Richard Morris, [32] is not the fully published correspondence and writings of Jay, but an edition primarily of the previously unpublished papers of Jay, making it a supplement to an earlier, selected edition of Jay's papers prepared in 1889–1892 by Henry P. Johnson.[33] If one is looking for documentation on a specific issue in the Morris edition there might be some surprise in not finding it, but a reading of Morris' introduction would have warned off the researcher looking for such documents, and informed the reader that a twentieth-century search turned up five thousand additional items in the Columbia University Library *plus* some "10,000 photocopied items" from other institutions.[34]

Researchers should also pay attention to the dates or time period covered by documentary editions, because many limit themselves to an active period of the subject's life. What most people offhandedly would refer to as the "Lafayette Papers" edition by Stanley Idzerda is formally titled *Lafayette in the Age of the American Revolution*, and is described as "Selected Letters and Papers, 1776–1790," of the French statesman and Revolutionary War officer, and thus covers only thirteen years.[35]

Many documentary editions are abbreviated not by time scale but by selection from a mass of material. *The Papers of Woodrow Wilson* project was able to finish its work in sixty-nine volumes (including series index) because the editor, Arthur Link, chose to document Wilson and not the presidency. The editors of *The Booker T. Washington Papers* elected not to fully document Tuskegee Institute, but Booker T. Washington, and thus limited themselves to thirteen volumes (plus an index), from the papers of Booker T. Washington in the Library of Congress, plus at least eighteen other collections there and elsewhere.[36]

Researchers should be aware of the designation of the editions as "comprehensive," "selective," or "highly selective," in the advertisements for them, and should know that "comprehensive" implies "most" but not "all" of the material related to the person or subject. There are some exceptions, such as the *Circular Letters of Congressmen to their Constituents, 1789–1829*, in which the volumes are advertised as "a comprehensive edition, complete in three volumes, of all such circular letters known to exist for the period."[37]

One of the largest editions attempting to be fully comprehensive is the *Documentary History of the First Federal Congress of the United States of America, March 4, 1789–March 3, 1791* ("a comprehensive edition of all known official and unofficial documents pertaining to the First Federal Congress").[38] Large comprehensive printed editions, however, have become unpopular among funding agencies upon which such projects depend for support.

Other limitations that should be looked for include restricted publication of only certain forms of original documents. A planned edition of the letters of the physician Thomas A. Dooley, III, covers six years from 1954 to 1960, and consists only of letters to his mother![39] Diaries are a common source for documentary editions, since they are circumscribed in length, do not require a search for additional material as letter projects do, and make the editor's life simpler by being in only one hand. The publication of a manuscript diary can be complicated, however, if the author revised and rewrote it over the years. In the edition *Mary Chesnut's Civil War*, editor C. Vann Woodward, as others before him, found it difficult to reestablish the original text of the Chesnut diary because of the many revisions that she made of the document over the twenty years after it was first penned, from February 1861 to July 1865.[40] The process employed was much like that of the literary editor, attempting to get back to the "pure" text of well-published authors such as Thoreau, Irving, or Emerson.

In a number of cases, editors (and their funding sources) have undertaken a two-pronged approach to the editing process as a result of their own practices and in response to critics of the limited editions. Their own practices have been to copy many more documents than they plan to publish, and then make a selection of what will go in the edition. This is especially true of projects that must rely on many repositories, with each providing them with limited numbers of documents so that they can assemble a corpus of materials on an individual or a subject. This process is not generally followed where the bulk of the material is in one place, such as the Library of Congress, the National Archives or some other holder of large collections. In such cases it is less expensive to select documents on-site, and copy only those selected.

One common criticism of limited editions is that the editor has made choices with which the researcher might not agree. In these circumstances some editors have found it desirable to film a significant body of materials that are scattered, and after producing a documentary microfilm that contains researcher aids, such as a table of contents, an index and perhaps even some headnotes or footnotes, a selected number of those documents are then edited for publication in book form. Thus, the editors have shared with the public all of the material collected, and have made it possible for researchers who find the published editions inadequate for their purposes to go to the microfilm for a fuller coverage of the subject. This process often results in accommodation of the "interested" researcher, who is satisfied with the printed, annotated and edited volumes, and also the technical or specialist researcher who wants in-depth access to the subject, without the editorial paraphernalia.

One of the more comprehensive mixed-media projects is the publication of the *Papers of Benjamin Henry Latrobe*. The editors, Edward C. Carter, II, and Thomas E. Jeffrey, produced a microfiche edition of the papers in 1976, consisting of 315 microfiche accompanied by a 129-page guide/index. A normal ninety-two-frame microfiche of 315 sheets would reproduce almost twenty-nine thousand pages of documents, but the Latrobe edition contains fewer than that because of the reproduction of charts and other graphics in larger than single-frame dimensions. Between 1977 and 1988 the editors then produced eight printed volumes of the *Papers of Benjamin Henry Latrobe* in four series: The Virginia Journals, The Architectural and Engineering Drawings, Latrobe's View of America (selections from his watercolors and sketches), and Correspondence and Miscellaneous Papers.[41]

Not as complicated, but serving a similar purpose, is the mixed media edition of Aaron Burr materials. In 1978 editor Mary-Jo Kline produced twenty-seven reels of microfilm and a one hundred-page guide/index to the *Papers of Aaron Burr, 1756–1836*, consisting of "Burr's papers, including legislative papers; his Revolutionary War orderly books; his European journals (1808–1812); and documents reflecting his activities in the New York City Mayor's Court, the New York State Supreme Court, and other judicial tribunals."[42] Then, in 1983, editor Kline produced a two-volume set of the *Political Correspondence and Public Papers of Aaron Burr*, which is advertised as a "highly selective edition."[43] Similar mixed media editions have appeared for Eugene Debs, Albert Gallatin, Philip Mazzei, Charles Willson Peale, Daniel Webster and others. Again, the researcher should be aware of what alternative sources are available if what has been found proves inadequate for the research project at hand.

There have been attempts at other forms of mixed media presentations, with mixed results. *The Documentary History of the Ratification of the Constitution* discovered many documents that were of research interest but that were too numerous to edit, set in type, and print in a bound volume. For the most part these consisted of printed materials—broadsides, tracts, posters, etc., that were part of the propaganda wars in the states at the time ratification of the Federal Constitution was under consideration. The editor of the first three volumes to reach publication (volumes 2, 3 and 10), Merrill Jensen, took an innovative approach to their publication by having the ephemeral material microcopied, and not placing the resulting microfiche (44 fiche in volume 2, 22 fiche in volume 3, and four fiche in volume 10) in a pocket inside the back cover, but shrink-wrapping it with the associated volume. Notes in the body of the printed text referenced the fiche where appropriate. It seemed like a good solution to the cry for adequate documentation, and it works well in private libraries (such as in the office of a faculty member). But in a large academic or public library the fiche either is separated from the text by librarians, who send it off to the proper media room, or by researchers, who are notoriously disruptive of order in loose materials. The idea never caught on, and the process of producing addenda in fiche appendices is rarely, if ever, used.[44]

Another process used at least once is reproduction of the original documentation photographically on the printed page, with added annotation in typeface. This obviously eliminates any editorial interference with the text, and yet provides explanatory and citational notes by the editors. It is thus a compromise between having to understand handwriting or having access to editorial assistance. A facsimile edition in five volumes of the *Records of the*

Johns Hopkins University Seminary of History and Politics, covering the years 1886 to 1912, was prepared by editor Marvin M. Gettleman between 1987 and 1990.[45] An analogous project is the *Plymouth Court Records, 1689–1859,* a facsimile edition that has no annotation (although there are extensive introductory essays included in volume 1).[46]

In summary, researchers using personal papers cannot afford to bypass the published editions, now numbering in the hundreds of titles and thousands of volumes. If the researcher/scholar questions the edition there is often the opportunity of locating documentation through the published volume indexes, reading the printed, edited version, noting the location of the original (if it is still extant) and going there or calling for a copy of it for closer inspection. Perhaps no researcher should take the word of another for content of documents not seen. Certainly no researcher should take another's word for the *interpretation* of documents not seen, but the high professional level of today's documentary editors instills trust in their products. The publication of documents in the editions mentioned here does not preclude the first option, nor force upon scholars the second.

One step closer to the original from the printed, edited version is a surrogate copy, probably photographic. The ultimate intimacy is direct inspection, but, as has been pointed out, the far-flung locations of personal correspondence make it almost impossible for any individual in one lifetime to travel to all of the cities, villages, towns and private homes where such materials are located.

Putting documentary editing in the context of historical studies, perhaps the work of the editors is the least controversial product coming from the historian's pen, or computer. While the historical philosophers dispute interpretation as either deconstructionist, relativistic, psychobabble, mythistory, realism, or any other departure from "truth" (which, of course, defines *their* interpretation), the documents remain to be interpreted as each generation sees fit. If the interpretive writing of history is a humanistic activity, modifying itself according to the mood of each generation, then documentary preservation, in original or surrogate form, is a scientific exercise to preserve the samples of that society's actions for others to interpret in the future. More than scattered shards of human activity, documentary evidence forms the terminal moraine of the societal glacier, left behind to be mined for an ex-post-facto understanding of what existence was like "back then."

Documentary editions, as the manuscripts that they reproduce, serve a much wider public than just historians, since much correspondence is not about events or people who ultimately will be declared to be "historic," but rather about everyday life and human activities. As such, the volumes have overtones of biography, or even autobiography without intent. One cannot read the volumes without gaining a sense of geography, including topographic features, place names, road conditions and transportation in general. One need only read Washington's diaries to get a sense of farming and crops in the middle Atlantic region, and the diaries of those who entertained in the great Southern mansions to get a taste of the choicest foods and their preparation. The letters between husband and wife or suitor and pursued are there in the love letters of Woodrow Wilson and Edith Bolling Galt, and Abigail and John Adams, and Julia Dent Grant and the general. The account books provide a sense of domestic economy, and those especially of large plantation slave holders may countermand the claims either of prosperity or near-destitution that come out of the correspondence of the master. Joseph Henry's volumes reveal the state of science, and especially electromagnetism, while *The Papers of Thomas A. Edison* is an insight to a keen mind and the blossoming of American technological genius, which developed at least in part out of the traditions set out by Benjamin Henry Latrobe and others half a century earlier.

In the past twenty years editors, other scholars, and funding sources have begun responding to the criticisms about publishing the papers of only "Great White Fathers." Although the criticism was never fully justified, the earlier editions were few in number and concentrated on the big names and topics. As research interests changed, and as collections of papers of less heroic figures were unearthed (often literally!) and brought to light, the edition contents began to reflect these research materials. In *Historical Documentary Editions, 1993*, published by the NHPRC, there are eleven projects relating to women, nine to African Americans, four to Native Americans, and four to the labor movement. One can anticipate that these numbers, and the percentage of the total number of projects, will grow in coming years.

As we move into the 21st century technological changes are being employed in documentary publications as in most other publications. In the 1970s many of the editors of documentary editions shifted over from manual typing and reproduction of texts to computerized formats. The projects began, in the spirit of the time, with word processors of varying capability, but within a few years had almost universally moved into personal computers. Since most of the projects are located at universities, they had access to communication networks, such as BITNET, and later to the Internet. In 1990 the Association for Documentary Editing created its own Internet listserve in order to enhance communication among members and any literary or documentary editors, archivists, historians or others who wished to join it. It was inevitable that this editorial confrontation with technology (see chapter 6) would have its advocates as well as its detractors, although for most it just seemed as logical as moving from the quill pen to the typewriter.

At the end of the 1980 decade some projects spoke of digitization of images rather than microfilming, while others considered the drawbacks of microfilmed text to be the same if they were digitized. Other projects felt that since their documents were being computer coded already as they typed them into their computers, it would be a simple technological step to copy the digitized typed text, annotation and all, onto CD-ROM format. A single disk could hold many volumes of text (often the entire publication), and the researcher could scan, search, and print the text. Since CD-ROM equipment is now becoming ubiquitous the process seemed a natural development in the evolution of editing from the scriptorium. At this writing, the George Washington papers have undertaken the preparation of a CD-ROM, as have all of the Founding Fathers projects and a number of others.

Yet to be solved is the role of the presses that have contracted to produce documentary editions. Questions of copyright loom large in the minds of many publishers, and visions of licensing agreements appear ethereally in discussions of the subject. Concerns are not over the copyright status of old documents, but the treatment of them in the editorial and publication process, where "means of expression" are in the annotation, index, design and other features. It might be simpler therefore to digitally reproduce the original, and present it to the user as one presents microfilm, but that takes us back to the question of the value of annotation and enhancement of the text.[47]

Notes

1. Thomas Jefferson to Ebenezer Hazard, February 18, 1791. Jefferson Papers, Library of Congress Manuscript Division; John P. Kaminski, ed.,

Citizen Jefferson. The Wit and Wisdom of an American Sage (Madison, Wis.: Madison House, 1994), 50.

2. Bradley Allen Fiske, of Washington, D.C., applied for a microfilm reading device patent on November 17, 1920, and patent 1,411,098 was awarded for the "Fiskescope" in March of 1922. Joseph N. Kane, *Famous First Facts*, 4th ed. (New York: H.W. Wilson Company, 1981), 388.

3. The ENIAC computer began functioning in 1946; the first commercially produced computer, the Univac I, was introduced in 1951. Ibid., 190.

4. Lester J. Cappon, "American Historical Editors before Jared Sparks: 'they will plant a forest.' " *William and Mary Quarterly* 30 (1973): 375–400.

5. Ibid.

6. Ibid.

7. Fred Shelley, "Ebenezer Hazard: America's First Historical Editor," *William & Mary Quarterly* 12 (January 1955): 44–73.

8. William Temple Franklin, *The Memoires of the Life and Writings of Benjamin Franklin*, 6 vols. (London: Henry Colburn, 1818–19).

9. Thomas Jefferson Randolph, *Memoir, Correspondence and Miscellanies from the Papers of Thomas Jefferson*, 4 vols., 1829.

10. Charles Francis Adams, *Letters of Mrs. Adams, the Wife of John Adams*, 2 vols., 1840.

11. Rothberg, Morey, and Jacqueline Goggin, *John Franklin Jameson and the Development of Humanistic Scholarship in America,* vol. 1: Selected Essays (Athens, Ga.: University of Georgia Press, 1993), 338–39.

12. See, for only one of many instances, Jefferson to Richard Henry Lee, 8 July 1775, *The Papers of Thomas Jefferson*, ed. Julian Boyd, 1: 455–456.

13. Harold C. Syrett, ed., *The Papers of Alexander Hamilton*, 27 vols. (New York: Columbia University Press, 1961–1987); Arthur S. Link, ed., *The Papers of Woodrow Wilson*, 69 vols. (Princeton: Princeton University Press, 1966–1993).

14. Philip M. Hamer (vols. 1–3), George C. Rogers, Jr. (vols. 2–9), David R. Chesnutt (vols. 5–13), eds., *The Papers of Henry Laurens*, 13 vols. (Columbia: University of South Carolina Press, 1968–); Leroy P. Graf (vols. 1–8), Ralph W. Haskins (vols. 1–6), Paul H. Bergeron (vols. 8–10), *The Papers of Andrew Johnson*, 10 vols. (Knoxville: University of Tennessee Press, 1967–); Robert A. Hill, ed., *Marcus Garvey and Universal Negro Improvement Association Papers* (Berkeley: University of California Press, 1983–); Robert L. Meriwether (vol. 1), W. Edwin Hemphill (vols. 2–10), Clyde N. Wilson (vols. 10–20), eds., *The Papers of John C. Calhoun*, 20 vols. (Columbia: University of South Carolina Press, 1959–).

15. G. Thomas Tansell, "The Editing of Historical Documents," in *Studies in Bibliography*, ed. Fredson Bowers (Charlottesville: University Press of Virginia, 1978), 1–56; Henry Graff and A. Simone Reagor, *Docu-*

mentary Editing in Crisis: Some Reflections and Recommendations (a report prepared for the National Historical Publications and Records Commission, 1981), 22 pp.; Thomas Etzold, "The Great Documents Deluge," *Newsletter of the Society for the Historians of American Foreign Relations* 8, no. 1 (March 1976): 14–21; Richard H. Kohn and George M. Curtis, III, "The Government, the Historical Profession and Historical Editing: A Review," *Reviews in American History* 9 (June 1981): 145–155; Richard J. Cox, "Archivists and the Use of Archival Records; or a View from the World of Documentary Editing," *Provenance* 9, nos. 1 and 2 (1991): 89–110.

16. *Using the Nation's Documentary Heritage: The Report of the National Historical Documents Study* (Washington, D.C.: National Historical Publications and Records Commission in cooperation with the American Council of Learned Societies, 1992).

17. David R. Chesnutt and C. James Taylor, eds., *The Papers of Henry Laurens*, vol. 11, *January 5, 1776–November 1, 1977* (Columbia: University of South Carolina Press, 1988); James W. Ely, Jr., and Theodore Brown, Jr., eds., *Legal Papers of Andrew Jackson* (Knoxville: The University of Tennessee Press, 1987); Clyde N. Wilson, ed., *The Papers of John C. Calhoun*, vol. 18, *1844* (Columbia: University of South Carolina Press, 1988). The Monroe papers project is in progress with no published volumes at this writing.

18. The Alexander Hamilton project deposited the project materials in the Low Library at Columbia University, the Booker T. Washington materials are in the McKeldin Library at the University of Maryland, and the Woodrow Wilson materials are in the Firestone Library, Princeton.

19. Pauline Maier, MIT (1994, December 8), "Re Documentary Editions" [Discussion]. *Scholarly Editing Forum* [On-line]. Available E-mail: SEDIT-L@UMDD.UMD.EDU.

20. Mike Sheehan (1994, December 15), "Re Presidential Papers" [Discussion]. *Scholarly Editing Forum* [On-line]. Available E-mail: SEDIT-L@UMDD.UMD.EDU.

21. Thomas Jefferson Randolph, ed., *Memoir, Correspondence and Miscellanies, from the Papers of Thomas Jefferson*, 4 vols. (Charlottesville: F. Carr and Company, 1829); Henry A. Washington, ed., *The Writings of Thomas Jefferson,* 9 vols. (Philadelphia: J. B. Lippincott and Company, 1864); Paul Leicester Ford, ed., *The Works of Thomas Jefferson*, 12 vols. (New York: G. P. Putnam's Sons, 1904–1905); Boyd, *The Papers of Thomas Jefferson*, vol. 1.

22. Charles Francis Adams, ed., *Familiar Letters of John Adams and His Wife Abigail Adams, during the Revolution* (Boston and New York: Houghton Mifflin Company, 1876); Lyman H. Butterfield, ed., *Adams Family Correspondence*, vol. 2, *June 1776–March 1778* (Cambridge, Mass.: The Belknap Press of Harvard University Press, 1963).

23. J. Franklin Jameson, "Correspondence of John C. Calhoun," *An-*

nual Report of the American Historical Association for 1899, vol. 2. (Washington: GPO, 1900).

24. Leila Avrin, *Scribes, Script and Books. The Book Arts from Antiquity to the Renaissance* (Chicago: American Library Association, 1991), 214.

25. Charles Francis Adams, ed., *Familiar Letters*, 97.

26. Lyman H. Butterfield, ed., *Adams Family Correspondence*, vol. 1, *December 1761–May 1776* (Cambridge, Mass.: The Belknap Press of Harvard University Press, 1963).

27. Charles Francis Adams, ed., *Letters of Mrs. Adams*, xliii.

28. The information on the editing by C. F. Adams comes from an as yet unpublished paper read by Adams editor Richard Alan Ryerson at the Annual Meeting of the Association for Documentary Editing, Tucson, Arizona, October 28, 1994.

29. Jane Turner Censer, ed., *The Papers of Frederick Law Olmsted*, vol. 4, *Defending the Union. The Civil War and the U.S. Sanitary Commission, 1861–1863* (Baltimore: The Johns Hopkins University Press, 1986).

30. Paul H. Bergeron, ed., *The Papers of Andrew Johnson*, vol. 8 (Knoxville: The University of Tennessee Press, 1989).

31. *Journals of the Continental Congress, 1774–1789*, 34 vols. (Washington: Library of Congress, 1904–1937).

32. Richard B. Morris, ed., *The Papers of John Jay*, 2 vols., with a third and final volume in progress (New York: Harper and Row, 1975–1980).

33. Henry P. Johnston, ed., *The Correspondence and Public Papers of John Jay*, 4 vols. (New York: Burt Franklin, 1890; reprint, Lenox Hill Publishing and Distribution Co. [Burt Franklin], 1970).

34. Richard B. Morris, ed., *John Jay, the Making of a Revolutionary*, vol. 1, *Unpublished Papers, 1745–1780* (New York: Harper and Row, 1975), 10.

35. *Lafayette in the Age of the American Revolution: Selected Letters and Papers, 1776–1790*, Eds. Stanley J. Idzerda (vols. 1–5); Linda J. Pike (vols. 1–4); Mary Ann Quinn (vols. 1–4); Robert Rhodes Crout (vols. 3–5); Stanley J. Idzerda (vol. 6, in progress) (Ithaca, N.Y.: Cornell University Press, 1977–).

36. Louis P. Harlan, *et al.*, eds., *The Booker T. Washington Papers*, vol. 2, *1860–1889* (Urbana: University of Illinois Press, 1972), xxix–xxx.

37. *Historical Documentary Editions* (Washington, D.C.: National Historical Publications and Records Commission, 1993), 10; Noble E. Cunningham, Jr., ed., *Circular Letters of Congressmen to Their Constituents, 1789–1829*, 3 vols. (Chapel Hill: University of North Carolina Press, 1978).

38. Linda Grant De Pauw (vols. 1–3), Charlene Bangs Bickford (vols. 4–6, 10, and 11), Helen E. Veit (vols. 4–6, 9–11), Kenneth R. Bowling (vols. 9–11), eds., *Documentary History of the First Federal Congress of the United States of America, March 4, 1789–March 3, 1791* (Baltimore: Johns Hopkins University Press, 1972–), in progress.

39. Anne R. Kenney, ed., *"Dr. America" Writes Home: The Letters of Thomas A. Dooley III to his Mother, Agnes W. Dooley, 1954–1960*. At this writing, however, actual publication is in doubt because of lack of funding for the project.

40. C. Vann Woodward, *Mary Chesnut's Civil War* (New Haven: Yale University Press, 1981), introduction.

41. Edward C. Carter, II, director, and Thomas E. Jeffrey, ed., *Papers of Benjamin Henry Latrobe* (Microfiche Edition) (Baltimore: Maryland Historical Society, 1976); Edward C. Carter, II, editor-in-chief, *The Papers of Benjamin Henry Latrobe*, 8 vols. (New Haven: Yale University Press, 1977–1988).

42. *Historical Documentary Editions* (NHPRC, 1993), 8.

43. Ibid., 7; also Mary-Jo Kline, ed., *Papers of Aaron Burr, 1756–1836 (Microfilm Edition)*, 27 reels (Ann Arbor: Microfilming Corporation of America, 1978); Mary-Jo Kline, ed., *Political Correspondence and Public Papers of Aaron Burr*, 2 vols. (Princeton: Princeton University Press, 1983).

44. Merrill Jensen (vols. 1–3), John P. Kaminski and Gaspare Saladino (vols. 8–10, 13–16), eds., *The Documentary History of the Ratification of the Constitution*, 18 vols. (Madison, Wis.: State Historical Society of Wisconsin, 1976-).

45. Marvin M. Gettleman, ed., *Records of the Johns Hopkins University Seminary of History and Politics* (New York: Garland Publishing Company, 1987–1990).

46. David Thomas Konig, *Plymouth Court Records, 1686–1859*, 16 vols. (Wilmington, Del.: Michael Glazier, Inc., 1978–1981).

47. See the comprehensive articles and "acknowledgments" by David R. Chesnutt, "Presidential Editions: the Promise and Problems of Technology," *Documentary Editing* 16, no. 3 (September 1994): 70–77. The anatomy of a specific CD-ROM application is dissected in Martha L. Benner, "*The Abraham Lincoln Legal Papers*: The Development of the Complete Facsimile Edition on CD-ROM," *Documentary Editing* 16, no. 4 (December 1994): 100–107.

· 11 ·

LAW, CURATORIAL ETHICS,
AND THE RESEARCHER

The public domain is a source of real social value, and
incursions on it should not be undertaken lightly.

Peter A. Jaszi[1]

Researchers who use collections of personal papers are confronted with far fewer government restrictions than are those
who use official records. Researchers who are working in collections of material that is over fifty years old face even fewer constraints. These conditions exist because one major federal
limitation on access—classified records—has little or no application
to private papers or records prior to the end of World War II.

THE FREEDOM OF INFORMATION ACT

If it does become necessary for a researcher to approach recent
federal records, it is possible to pry open those that are closed by
invoking the Freedom of Information Act (FOIA),[2] but before taking that step researchers should be aware of the extent and limitations of the act.

Access to most federal records is unrestricted, and those that
are limited have restrictions at various levels. National security information records restrictions range from *confidential* to *top secret*
and beyond for some nuclear-related information. Therefore, if
records are not encumbered by restrictions it should not be necessary to use the FOIA to obtain access to them. In fact, however,
most agencies will not provide information to individuals unless
the request is filed as an FOIA request, except for specific "information products" that agencies package for general distribution.

237

The exceptions are the National Archives and certain other research institutions within the Executive Branch.

Researchers should be aware of the fact that the FOIA applies only to federal records of the Executive Branch, and does not affect records of the Congress or the judiciary. An attempt to invoke FOIA in order to see records of a congressional committee, or *in camera* deliberations of a justice, would be rebuffed. All of the states have their own versions of FOIA for state records, but they, too, apply to the executive records only. None of the FOIA laws applies to personal papers of an individual.

At the federal level, most records over fifty years old that were classified have been declassified. If they have not, restrictions on access to them fall under the first of the nine exemptions to free access that apply to the bulk of government records:

> 1. (1)(A) [matters] specifically authorized under criteria established by an Executive order to be kept secret in the interest of national defense or foreign policy and (B) are in fact properly classified pursuant to such Executive order.

The main points of the other exemptions to access, as listed in the most recent version of the FOIA (complete text is in the Appendix, p. 287), are matters:

2. solely relating to internal personnel rules and practices of an agency;

3. specifically exempted by an overriding statute (such as the Internal Revenue Service statutes, or laws relating to intelligence activity that are usually referred to as "protection of sources and methods");

4. trade secrets and commercial or financial information obtained from a person and privileged or confidential;

5. certain interagency or intra-agency memoranda (the courts have not allowed agencies to expand or use this very much, and it probably applies mostly to drafts and developmental papers where a final product exists and can be made available);

6. personnel and medical files and similar files the disclosure of which would constitute a clearly unwarranted invasion of personal privacy;

7. many, but not all, investigatory or law enforcement records;

8. certain records relating to regulation or supervision of financial institutions;

9. geological and geophysical information and data, including maps, concerning wells.[3]

Agencies provide information about how to request access to records that fall under these restrictions. The process involves sending a request to the agency indicating that it is an FOIA request. Since there are many such requests, agencies have established FOIA offices where the requests are processed. The agency has an initial ten days to respond to the request, although that does not mean that the response will provide the information—in many cases it merely acts as a notice of receipt and an indication of when action on the request is beginning. The request then goes to the appropriate unit of the agency where the information is maintained, and a search and evaluation is then performed at that unit. There may then be internal reviews of that unit's decision. If the information is released the inquirer is either sent copies or is informed where it can be seen; if it is denied, the inquirer is notified of the grounds for denial and of his or her rights to appeal. The appeal process can go all the way up to the courts, with the process occasionally lasting for years before a final decision is reached. An agency's application of the exemptions, however, is discretionary, not mandatory, so that in some cases all of the information that might be covered by an exemption is not necessarily withheld.

The processes involved in FOIA can be complex, and from time to time they are revised by legislation. Researchers who find a need to access recent government information should therefore request the latest brochure on the process from the government involved—federal or state. Important sidelights to remember about FOIA are that it is not limited to citizens of the United States, and the requestor need not state *why* a request is being filed.

THE PRIVACY ACT

If the Freedom of Information Act guarantees that most government records will be open unless specifically and purposefully closed, its counterpart—the Privacy Act[4]—provides for the definition of certain categories of records that relate to individuals, with twelve reasons why they may be opened, or at least made available within limits. The act itself does not close any records, but provides the basis on which the FOIA exemptions may be invoked, such as exemption 6 relating to personnel and medical records of an individual.

Like FOIA, the Privacy Act applies only to federal records of the Executive Branch. It, too, has its counterpart in the states.

If FOIA is meant to guarantee open government through the revelation of government business, the Privacy Act is meant to guarantee the privacy of individuals who must, under law, reveal personal information to the government. The Privacy Act, like FOIA, does not apply to collections of personal papers.

The Privacy Act does not guarantee that *all* records held by the government that relate to individuals will be closed, but merely establishes definitions for *systems of records* containing personal information that can be retrieved with reference to an individual. Thus, the act defines what is meant by a system of records as: records that are accessed by personal name, such as personnel or medical records; records accessed by a number which equates with an individual, such as a social security number, military service number (now universally the same as the SSN), or an account number unique to an individual. The act also restricts access to records in which an individual could be identified by a photograph or symbol, such as fingerprints, voice prints, or DNA codes. The act does not protect personal information contained in files that are accessed by other identifiers, such as property owners where the file scheme is arranged by plot or lot numbers or other personal property, such as private aircraft, where the files may be accessed by the aircraft registration number, regardless of current owner.

The Privacy Act provides each person named in such systems of records a right of access to the information about him/herself, and a right to demand modification or correction of the information. By conveying this right, the act does not extend the right of a person to have access to information about other persons named in the records. It is not, however, the Privacy Act that closes those records, it is the link of the Privacy Act to the Freedom of Information Act that makes it possible to close personal records under an FOIA exemption. The courts have generally held that if records have been opened under FOIA they cannot be closed for privacy reasons.

The Privacy Act allows for exceptions, essentially to serve the purposes of government for which the records have been assembled. The act states:[5]

No agency shall disclose any record which is contained in a system of records by any means of communication to any person, or to another agency, except pursuant to a written request by, or with the prior written consent of, the individual to whom the record pertains, unless disclosure of the record would be—

(1) to those officers and employees of the agency which maintains the record who have a need for the record in the performance of their duties;

(2) required under section 552 of this title [the FOIA];

(3) for a routine use as defined in subsection (a) (7) of this section and described under subsection (e) (4) (D) of this section;[6]

(4) to the Bureau of the Census for purposes of planning or carrying out a census or survey or related activity pursuant to the provisions of Title 13;

(5) to a recipient who has provided the agency with advance adequate written assurance that the record will be used solely as a statistical research or reporting record, and the record is to be transferred in a form that is not individually identifiable;

(6) to the National Archives of the United States as a record which has sufficient historical or other value to warrant its continued preservation by the United States Government, or for evaluation by the Archivist of the United States to determine whether the record has such value;

(7) to another agency or to an instrumentality of any governmental jurisdiction within or under the control of the United States for civil or criminal law enforcement activity if the activity is authorized by law, and if the head of the agency or instrumentality has made a written request to the agency which maintains the record specifying the particular portion desired and the law enforcement activity for which the record is sought;

(8) to a person pursuant to a showing of compelling circumstances affecting the health or safety of an individual if upon such disclosure notification is transmitted to the last known address of such individual;

(9) to either House of Congress, or, to the extent of matter within its jurisdiction, any committee or subcommittee thereof, any joint committee of Congress or subcommittee of any such joint committee;

(10) to the Comptroller General, or any of his authorized representatives, in the course of the performance of the duties of the General Accounting Office;

(11) pursuant to the order of a court of competent jurisdiction;

(12) to a consumer reporting agency in accordance with section 3711(f) of Title 31.[7]

These exemptions seem to leave out release of privacy files to the individual who is the subject of the file. Section (d) of the act, "Access to records," however, addresses that question:

> Each agency that maintains a system of records shall—(1) upon request by any individual to gain access to his record or to any information pertaining to him which is contained in the system, permit him and upon his request, a person of his own choosing to accompany him, to review the record and have a copy made of all or any portion thereof in a form comprehensible to him, except that the agency may require the individual to furnish a written statement authorizing discussion of that individual's record in the accompanying person's presence.[8]

The rest of the access section deals with procedures for individuals to follow when requesting amendment of their record by making "any correction of any portion thereof which the individual believes is not accurate, relevant, timely, or complete."[9]

There are also "general exemptions" that relate to access to privacy files by the Central Intelligence Agency and any other agency "which performs as its principal function any activity pertaining to the enforcement of criminal laws," with an elaboration of limitations.[10]

Researchers who are concerned about restrictions imposed by the Privacy Act should know that the act makes three distinctions among records that are under the custody of the National Archives. The first category covers those records that are being stored by the National Archives for an agency, mostly in one of the National Archives Federal Records Centers. Those records are still legally records of the agency, and the act notes that:

> The Archivist of the United States shall not disclose the record except to the agency which maintains the record, or under rules established by that agency which are not inconsistent with the provisions of this section.[11]

However, once records have been transferred to the National Archives (accessioned, in archival terminology), control of access moves to the archivist of the United States and is no longer subject to the access limitations of the Privacy Act, although some records may be exempted from disclosure under the privacy exemptions ((b)(6) and (b)(7)(c)) of the FOIA. There are minor differences delineated in the act between records transferred *prior* to the act's effective date, and those transferred after that date.[12] What this means is that records in the National Archives are generally exempt from the Privacy Act, although access to them may be restricted under other laws or legal agreements, such as the terms of a deed of gift for nongovernment material in the Presidential libraries or any of the "gift collections" in the National Archives proper.

The most dramatic illustration of this principle of archival/nonarchival material is the Internal Revenue Service (IRS) personal income tax records. Each year the National Archives records centers receive some two hundred million personal income tax forms that have gone through the IRS for processing. When deposited in the federal records centers the forms are still considered to be held by the IRS, which reimburses the National Archives for their storage and processing. Most of those forms are declared to be nonpermanent records by the IRS, are protected under the Privacy Act, and shortly before they are eight years old the IRS destroys them. Technology is changing the way in which IRS records are maintained, and the association with Federal Records Centers will probably be considerably reduced in the next decade.

On the other hand, the decennial records of the Bureau of the Census are maintained by the bureau for a period of time, then transferred to the National Archives where they are formally accessioned. They are then administered by the National Archives in accordance with an agreement originally negotiated in 1952, long before the advent of the Privacy Act, and which is supported now by a provision of the law relating to the census. They may be held under exemption (b)(3) of the FOIA. Decennial census records are normally opened to the public seventy-two years after the census was taken.

There has been a considerable amount of literature on both the FOIA and the Privacy Act, and that literature expands annually. The expansion may reach geometric proportions as questions of electronic records become more and more prominent in the affairs of government. At this writing bills are being fashioned in Congress to deal with public access to electronic records and also with questions of electronic "systems of records" and electronic transfers of information in records that may be subject to the Privacy Act. A literature search on these topics can be overwhelming, and it is becoming clear that researchers are going to need more assistance than they have in the past from lawyers knowledgeable about recent legislation and regulations.

Of course, research in purely "personal" papers will not be affected by these regulations, which are meant for documents created, received or maintained by government. But it is difficult to think of any historical work being written today that will not, at some point, have to contain some government material to supplement or complement the manuscript sources. Although most historical research is in historical records that are not affected by issues of personal privacy, medical/genetic studies and similar research may require adherence to special procedures for the protection of privacy.

THE COPYRIGHT ACT

Researchers who use personal papers cannot be totally unconcerned about federal law, therefore. The most important law that affects them is copyright legislation. The Copyright Act, Title 17 of the United States Code, underwent a major revision by Public Law 94-553 in October 1976, effective on January 1, 1978.[13] Copyright does not limit *access* to material, or even use of the information that such sources contain. It does, however, protect the author's "means of expression," and in so doing puts limits on how much of the copyrighted text can be employed in a secondary work.

Prior to the passage of the Copyright Act revision of 1976 copyright did not apply to as yet unpublished material. Manuscripts were protected under "literary property rights," or common-law copyright. As such, cases arising out of these rights were confined to state courts.

Literary property rights applied to an author's work prior to publication, if publication was even considered. Thus, the rights to *any* material created but not published, including personal letters, diaries, poetry, and other "works," remained in a status of ownership by the originator or his or her heirs and assigns that was both complete and perpetual. Additionally, such rights descended to all heirs in equal portion over generations. This condition presented almost insurmountable problems for researchers who wished to quote extensive portions of such works centuries after they were created.

Yet, there are regularly published volumes containing letters and writings of American political, literary, scientific and corporate figures, and scores of others, for the most part without formal consent of any known heirs. The explanations of the editors and publishers are many. One is that it is no longer possible to determine who holds the rights to ancient material. Another is that in many cases some of these documents have previously been published, individually or collectively, in which case the test of copyright moves from that of unpublished to that of published material. There is, however, the question of ownership of copyright in material previously published without regard to the concept of literary property rights. Most present-day editors will argue that the publication of letters does not convey to the publisher the sole use of the letters, which were considered to be in the public domain by the publisher in the first place. Therefore, the reasoning goes, the publisher may copyright the style, format, index, and other editorial or substantive textual additions to the documents, but not the documents themselves, thus leaving them open to publication in other formats by others.

In some cases editors have made a good-faith effort to search out heirs or assigns of the author of correspondence before publishing such materials, but modern editions contain not only the letters of a single individual, such as Franklin or Jefferson, but also the letters of those with whom they corresponded. A single volume of the Jefferson papers might include letters from two hundred or more correspondents. It is certain that the editor has not obtained permissions from the heirs of all of these other "authors." The problem is compounded in publications centered on a topic, rather than an individual, such as the *Documentary History of the Ratification of the Constitution*, which contains petitions, letters from the general public, and other material from the so-called inarticulate populace, which may be our most articulate source of public opinion. While it *may* be true that clearance to reproduce has been received from the owner of the rights to the collection (presumably the donor), it is difficult to imagine that such clearance has been received from all of the correspondents within the collection. Thus, it would appear that many institutions that published their collections in print or in microcopy for sale and distribution were in technical violation of common law copyright.

The Copyright Act of 1976 changed all of that by including unpublished writings and other materials under the act, effective January 1, 1978. The language of that part of the act reads:

Copyright protection subsists, in accordance with this title, in original works of authorship fixed in any tangible medium of expression, now known or later developed, from which they can be perceived, reproduced, or otherwise communicated, either directly or with the aid of a machine or device. Works of authorship include the following categories:[14]

    (1) literary works;

    (2) musical works, including any accompanying words;

    (3) dramatic works, including any accompanying music;

    (4) pantomimes and choreographic works;

    (5) pictorial, graphic, and sculptural works

    (6) motion pictures and other audiovisual works;

    (7) sound recordings

    (8) architectural works[15]

The text of the 1909 Copyright Act that this section revised applied the act only to books, periodicals (including newspapers), lectures, sermons, addresses (for oral delivery), musical composition, maps, works of art, models or designs for works of art, reproduction of a work of art, and a variety of audiovisual representations.[16] Unpublished personal correspondence was not subject to copyright.

The 1976 act allowed twenty-five years for transition from the unlimited common-law copyright of unpublished works to a fixed duration of copyright for these materials. It grandparented all existing unpublished materials into a category that would have their status remain protected until December 31, 2002, with some exceptions. Thus, any unpublished letters sent to Madison by obscure correspondents would officially fall into the public domain on January 1, 2003, as would most similar material in that category. However, another part of the act provided protection for the life of the author plus fifty years. Therefore, unpublished writings of Ernest Hemingway, who died in 1961, would be protected until 2011.

The 1976 act did permit *some* copying of material from protected works, however, and it is in the area of "fair use" (Sec. 107) that the lumping together of published and unpublished material began to unravel.

The House of Representatives Report on the copyright law revision, issued in 1976, notes that traditionally, fair use of copyrighted material has been applied to:

quotation of excerpts in a review or criticism for purposes of illustration or comment; quotation of short passages in a scholarly or technical work, for illustration or clarification of the author's observations; use in a parody of some of the content of the work parodied; summary of an address or article with brief quotations, in a news report; reproduction by a library of a portion of a work to replace part of a damaged copy; reproduction by a teacher or student of a small part of a work to illustrate a lesson; reproduction of a work in legislative or judicial proceedings or reports; incidental and fortuitous reproduction, in a newsreel or broadcast, of a work located in the scene of an event being reported.[17]

These traditions and the precedents established by the courts led to the text of Section 107 of the 1976 act:

> Notwithstanding the provision of section 106, the fair use of copyrighted work, including such use by reproduction in copies or phonorecords or by any other means specified in that section, for purposes such as criticism, comment, news reporting, teaching (including multiple copies for classroom use), scholarship, or research, is not an infringement of copyright. In determining whether the use made of a work in any particular case is a fair use the factors to be considered shall include—
>
> (1) the purpose and character of the use, including whether such use is of a commercial nature or is for non-profit educational purposes;
> (2) the nature of the copyrighted work;
> (3) the amount and substantiality of the portion used in relation to the copyrighted work as a whole; and
> (4) the effect of the use upon the potential market for or value of the copyrighted work.

Although the language of the act implies that these four tests are given as examples ["the factors to be considered shall *include*—"], the door is left open for other tests. The courts, however, have consistently cited only these four tests in their opinions.

The language of the section on tests means that the courts will apply an equitable rule of reason, because no definition of these tests is possible for general applicability, so each case must be based on its own facts. The first test is clear, distinguishing between commercial and noncommercial works as a "consideration"; the second test relates to the work as fact or fiction, published or unpublished, available or out-of-print. Quotation of a factual work (a manual, reference work, bibliography) might be treated more liberally by the court than quotations from poetry, novels, political speculation, and similar "creative" material.

The amount and substantiality test for "fair use" sometimes leads the courts to count pages and calculate percentages of the total used. The key here is what is considered to be the copyrightable "work." In one case concerning copying of an article from a journal, the court found that since each article was copyrightable, the defendant could not claim that one article out of an entire journal met the fair use provision.[18] Thus, since letters, poems, and other short works may hold copyright individually, republishing them in full cannot be considered to be fair use.

The effect of republication on the market value of a work usually relates to the rarity of the original, which may be a factor of its age, price, or uniqueness. There is also a consideration of the original work having been "abandoned," or, in the case of correspondence, inaccessibility to the author or any of the presumed heirs or assigns. The insignificant effect of republication on the market value of a work is the rationale that most editors would use when freely publishing aged letters from historically obscure individuals. The general feeling among documentary editors is that the few letters of an individual that are published in association with the main corpus of papers of the targeted subject (e.g., four letters of Stephen Cathalan, Jr., to Madison in the *Papers of James Madison* publication, or three letters of August Delabar to Samuel Gompers in the *Samuel Gompers Papers*) will have little or no effect "upon the potential market for or value of" the Cathalan or Delabar documents. Although that may be a valid assumption for older materials, where the heirs or assigns might be lost in generational obscurity, it has been challenged as a concept in recent material, where the author of the letters is still alive and active, and, as we shall see, questions of an author's rights of first publication may outweigh claims of denied revenue.

A significant problem for researchers has arisen through four court cases which provide judicial thinking on the subject of fair use of unpublished material. These four cases, dating from 1985, are frequently cited in the literature on recent copyright issues, and I need not go into great detail here, but a chronological overview may be instructive.

Harper and Row v. Nation Enterprises

Harper and Row contracted to publish the memoirs of President Gerald Ford, and the publisher also contracted with *Time* magazine to publish a 7,500-word extract of the work for a fee, consisting of passages agreeable to both parties. *The Nation* magazine had access to a purloined copy of the Ford manuscript and published excerpts of 2,250 words from it.

Time felt that it has been "scooped" and canceled the agreement with Harper and Row, thus denying the publisher of the fee. Harper and Row sued *The Nation* for unfair use in violation of copyright.

The District Court for the Southern District of New York ruled in favor of the plaintiff, Harper and Row. The defendants appealed, and the Court of Appeals for the Second Circuit reversed the lower court's decision. Harper and Row appealed to the Supreme Court.[19] The court cited one of its earlier rulings that "every commercial use of copyrighted material is presumptively an unfair exploitation of the monopoly privilege that belongs to the owner of the copyright."[20] In short, Ford and Harper and Row, as copyright holders, could decide who could excerpt, and that "a fair use doctrine that permits extensive prepublication quotations from an unreleased manuscript without the copyright owner's consent poses substantial potential for damage to the marketability of first serialization rights in general."[21]

In other remarks, the court noted that "the unpublished nature of a work is '[a] key, though not necessarily determinative, factor' tending to negate a defense of fair use,"[22] and further, "under ordinary circumstances, the author's right to control the first public appearance of his undisseminated expression will outweigh a claim of fair use."[23]

Salinger v. Random House, Inc.

The concept of an author's right to first public appearance was soon tested in the case of an unauthorized biography of J. D. Salinger written by Ian Hamilton, who used manuscript collections at Princeton, Harvard and the University of Texas at Austin. The collections were papers of people with whom Salinger corresponded. Although Hamilton had signed agreements with the libraries not to publish without permission of both the libraries and Salinger himself, he completed his work and submitted the manuscript to Random House with extensive citation from the Salinger letters.

Random House rejected the manuscript, asking for fewer direct quotes, and Hamilton reformed the quotes to become close paraphrases.

Salinger obtained a prepublication version of the manuscript and brought suit on the basis that his rights of first publication were being violated and that he was a third-party beneficiary of the use agreements signed by Hamilton.[24]

Hamilton claimed that he was not infringing copyright, but operating under the fair use provision of Section 107 of the U.S. Copyright Act. The Second District Court (New York) ruled for Hamilton and upheld his fair use claim, stating that "the wound [Salinger] has suffered is not from an infringement of his copyright but of the publication of a biography that trespasses on his wish for privacy. The copyright law does not give him protection from that form of injury."[25]

The Second Circuit Court reversed this decision on appeal by stating that the right of first publication outweighs the author's claim of fair use, and further stated that normally unpublished letters enjoy "insulation" from fair use copying.

One of the significant differences between *The Nation* case and *Salinger* is that Gerald Ford was going to publish his letters, and therefore it was not a matter of not wanting them made known, but *The Nation* scooped his publisher, infringing his copyright. Salinger did not know the letters existed in the collections used by Hamilton, but when he learned of them he did not want them published, so he insisted on his right to first publication. In Ford's case he had already secured first publication rights, through Harper and Row. The significance of the court statement in *Salinger* is that it implied the authority of the author to exercise a right to first publication over all fair use applications.

Salinger revealed a dilemma in the new copyright law. Copyright was intended "to promote the Progress of Science and useful Arts by securing for limited Times to Authors and Inventors the exclusive Right to their respective Writings and Discoveries,"[26] thus encouraging publication. Salinger was using the act to *prevent* publication, but could do so only until fifty years after his death. In that regard, the new copyright law is more liberal than the old common law of literary property rights, which had no time limit on protection.

There are many considerations here. Hamilton did not honor the agreements that he signed with the libraries that provided the papers. Salinger, on the other hand, was not protesting the publication of what he would consider a "work" but, rather, his personal communications. To him it was a privacy issue, as the court of original jurisdiction had noted. The Copyright Act, by applying to any "original works of authorship fixed in any tangible medium of expression," now encompasses personal and confidential expressions, which many would claim are not "works" at all. The case reignited the old debate in literary circles as to how much of the private life and authorial motivation is important in order to understand or appreciate an author's published work. Among archivists it led to a spate of articles on the approach that curators should take to third-party correspondence access in their collections, which was discussed in another context in chapter 3.

The Salinger case also led to an amendment to the fair use language of the Copyright Act. P.L. 102–492 of 1992 stated: "The fact that a work is unpublished shall not itself bar a finding of fair use if such finding is made upon consideration of all of the above factors."[27] This amendment, originally introduced by Senator Paul Simon of Illinois, followed concerns that *Salinger* and *New Era* (*infra*) would prevent fair use of *any* unpublished material.

New Era Publications v. Henry Holt[28]

Russell Miller, author of *Bare Faced Messiah: The True Story of L. Ron Hubbard*, used a significant amount of paraphrased and quoted material from unpublished letters and diary entries of Ron Hubbard, the founder of the Church of Scientology, published by Henry Holt. New Era sued.

The court determined that fair use was applicable to all types of unpublished materials. Looking back at the *Nation* case, the court decided that the key factor there had been the pirated or purloined nature of the material, making it unfair. The court looked favorably on the Salinger case as injurious to the plaintiff, but held that "to conclude that the author's commercial interest in controlling the circumstances of first publication is an absolute right would be incompatible with First Amendment interests."[29]

The decision was based on what was used, and why. Thus "the use of the protected expression must be reasonably necessary to the communication and demonstration of significant points being made about the subject and must have no significant adverse effect on the market for the copyrighted work."[30] The court concluded that the use of Hubbard's words was to prove the author's case against him, not to exploit his literary rights. The amount used was insubstantial, and the impact on the market minimal. Yet the court held that since the material copied was never before published, the use was not fair; but it refused to order an injunction to stop publication, on the grounds that it would constitute prior restraint, and recommended action for an award of damages.

The Second Circuit again reversed, stating that just because citations are facts does not make them any less vulnerable to charges of usurpation of first publication rights. It indicated its concern was primarily with the property interest of the creator, and not with the public's right to know.[31]

The Second Circuit, in reiterating its original stance on *Salinger*, seemed to close the door on any other cases where copyright property interests were threatened. However, since the issues in copyright were considered to be judged on the equitable rule of reason, each new case was to be judged on its merits, and not on precedent. The next case put *Salinger* in doubt for broader application.

Wright v. Warner Books[32]

Author Margaret Walker employed paraphrased excerpts from unpublished Wright journals in Yale's Beinecke Library, and from unpublished letters Wright had written to others. The biography that resulted was published by Warner Books as *Richard Wright, Demonic Genius*. Although earlier drafts had contained many verbatim quotes from Wright's letters, the published version had been recast without direct quotes.

Yale had purchased the Wright collection from the widow, and had a contract that allowed for use of the collection, but she still retained copyright. On publication, she sued Warner Books, on a claim of breach of contract and infringement of copyright.

The court found that the purpose of the use was in favor of the publisher/author because the purpose was a work by an accredited biographer, but concurred that "the scope of fair use is narrower with respect to unpublished works."[33] As opposed to *Salinger*, where the documents in question were located in someone else's collection, the court noted that in this case the focus was on the primary material sold to Yale by the widow with little or no restriction on use, and even encouragement that they be opened for research. With the purchase and the maintenance of the collection

Yale had authority "to share Wright's work with interested scholars."[34] It upheld Walker and Warner.

The Second Circuit this time affirmed the District Court decision, noting Walker's sparing use of Wright's creative expression.[35] It did not apply Salinger because it indicated fair use had to be judged ad hoc on the four tests, not on the precedent of an earlier case. The court said that the manuscript passed all four tests for the defendant. One of the key points vis-à-vis *Salinger* was that Wright was dead, and privacy issues could not be claimed. Of interest to researchers is the Second Circuit's statement that "it defies common sense to construe this agreement as giving scholars access to manuscripts with one hand but then prohibiting them from using the manuscripts in any meaningful way with the other."[36]

There will undoubtedly be more challenges and court cases relating to the publication of unpublished recent documents. The most recent amendment to the fair use clause is very weak and does not really change the original language, but rather expresses the opinion of Congress that the courts can take into consideration. While attempting to remedy the perpetuation of literary property rights in the pre-1976 system, the law has complicated the process of defining a "work" by bringing under that definition anything written by anyone at any time for any reason.

The issue of copyright affects the researcher in the copying of research material that is covered by it. Limitations on exclusive rights are covered in Section 108, in which it states that it is not to be construed that a library or archives or its employees are subject to liability for copyright infringement if equipment located at the library or archives is used unsupervised, "provided, that such equipment displays a notice that the making of a copy may be subject to the copyright law." It goes on to state that nothing in Section 108 should be construed as excusing

> a person who uses such reproducing equipment or who requests a copy or phonorecord under subsection (d) from liability for copyright infringement for any such act, or for any later use of copy or phonorecord, if it exceeds fair use as provided by section 107.

The fair use section declares:

> Notwithstanding the provisions of section 106, the fair use of a copyrighted work, including such use by reproduction in cop-

ies or phonorecords or by any other means specified by that section, for purposes such as criticism, comment, news reporting, teaching (including multiple copies for classroom use), scholarship, or research, is not an infringement of copyright.

However, after five years of the new copyright law, the Register of Copyright was required to review its operation, and in a 1983 report indicated that "since the copyright owner has elected never to publish the work . . . there is no fair use copying permitted beyond that authorized by 108(b)." That section states:

> The rights of reproduction and distribution under this section apply to a copy or phonorecord of an unpublished work duplicated in facsimile form solely for purposes of preservation and security or for deposit for research use in another library or archives of the type described by clause (2) of subsection (a), if the copy or phonorecord reproduced is currently in the collections of the library or archives.

This section would imply that there is no legitimate reason for copying unpublished manuscripts, without permission of the owner to the rights of the unpublished material, except for preservation or security. All of the rest of Section 108 applies to published material. Since there is no time limitation in this section, it implies that unpublished manuscript material of any kind is protected until published by or with the consent of the copyright holder, or, according to Section 303, at least until December 31, 2002. The 1991 amendment of the act not to exclude unpublished materials from the fair use clause may nullify this interpretation, but at this writing there have been no tests of that amendment.

Title 17 of the U.S. Code has provided a complex schedule of times for the expiration of copyright. Some of this complexity is transitional, and on January 1, 2003 much of the problem will disappear, as almost all material more than seventy-five years old will enter the public domain. If the manuscript is created on or after January 1, 1978, Section 302 declares that copyright in it "subsists from its creation and, except as provided by the following subsections, endures for a term consisting of the life of the author and fifty years after the author's death."

It is apparent, therefore, that any unpublished manuscript material created before 1978 located by researchers *today* could not be reproduced without consent of the holder of the copyright, except for preservation or security reasons, thus implying that all publications of documentary sources without such permissions are in violation of this act. The big change will come in 2003.

As this is being written, however, legislators are discussing the prospect of extending general copyright protection from fifty years after the author's death to seventy years, and in the case of older unpublished material, extending the 2003 opening date by ten years, to 2013. These moves are being considered in order to bring the act into accord with the Berne Convention on Copyright. The Senate ratified the treaty document for U.S. adherence to the Berne Convention for the Protection of Literary and Artistic Rights, and the Berne Convention Implementation Act of 1988 modifies the U.S. Copyright Law to bring it into accord. Current legislation is aimed at addressing differences between the two. Congress is also looking at the questions of digitization technology and networked information as a basis for another revision of the law.

Forces on each side of the discussion are again lining up to debate the pros and cons of the issues.[37] The statements of various members of Congress about extending the copyright for unpublished material created *before 1978* for ten years indicates a lack of understanding of the time periods already imposed by law on the material involved. A contemporary, living author who has unpublished material prepared in 1977 would be affected, but so would Jefferson's *unpublished* letters, or those of any lesser historical figure which fall in the pre-1978 time frame. The contemporary writer's works, however, would be covered under the "life of the author plus 50 years" language of Section 303, thus protecting the rights of an author who died on January 2, 1978, until 2028. Considered judgment would suggest not adding ten years to the expiration of copyright coverage on Franklin, Jefferson and Lincoln, or the unpublished letters of one's great-aunt from the Wilson era.

It will not be surprising to see additional cases on this complex issue, and it appears that when revising the Copyright Act in 1976 Congress did not fully evaluate the nuances of difference between published and unpublished, or public and personal material.[38]

NATIONAL SECURITY EXECUTIVE ORDERS

Presidential Executive Orders are a form of governance not enumerated in the Constitution, but the practice of issuing them stems from the fact that if the executive is to administer and enforce the laws passed by Congress there must be some mechanisms to forward that goal. The president must administer the employees of the Executive Branch, and must also carry out his duties as commander in chief of the armed forces. The tools available to the president include regulatory powers authorized by Congress, where regulations have the force of law; and the authority to issue proclamations, some of which are ceremonial and insignificant, but others of which have broad impact, such as the Emancipation Proclamation.

Executive Orders are not defined by law but policies established by them have the force of law, violation of them may cause loss of government benefits, and ultimately they are subject to congressional oversight if they require funding or implementing legislation. They cannot conflict with provisions of either the Constitution or statute, or even with the implied intent of Congress, which, in addition to recognition through financial support, can recognize them by ignoring them. Implementation of an Executive Order over time without congressional protest has been taken by the courts as implicit ratification.

Executive Orders originate with the president and need no official affirmation by Congress or the courts unless they are brought into question. They remain in force until amended or canceled, from president to president, with each president having the authority to cancel, amend, or completely replace an order of a predecessor. Documents relating to national security have traditionally been the subject of Executive Orders, and researchers who have a need to consult materials should be aware of the most recent issuance and its provisions.

Executive Orders (EOs) on classification of documents date to EO 8381, issued March 22, 1940 by President Franklin Roosevelt and related to "vital military and naval installations and equipment."[39] Earlier versions of the EO form, however, go back at least to Lincoln's issuance of an order regarding military courts in Louisiana in 1862. There is no set form to an EO, but it usually cites the authority under which the president feels he is acting, and since 1948 there has been a requirement that they be published in the *Federal Register* on issuance. Executive Orders are also issued by state governors for areas within their jurisdiction.

EO 8381 was issued by FDR as commander in chief of the armed forces, and expanded on earlier orders that usually related to photographs, pictures, drawings, maps or geographical representations. The FDR EO included "all official military or naval books, pamphlets, documents, reports, maps, charts, plans, designs, models, drawings, photographs, contracts, or specifications" and established three classes of coverage: secret, confidential, or restricted.[40] Since then there have been eight EOs on classification of national security materials issued by Truman (EO 10104, Feb. 1, 1950; 10290, Sept. 24, 1951); Eisenhower (10501, Nov. 1953); Kennedy (10964, Sept. 22, 1961); Nixon (11652, Mar. 8, 1972); Carter (12065, Dec. 1, 1978); Reagan (12356, Aug. 1, 1982); and Clinton (12958, Apr. 17, 1995). Most of these were in response to some national security threat, usually of a military nature, including the Korean conflict, the Berlin crisis, the leak of the Pentagon papers, and other intelligence or military–related activities. Some orders were issued in order to lessen tensions and clear out a backlog of classified records. The Nixon, Carter and Clinton EOs are examples of presidential attempts to lessen the burden of such records on the Executive Branch. An EO applies *only* to Executive Branch records, although it applies to them even if they are in the hands of other branches or in the private sector.

Although early EOs, including the FDR, Truman and Eisenhower issuances, authorized *classifying* sensitive records, the Kennedy EO was the first to address the question of downgrading and *declassifying* those for which classification was no longer necessary. An attempt was made to set automatic declassification schedules, so that some records would systematically be downgraded and ultimately attain automatic declassification after twelve years.

One of the difficulties under the EOs before Nixon was that a positive action on the part of the classifying agency was required in order to declassify its documents, and the backlog of work in what to many agency people seemed like useless old records led to low priorities for the use of staff to attack the task. The Nixon EO accomplished several things that were revolutionary. It removed classification authority from most agencies, thus "taking away their rubber stamp"; it continued Kennedy's stress on automatic declassification but shifted the responsibility, telling the agencies that unless they could justify keeping something classified it would automatically be downgraded without their assistance. To assist in this effort, the Nixon administration authorized the National Archives to hire one hundred declassifiers and begin attacking the problem. The Carter EO pushed the declassification idea even further, and set almost unattainably short time periods for downgrading, but it replaced a Nixon-created cumbersome review board that largely represented the interests of the classifying agencies, with an independent Information Security Oversight Office (ISOO), whose director is appointed by the president.

The Kennedy-Nixon-Carter trend to apply minimal classification levels to documents and to declassify in borderline cases was reversed by Reagan's EO 12356, which tightened up by classifying in questionable cases, and classifying at the highest level appropriate to a document, rather than the lowest. The Reagan EO also permitted *reclassification* of documents that had already been released to the public. The Clinton EO returns to the tradition of Nixon-Carter by instructing agencies to set:

> A.) the date or event for declassification, as prescribed in section 1.6(c); or
> B.) the date that is 10 years from the date of original classification, as prescribed in section 1.6(b); or
> C.) the exemption category from declassification, as prescribed in section 1.6(d); and
>
> 5) a concise reason for classification which, at a minimum, cites the applicable classification categories in section 1.5 of this order.[41]

Through the years since 1942 the original classification levels have changed, but in the recent EOs they are top secret, secret, and confidential. The differences are whether unauthorized disclosure of information could reasonably be expected to cause "exceptionally grave damage," "grave damage," or just "damage" to the national security. Classification can be downgraded from one category to a lesser one as time goes by.

Classified material is subject to the Freedom of Information Act, but its release may be disallowed under Exemption 1 of that act. EO 12958 spells out the reasons why that exemption could be claimed on the grounds that the release could reasonably be expected to:

> 1) reveal an intelligence source, method or activity, or a cryptologic system or activity;
> 2) reveal information that would assist in the development or use of weapons of mass destruction;

3) reveal information that would impair the development or use of technology within a United States Weapons system;

4) reveal United States military plans, or national security emergency preparedness plans;

5) reveal foreign government information;

6) damage relations between the United States and a foreign government, reveal a confidential source, or seriously undermine diplomatic activities that are reasonably expected to be ongoing for a period greater than that provided in paragraph (b) above;

7) impair the ability of responsible United States Government officials to protect the President, the Vice President, and other individuals for whom protection services, in the interest of national security, are authorized; or

8) violate a statute, treaty, or international agreement.

The most radical change wrought by EO 12958 is the so-called drop-dead-date feature, in which the EO provides for the automatic declassification of all permanently valuable information after twenty-five years if the classifying agency takes no action to extend the coverage. Unlike the automatic declassification of Nixon's EO 11652, which applied only to material classified under that order, EO 12958 sets automatic declassification, with some stipulations, to affect *all* records more than twenty-five years old, which implies everything prior to 1970. Government officials are predicting that some 50 percent of all classified records before 1970 will be quickly declassified under this order.[42]

Section 3.6 of the EO describes mandatory declassification review when there is a request for information that is classified, and Section 3.7 discusses processing requests for information under the Freedom of Information Act. Section 3.8 discusses the establishment of a "Declassification Database" by the archivist of the United States, and the availability to the public of any information in that database.

Although it may seem that researchers using personal papers collections may not be in need of access to classified government documents, it should be remembered that *information* is classified, regardless of the form of the document in which it is contained. Therefore, if a biographer is preparing a study of the life of a recent military officer or government official, any papers that are duly marked as containing classified information that are in the "personal papers" of that person are classified the same as the record copies in agency files. Manuscript curators who have such material in their holdings must themselves be cleared for access to the information, the papers must be held under security conditions comparable to those within an agency, and authorized physical access to them must be in research areas that also meet the standards of agency classified research areas. Researchers who successfully demonstrate a "need to know" information that is classified must obtain a security clearance to view such materials, but that does not imply the right to reveal the contents. Such researchers, however, are in an excellent position to pursue FOIA action on the classified material because they can cite specific document-identifying data on the request for mandatory review.

With all of the rights, restrictions, classifications and other legal restrictions on documentary materials, plus the limitations on access imposed by donors of personal papers, it might seem to be an impossible task to pursue any historical research in original sources. The response to that statement depends on the type of research undertaken. Many, but certainly not all, government documents created or received prior to World War II are free of national security restrictions; within the next decade almost all unpublished materials prior to 1978 will be freed from copyright restrictions, except those created by people who are still alive or who died after 1953.* The Freedom of Information Act ultimately provides most of the records needed for research, except in the nine restricted categories, and even some of those are penetrable through dogged application for entrée. The Privacy Act rightly protects an individual's personal information, but much of what is in those files that are part of the "systems of records" under the act can be obtained through other sources, including vital statistics records at local, county and state levels and records of religious institutions. What remains hidden is material relating to a person's direct relationship with the government, dealing with employment, behavior, crime, or role in investigative or security areas.

The Archivist and Ethics

How do archivists and manuscript curators deal with all of the limitations placed on access to their materials? Do they consider

---

*The year 1953 relates to the life of the author plus fifty years duration statement in the Copyright Act. Thus, the works of authors who died as late as 1953 would be protected until 2003, with some exceptions for works of joint authorship or works made for hire.

themselves "gatekeepers" whose role is to keep out all but the favored? Or would they prefer to be thought of as cultural "ushers" who try to guide patrons to their goal, sometimes down a dark aisle? The answer is that both types exist, sometimes within the same repository. In consideration of human frailties when overseeing patrons, there are legal obligations as well as institutional rules that exist in order to level out personality variations among staff.

Archivists who deal with security classified material must receive security clearances, which require background investigations of character and personal history. The clearance process requires that the archivist take an oath to abide by the laws and regulations. Violations can result in reprimands, disciplinary action, or in extreme cases, prison.

Government agencies have rules and penalties relating to the administration of the Privacy Act and the Freedom of Information Act by government employees, with supervisory oversight of these rules and regulations. Patron grievances can be pursued for redress by reference to published processes. Ultimately, court intervention is an option available to the patron.

But all of these processes and procedures constitute a sort of "ethics through law," and there are few if any laws relating to the day-to-day function of service in the reading room of a historical society, a genealogical research facility, or a department of special collections in a research library. Institutions, especially private institutions, can make their own rules on how to deal with patrons, as long as they are not in violation of some overriding civil law. An institution, therefore, could restrict access to its collections to recognized members of the institution. It could place restrictions on the use of private papers in order to permit a biographer or historian sole right of use for a period of time. A religious repository could limit access to certain materials only to individually "approved" members of the research community, just as a corporation could close its archives to anyone who does not have corporate approval for entrée. A locally elected library control board may have its own ideas on what materials should not be in the county libraries, or who should be permitted to use certain collections. The varieties of donor, institutional, corporate, local, state, and federal administration of restrictions may be a burden to researchers, but they are also often a burden to those who must apply those limitations on access.

The major organizations of manuscript curators and archivists, that is, the American Library Association (ALA),[43] one of its divisions, the Association of College & Research Libraries (ACRL), [44] and the Society of American Archivists (SAA),[45] have attempted to address these conflicts through their issuance of statements on ethical behavior of their members. Many manuscript curators hold library science degrees and work in library settings; many archivists also have a library science education, but a large proportion are educated as historians and work in settings where professional colleagues are also historians. For federally employed archivists the overriding document on their behavior comes, not from the professional organizations, but from the U.S. Office of Government Ethics.[46] The document does not concentrate on, or even mention, libraries and archives, but its standards of professional behavior echo some of those in the professional standards when discussing conflicts of interest, gifts, outside employment, etc.

The ethical questions addressed by the SAA and ACRL codes center on the acquisition of new material, restrictions on use of collections, personal collecting and dealing in manuscripts, personal gain through gifts, authenticating the validity of their holdings,* respect for the privileged position they hold as caretakers of sometimes private information, and caring for their documentary wards for the benefit of future generations of users.

Much of what goes under the rubric "ethics" is, in reality, standards of professional conduct. Thus, the SAA code calls for archivists to guard their collections "against defacement, alteration, theft, and physical damage"; and, further, to "cooperate with other archivists and law enforcement agencies in the apprehension and prosecution of thieves." There are other sections that deal with relations among archivists, pledging them to "avoid irresponsible criticism of other archivists and institutions," or to "share knowledge and experience with other archivists through professional association and cooperative activities and assist the professional growth of others with less training or experience." The ALA 1995 statement includes the dictum: "We provide the highest level of service to all library users through appropriate and usefully organized resources; equitable service policies; equitable access; and accurate, unbiased and courteous responses to all requests."

---

*As mentioned in an earlier chapter, this does not imply authentication of the contents, but only the provenance of a document.

One may well ask if "usefully organized resources," or "accurate . . . and courteous responses to all requests" are ethical or merely service standards.

The problem confronting the ALA and the SAA when considering ethical behavior is that their members are essentially interdisciplinary and function professionally in security agencies; law firms; international corporations; community historical or genealogical societies; federal, state, and local agencies; hospitals; churches; and all other institutions that have reference collections, records, or both.

With this broad spectrum of membership it is difficult to state that curators and archivists should provide freedom of access to the materials in their care as an ethical norm. It is difficult to state that all persons should be treated equally, or that the sanctity of the researcher's use of material should be sacred.

The best that usually comes from such statements is that all persons of equal authorization should be treated equally—that there should be "equitable access": in other words, if a collection is restricted only to members of the organization, then all members of the organization should be treated equally. The message that primarily comes across is that curators should not refuse access based on a researcher's "scholarly merit or appropriateness."[47] Because of the kinds of material most of their members deal with, the ALA and the SAA have differences in their philosophical priorities. The ALA is a staunch opponent of censorship, and especially prior restraint, and its ethics statement declares emphatically: "We uphold the principles of intellectual freedom and resist all efforts to censor library resources." Archivists of government records live with access restrictions every day and, in fact, implement their imposition under law. The rare book and manuscript librarians of ACRL take a balanced approach to the question:

> The library must provide reasonable access to the collections on a nondiscriminatory basis in accordance with pertinent professional standards governing access policies and procedures. To the fullest extent permissible by donor and legal requirements, library access policies should further the goals of scholarship for which the collections are maintained.[48]

The *ALA Code of Ethics* admonishes members to "protect each library user's right to privacy and confidentiality with respect to information sought or received, and resources consulted, borrowed, acquired, or transmitted." The archivist's code states that "archivists endeavor to inform users of parallel research by others using the same materials, and, if the individuals concerned agree, supply each name to the other party."[49]

In some of their activities, the ethics of archivists are imposed by the institution that employs them. Thus, the SAA ethical statement that "if archivists use their institutions' holdings for personal research and publication, such practices should be approved by their employers and made known to others using the same holdings." This seems to be more an imposition by the employer, rather than one self-imposed by the archivist, and many employers do impose it. The ACRL statement echoes this sentiment: "Any perception of possible conflict of interest can be avoided by making this activity [personal research] known publicly or by notification to the proper administrative authority."[50]

In the area of restrictions, First Amendment rights, collecting competitiveness and other questions relating to the administration of their collections, many if not most archivists and curators are more liberal in their personal attitudes than the rules under which their work would allow, but they also realize that the rules are legal and their validity is supported by law or legal contract. The ACRL *Standards for Ethical Conduct* state this as:

> Special collections librarians should not reverse, alter, or suppress their professional judgment in order to conform to a management decision, but they must be accountable for making themselves familiar with and adhering to institutional policies as well as applicable laws.[51]

Archivists may urge or wish for declassification but recognize the validity of the laws that keep material classified. They probably side with unrestricted access to old correspondence files, but recognize the validity of a deed of gift that will keep them closed. They may even believe that a collection in their possession probably would be better placed elsewhere, but recognize the sanctity of the donor's purposeful decision to place it with them. There is even a case on record where the curator strongly informed a donor of the consequences of unrestricted access to his collection of recent material, but then publicly defended the donor's expressed desire to have it opened.[52] With all of these qualifications, archivists and manuscript curators profess above all the critical importance of preservation of sources for the study of the past and their role in that task. Indeed, they feel fervently that incursions on the public domain of history should not be undertaken lightly.

NOTES

1. "Statement of Peter A. Jaszi, Washington College of Law, American University, on S. 483, the Copyright Term Extension Act of 1995, September 20, 1995, before the Senate Judiciary Committee, September 10, 1995," 1.

2. 5 U.S.C. 552.

3. Ibid., (b).

4. 5 U.S.C. 552a.

5. Ibid., (b).

6. Ibid.,(a)(7), "the term 'routine use' means, with respect to the disclosure of a record, the use of such record for a purpose which is compatible with the purpose for which it was collected." Subsection (e) (4) (D) states: "Each agency that maintains a system of records shall—subject to the provision of paragraph (11) of this subsection, publish in the Federal Register upon establishment or revision a notice of the existence and character of the system of records, which notice shall include—each routine use of the records contained in the system, including the categories of uses and the purpose of such use."

7. 552a (b).

8. Ibid., (d)(1).

9. Ibid.,(d)(2)(B)(i).

10. Ibid., (j)(1)(2).

11. Ibid., (l)(1).

12. Ibid., (l)(2)(3).

13. PL 94-553 (Oct. 19, 1976) (90 STAT. 2541), codified at Title 17 United States Code.

14. 17 U.S.C. 102(a).

15. Added under the Architectural Works Copyright Protection Act [PL 101-650, Title VII 703, Dec. 1, 1990, 104 Stat. 5133 (codified at 17 U.S.C. 102 (Supp. IV 1991)).].

16. 17 U.S.C. 1(5) (1909).

17. U.S. House of Representatives, 94th Cong., 2d session. Report No. 94-1476. *Copyright Law Revision* (Washington: GPO, September 3, 1976), 65.

18. *American Geophysical Union v. Texaco, Inc.*, 802 F. Supp. 1 (S.D.N.Y. 1992). Cited in Laura N. Gasaway and Sarah K. Wiant, *Libraries and Copy-*

right: A Guide to Copyright Law in the 1990s (Washington, D.C.: Special Libraries Association), 29.

19. The original suit and the appeal are summarized by the Supreme Court ruling, *Harper and Row v. Nation Enterprises*, 471 Sup. Ct. 542 (1985).

20. Ibid., 562.

21. Ibid., 569.

22. Ibid., 554.

23. Ibid., 555.

24. *Salinger v. Random House, Inc.*, 650 F. Supp. 427 (1986).

25. Ibid., 426.

26. U.S. Constitution, art. I, sec. 8.

27. PL 102-492, Oct. 24, 1992, 106 Stat. 3145, codified at 17 U.S.C. 107.

28. *New Era Publications International v. Henry Holt and Co.*, SNY No. 88 Civ. 3126 (PNL), 8/9/88; 695 F. Supp, 1493, at 1498 (S.D.N.Y. 1988).

29. Ibid. at 1502.

30. Ibid. at 1504.

31. *New Era Publications v. Henry Holt*, 873 F. 2d 576 (2d Cir. 1989).

32. *Wright v. Warner Books*, 748 F. Supp. 105 (S.D.N.Y. 1990).

33. Ibid., 108.

34. Ibid., 110.

35. *Wright v. Warner Books*, 953 F.2d 731 (2d Cir. 1991), 734.

36. *Ibid.*, 741.

37. "Historians Oppose Copyright Extension for Unpublished Material," *Archival Outlook*, newsletter of the Society of American Archivists, September 1995, 27. The article reports on hearings for H.R. 989 held on July 13, 1995, to consider the extension of copyright duration. Marybeth Peters, Register of Copyright, supported much of the bill but objected to extending the duration on unpublished material created before 1978. Michael Les Benedict, professor of history at Ohio State University and author of a number of articles on copyright issues (see next footnote), submitted testimony on behalf of the National Coordinating Committee for the Promotion of History in opposition to the extension. On September 20, 1995, the Senate Judiciary Committee held a hearing on S.483, the Copyright Term Extension Act of 1995. The Register of Copyright repeated her testimony of July 13 before the House committee relating to unpublished manuscripts. While most of the discussion related to published works, and the extension to seventy years was favored by entertainment industry representatives, Professor Peter A. Jaszi of The American University had strong reservations about the bill, and stated: "The public domain is a source of real social value, and incursions on it should not be undertaken lightly." Jaszi, ibid.

38. The literature in the field is overwhelming. I have found especially

useful the essays in Mary Boccaccio's *Constitutional Issues and Archives* (n.p.: Mid-Atlantic Regional Archives Conference, 1988), containing a discussion between Christopher M. Runkel, "Salinger v. Random House: The Case," 49–60, and Michael Les Benedict, "Salinger v. Random House: Implications for Scholars Use," 61–70. Benedict also wrote "Historians and the Continuing Controversy over Fair Use of Unpublished Manuscript Material," *American Historical Review* 91(October 1986): 859–881, and "Copyright I. 'Fair Use' of Unpublished Sources," *Perspectives* (American Historical Association Newsletter) 28, no. 4 (April 1990): 9–13; Jerry G. Henn, "Fair Use," *Copyright Law. A Practitioner's Guide*, 2d ed. (n.p.: Practicing Law Institute, February 1988), 179–215; Peterson and Peterson, *Archives and Manuscripts: Law* 81–89; Alan Latman, Robert Gorman, and Jane C. Ginsburg, *Copyright for the Nineties: Cases and Materials* (Charlottesville, Va.: The Michie Company, 3rd ed., 1989), 49–56; L. Ray Patterson and Stanley W. Lindberg, *The Nature of Copyright. A Law of Users' Rights* (Athens: University of Georgia Press, 1992), 19–46, 191–224. These have proven appropriately provocative to stimulate classroom discussions.

39. Arvin S. Quist, *Security Classification of Information. Vol 1. Introduction, History, and Adverse Impacts.* (Oak Ridge, Tenn.: Oak Ridge Gaseous Diffusion Plant, Operated by Martin Marietta Energy Systems, Inc. Report K/CG-1077/VI, September 1989), 26.

40. Ibid.

41. Executive Order 12958, April 17, 1995, Sec. 1.7.

42. Conversation with Steven Garfinkel, director of the U.S. Information Security Oversight Office, November 13, 1995.

43. "ALA Code of Ethics," *American Libraries*, July/August 1995, 673.

44. Association of College & Research Libraries (a division of the American Library Association), *Standards for Ethical Conduct for Rare Book, Manuscript, and Special Collections Librarians* (Chicago: ACRL, 1994), 8 pp.

45. Society of American Archivists, *Code of Ethics for Archivists* (Chicago: SAA, 1992), 4 pp.

46. United States Office of Government Ethics, *Standards of Ethical Conduct for Employees of the Executive Branch* (Washington, D.C.: United States Office of Government Ethics, August 1992).

47. ACRL *Standards*, 4.

48. "Access to the Collections," ibid.

49. *ALA Code of Ethics*, III.

50. *Code of Ethics for Archivists*, IX

51. Ibid., X.

52. ACRL *Standards*, 3.

· 12 ·

PERSONAL COMMUNICATION IN THE
ELECTRONIC AGE

Littera Scripta Manet[1]

This book has been dedicated to the past. All of the examples given, and the processes discussed, have related to historical material already in manuscript collections, or on its way to them. And yet, the coverage has only touched the surface of the mass. The 72,000-plus collections listed in *NUCMC* represent the holdings of only 1,400 repositories, but *DAMRUS* lists more than 4,000 repositories. Nor does *NUCMC* profess to include material in the major archives of the country, leaving out government, corporate, business, religious, educational, and other institutions that maintain their own records. Certainly, there is no paucity of sources for today's researchers to probe and exploit. If we allow a lag time of twenty to thirty years before active collections enter manuscript repositories, there is enough recent material still outstanding to keep archivists and manuscript curators occupied for the foreseeable future, and older collections continue to flow in.

But what about tomorrow? Are the materials being created today the stuff that will enhance collections tomorrow? Given the unstated mandate of the profession to collect documents of contemporary society for future generations, will tomorrow's curators be able to carry it out?

There is a general belief that the age of the telephone began the decline of personal written communications of the kind that one finds prior to its common use, and the assumption holds up for certain kinds of communication—the one-on-one confidential revelation, preliminary planning, or idle gossip that often reveals an underlying text. This may be true, but it is an untested theory, because no one has attempted to document it.

The telephone did not substitute for person-to-person written communication, but changed it. In business and politics it is common to find letters of affirmation or confirmation that begin: "In re our recent phone conversation." What has been lost is the banter, the give-and-take, the confidences, the nuances, and the decision process. By the time the letter is written the decision has been reached, and the written word merely confirms what it is. Unfortunately, only the written word endures, and we must rely on *ex post facto* memoirs, letters to others explaining the rationale for the decision, or diaries, all of which permit the writer to expand or reduce the reality of the telephone discussion.

But, certainly, the telephone has not replaced all written communication! If the soldier serving far from home in the Persian Gulf, or Haiti, or Bosnia now has an opportunity, through satellite communication, to call home rather than write; and if the progress of the grandchildren located across a continent are reported via phone and videotapes rather than in letters, some communication still uses the mail. But how much will it tell our great-great grandchildren about us?

Much personal writing has been reduced to the prefabricated sentiments of the greeting card, which "says it all" for those who do not have the time, energy or inspiration to say it themselves. There are greeting cards for every occasion—not just birthdays, but each birthday, including the one hundredth. There are targeted greeting cards, not just to mother, dad, sister, or brother, but to "Dad's new wife," "my other mother," "son and his companion," and just about any combination required to eliminate the sender's need to be definite about the recipient's identity. Similarly, members of both houses of Congress receive millions of pieces of printed postcards as impersonal as a greeting card; only the signature *seems* to be authentic. They also receive electronic mail and they respond by electronic mail with formula responses. This glut of "information" is a far cry from nineteenth-century petitions in terms of historical value.

The greeting card companies employ verse both florid and cute, humor, cant, eroticism, innuendo, and every human means of expression that permits the sender to convey sentiments without personalizing them. If it appears on a published card, the expression is presumed to be acceptable and universal, but distances it from the individual sender at the same time that it suggests an association. These cards leave little for future analysts to uncover about people of the 1990s. It is no longer necessary to express one's self in writing, and greeting cards are to written personal sentiment what frozen dinners are to culinary skills. A corporate initiative has selected the ingredients and prepared them for packaging.

The greeting card surrogates also cloak many of the social graces, since they substitute for invitations, expressions of sympathy, or appreciation for kindnesses rendered. They might well tell a future researcher something about the recipient and what others thought of him or her, but they tell nothing about the senders, except their taste in greeting cards. In an impressive display of rationality, Judith Martin, a.k.a. Miss Manners, urged upon her readers a "list of obligatory handwritten letters and their contents," and included the love letter, the condolence letter, the letter of thanks, and the letter of apology. She comments incisively: "On certain occasions, a letter is the only way to show that you are sincere, which is sometimes necessary whether you are or not. Even without tear stains, there is just something earnest-looking about those wandering lines and shadings of ink."[2]

Even that old standby, the note or letter of congratulation, is now suspect. The contents were always largely unrevealing, but at least there was an indication of enough personal involvement by the sender to express sentiments of congratulation to the recipient. Even that pretense has fallen, as congratulatory letters are now solicited, for retirees for instance, so that they can be bound and presented to the honored person at an appropriate ceremony.[3]

One form of personal communication whose *composition* has not (yet) been mechanized is the annual family holiday letter. But the mechanized copying devices and the low cost of running off a required number have provided another incentive for the "stressed-out" generation to take the shortcut to impersonal communications. These formalized epistles may, in spite of their lack of personal insight, be one of the few sources of family communication available in the future. But, like corporate annual reports, which they seem to emulate, they reveal no hardship, disturbing trends, dissension or family problems, except between the lines. The genre also prevents any form of sentimental expression between sender and recipient, except perhaps a hurriedly penned note at the end, generally along the lines of "Hope all is well with you and your family." At least with a corporate annual report a researcher can go back into the retained records of day-to-day activities to probe reality.

In the area of social communication, invitations, announcements, expressions of sympathy, personalized family news, and other sources for studying society, the decline of writing may be largely attributed to the changing role of women in society. When they were home, raising the family, tending to domestic affairs, and socializing, it fell to the woman to perform the social graces. The transition to career woman, breadwinner, single parent, or working married partner has reduced the time for these niceties in the scheme of priorities, and the premanufactured sentiment or format, like the frozen meal, has provided a substitute for "the real thing."

As we move further into the electronic age it is the cellular phone, the beeper, automatic redial, home voice mail with multiple mail boxes for family members, and other forms of voice communication that cause further decline in the need to write. But, ironically, another form of written communication is springing up among the computer-privileged class in the form of electronic mail, or E-mail. Among academics, corporate employees, students and teachers at all levels, and communication professionals, E-mail has all but replaced other forms of personal communication — even the telephone. These groups may constitute less than ten percent of the population, but their numbers grow dramatically, and there is promise of even faster expansion as schools, aided by local corporations, increase the number of computers found in the classroom.[4] The generational tide should reach storm-surge proportions within a decade, as those students move behind the teachers' desks or terminals.

It is so much easier to sit down to a keyboard, throw a few switches, jiggle a mouse or punch a few keys, and go on-line, access a personal mailbox, and read, delete, save, print, or perform any number of processes in communication with others than it is to wait for the mail carrier or find a piece of paper, an envelope, an address and a stamp, and then go to the post office or wait for the letter to be picked up for delivery. E-mail permits almost-instant communication—unlike the postal service—or what might be even more desirable, communication at any time of day or night, whether the recipient is available or not—unlike the telephone. E-mail permits international communication without worrying about postage calculations, weight or bulk. E-mail permits broadcast to many, or narrowcast to a few recipients. Messages can be dispatched to *all* members of Congress in one transmission. E-mail is written but can be informal. Acknowledgment can be instantaneous, or delayed pending contemplation or advice-seeking. Today's electronic communication through the Internet, that great information landfill, can, with some digging and patience, bring forth vast amounts of information (some quite useless), without so much as reaching over one's shoulder for a book.

E-mail has many of the attributes of traditional correspondence. There is a sent copy and a retained copy, at least electronically. For archivists the question is whether either or both of those copies are transferred to a hard medium that can be retained, maintained in the soft medium of electronic nonsubstance, or deleted before attaining either form. If retained on paper, E-mail can be a direct substitute for traditional correspondence files. If maintained electronically, ironically the file can provide *more* to a future researcher than either traditional correspondence or printed E-mail because of imbedded "metadata" (on more of which, below). If deleted, depending on the equipment and operating system used, the information may be recoverable; this is comparable to riffling through a wastebasket that has not yet been emptied and the contents destroyed.

One other form of communication that still appears to be employed by a few is the diary. Diaries require discipline if they are to be kept systematically, and few people have the patience and stamina to be successful diarists. It is a form of communication in that the diarist is communicating with the future, either introvertedly for him or herself alone or extrovertedly to share information with others when conditions seem to call for it. Diaries are resorted to probably most often during times of momentous activities in the life of the diarist—at work, at war, in love, or in personal crisis. Diaries may be kept for "proof" when one has a feeling of being wronged, or to indicate self-importance when little recognition is coming from others. As noted in chapter 2, belief in the contents of a diary depends on an understanding of the motivations and circumstances of the diarist.

With the growing paucity of direct personal expression through the traditional form of correspondence and other personal writings, the researcher of today, and more so of tomorrow, will turn to sources other than personal communication in order to understand society. The communications media, both print and electronic, become more important if one is to get a sense of style, mood, purpose, and expression of the community being studied. In reaction to this need, archival preservation of the media has become increasingly important for research, but essentially for research of the twentieth century, and even there the emphasis is on the post–World War II era, that defining period of the century itself. Researchers concentrating on earlier eras must still rely on the traditional documentation media of personal communication and official records. Even the lessons brought to us by Ken Burns in his Civil War series of documentaries made from contemporary photographs did not suggest that they could stand alone as historical sources. Photographs do not document themselves or put themselves in context, and their accompaniment by written documentary evidence is basic to an understanding of what role the photograph plays in any story.

If personal communication is undergoing a major transition at the end of the twentieth century that will affect how people of the twenty-first will view us, creative writing is also undergoing a transition that will affect future researchers. Every author has personal work habits, wherein some still draft in longhand and then transcribe and edit. Others still compose and create on a typewriter, although a sign of the times is that the last American-made typewriter was produced in 1995. Some may continue to dictate text verbally into a tape recorder, to be transcribed later in preparation for editing. But, more and more, authors turn to word processing programs run on a personal computer. After all, the scrolling feature means no more stopping for a carriage return and calculating word breaks; no more messy erasing or crossing out of unwanted text or misspellings; no more feeding in new sheets when the page is full; and no more worrying about a lost manuscript left behind at an airport. The art of the writer is to write, not to fool around with equipment that impedes progress and distracts chains of thought.

For the researcher interested in authorial process, in creative development, in the imposition of external editors on an author's work, in understanding the agony and ecstasy of expression, much can be lost if the author has produced a word-processed text. The computer and advanced word processors have the capacity to store and compare all versions of a manuscript in progress, and researchers interested in studying textual drift should therefore be able to enter variant texts of literary figures and let the machine sort out the differences between them. But, as the historian must find new ways to ply his or her trade as communication methodology shifts, so must the literary researcher of tomorrow looking at today's authors. For both, it may be necessary to rely on interviews, or oral history, to pry from artists the tales of their search for their personal muse.

There is another consideration to be given to the question of the writer in an electronic era. A novelist or poet may not use the Internet as a source of information or inspiration, but it is clear that for some who may not feel that they are properly appreciated in the commercial marketplace, the Internet becomes an electronic vanity press, where they can load up their outpourings for all to see and, of course, to appreciate. It is a temptation to some to take advantage of an opportunity to distribute one's own work to hundreds of thousands of people throughout the world without the interference of editors, the barbs of prepublication reviewers, the constraints of publishers, or the costs of self-publication. In those cases, celebrity comes with the establishment of one's own "home page" on the World Wide Web. And so the great information landfill is piled higher and higher while university and commercial presses try to figure out how to use this distribution process and yet maintain copyright protection and its concomitant financial compensation. Archivists, meanwhile, wonder what to save.

While scholars may caution against the ready acceptance of digitized documentary sources without applying the usual tests for verification,[5] the time is rapidly approaching when the digital text is all that exists because it *is* the original text, and not a surrogate for one on paper.

What survives may skew an understanding of our society by future generations. It is likely that personal communication will constitute less and less of the source, and corporate records more and more. Manuscript curators have always collected the "corporate person's" files as "personal papers." Although some family and noncorporate activities are generally included, the bulk of such collections traditionally is made up of the individual's activities on behalf of the corporate body, be that a church, a business, a philanthropy, a university or a government. These files are personal only in that they have been segregated from the corporate mass and portray only (or mainly) the role of the individual. They are distinguished from the corporate archives because they do not reflect functions and processes of an office, but activities of an individual within that office. Examples are numerous, such as Herbert Claiborne Pell (1884–1961), whose papers at the Franklin D. Roosevelt Library include:

Correspondence, memoranda, reports, cablegrams, telegrams, article file, and newspaper clippings documenting Pell's service as Democratic party leader, U.S. representative, minister to Portugal (1937–41) and Hungary (1941–42), and American member to the United Nations Commission for Investigation of War Crimes (1943–45). Includes personal and business papers.[6]

By substituting the names of other individuals and places this description could be applied to hundreds of collections in the Presidential libraries, the Library of Congress, and historical society and university collections nationwide. If that fact tells us anything, it is that these quasi-personal collections are the products of corporate life; the "papers" (read "records") were created through corporate mechanisms, and form by-products of the corporate communication process.

With those facts established, it is easy to predict what the form of future collections of "personal" papers from corporate members will look like: for the most part they will reflect the corporate production methods and will be digital. The U.S. Department of State began digitizing its communication with overseas posts in the 1970s, when the daily "cable traffic" was computerized. The files that resulted, however, consisted of printouts on paper. The advance of bigger and better electronic communication systems and the rise of E-mail and the Internet have all pushed that process forward to the point where, soon after entering office, the Clinton administration publicized the E-mail addresses for the president and vice president. Agencies soon followed suit or were instructed to modernize, and they created gopher sites and home pages available to all. Publications of the agencies, the Office of the Federal Register, the GPO and even the Congress were made available to anyone with the computer capability to access them, and newspapers, newsletters, academic programs, travel rates and schedules, and masses and masses of other information sources joined the crowd. Politicians found that they could reach many of their constituents by broadcasting their accomplishments (never their failures) to them electronically, depending on the electronic sophistication of their districts. The U.S. Senate World Wide Web home page was activated in October 1995.

The Reagan White House had earlier grasped the advantages of speed and easy communication, and installed a central computer that ran on a system developed by IBM called PROFS, which permitted internal, secured communication between and among offices of messages, document texts, calendars, reminder notes, notices, and all of the records accoutrements of office life in a corporate setting. Naturally, when the administration ended, the staff wanted to take their electronic files with them or delete them as insignificant— in archival terms, "of no enduring value." The succeeding Bush administration followed the same path but, because there had been a Citizen's Committee (for litigation purposes) that was trying to reverse the Reagan document disposal process, the Bush staff (and the president) convinced the archivist of the United States that the removal of the files on January 19, 1993, was legal and asked him to sign off on the proposed action, which he did.

The Citizen's Committee reacted negatively, called for an injunction on the removal, and the case came before District Court Judge Charles Richey. Judge Richey then did something that astounded the archival community, and has had repercussions since. In his judgment, Judge Richey denied two archival principles that had been put forward in defense of the White House actions. One stated that not every file in an office constitutes a "record," thus creating "nonrecord material." The second archival premise was that the "record" remains one, and in fact probably attains status as a record only when it is printed out from the electronic database. Therefore, if the archivists could separate the record from the nonrecord material, and then print and file the former, their obligations to the Federal Records Act would be fulfilled.

Judge Richey demurred, and declared that the electronic file *is* the record, and is endowed with that status because only it contains the metadata of the record itself. These metadata are electronic "stamps" imposed by the medium on everything entered into the system, which form the true provenance of the message. That provenance data provides the date and precise time of creation, the office that created it (and sometimes the very machine used), the routing of the information, the electronic transfer points through which it passed on the way to its destination, whether it was a message of origin or a reply, and the length of the text. And the system could even replay the alterations made to the text, or whole texts that the creator had "deleted." Without explicit reference to Marshall McLuhan, Judge Richey was stating that, indeed, "the medium is the message."[7]

What all of this implies is that records officers and corporate officials may take Judge Richey's message to heart and dispute the need for keeping paper in addition to, or in lieu of, the electronic data base from which it is created. The acceptance of electronic records in court has probably tolled the death knell for large accumulations of paper files and, indeed, their speedy digitization, not only as a space-saving, economical move (which has always been the rationale for corporate microfilming) but also for their rapid retrievability. Law firms that represent corporate or institutional clients have already begun the process of text conversion of masses of files, and other types of offices are following suit.

While it was relatively simple for a Herbert Claiborne Pell, an Averell Harriman or a Colin Powell to have a secretary retain a carbon or photocopy of all of their correspondence and keep them in a "personal" file for later reference after retirement, what will the dynamic executives and managers of the future do with the electronic files in which their life's work and accomplishments have been recorded? Will they ask for a duplicate copy, to be retained by them on tapes or disks? Will they have the equipment needed to play back the medium? Will they retain the operating system and the application program needed to understand what is being played back? Will they order that every document of theirs be printed for retention in paper form, important or not?

If we include in the term "corporate" all members of the legislatures of the country, we are then including a large segment of the voice of the people through the accumulation of constituent mail, which can be an important source for understanding society at any one time. At least it provides some understanding of "issues" and public problems. Whether the digitization fever will infect this source or not can only be speculated on.

If all of these options are possible, then there must be a question of what happens when these corporate or agency files from many origins are retired to a collecting institution. We could expect that the Library of Congress, the Presidential libraries (which are part of the National Archives and Records Administration), and the major research libraries *may* be in a position to receive, store and preserve the electronic record as "personal papers." But such institutions will find their practices complicated by the varieties of electronic equipment and software used to create the records of the captains of industry, government, and the arts and sciences. Until now all paper documents have been created equal: they can be handled, perceived and (depending on the language or graphic image) read, regardless of source. Additionally, all photographs can be viewed, all transparencies projected, all sound recordings heard, because of standards among the manufacturers of those media. The electronic media at the personal computer level are staggering towards standardization but are not there yet. Information that was created on mainframe or minicomputers may require considerable manipulation to become compatible with new state-of-the-art equipment. Will there still be the equivalent of a Manuscript Division to treat with these electronic files? Although one could surmise that all electronic sources would be administered by a centralized electronic computerized information office, with transmissions of text and images to terminals in the various research rooms, or to a single, large research complex, we can only hope that the admonition of one researcher is heeded: "We need to pay greater attention to the content of the message, rather than be dazzled by the medium."[8]

My concern here is not with the progress of electronics, which is inevitable, but with the combination of declining personal communications and the shift of "personal" corporate communication to electronics, because it may be only news media and the organized, mandated, efficient corporate record that will be left to inform the future of the nature of our society. And in those records we will be known for *what* we were, but not really for *who* we were, and the personal record of the individual in society may only survive in the archives of Ann Landers.

It is apparent, however, that for pre-twenty-first-century social documentation we will be relying on the paper source for a long time to come. The professional literature is full of excited news about digitization, but little space is given to considerations of effort and cost. Fifty years ago the archival and library literature was touting the qualities of microfilm, and the prospect of our reducing storage needs through conversion from paper. It has not happened in archives and manuscript collections. Where microfilm has been used to create surrogates, the originals have been retained, both for intrinsic value and as the "master copy" that one could fall back on. A recent informal survey that I conducted among the 1,700 members of an archives listserve indicated that only a few of the larger research libraries had approached having ten percent of their collections on microfilm: the smaller institutions generally reported that none had been filmed. If, after fifty years of the technology, such a small percentage of our national documentary heritage has been transferred to film, why should we anticipate a major move to digitize the same collections? Cost is the greatest deterrent, but the lack of a rationale for carrying out a digitizing program is also a strong factor.

What, then, is the future of the past? I often say that I like writing about the future because it does not require endnotes, and I will not be defrocked if I am proven wrong. It is also a great gamble to make a prediction when all of the possible variables are not known. But there are some verities that deserve consideration, perhaps to show that the future never is as dramatically different from the present as might be imagined.

First, there is the nature of historical research. Is it to establish facts? Perhaps, but archival records, if empirical, neutral, and detached, can establish certain facts of the past, such as the price of grain, the condition of roads, the winners and losers of public contests, and the status of various segments of society. The role served by collections of personal papers is to provide motivations for and reactions to events. Why something happened is as instructive as knowing what happened. The Mearns enumeration at the head of chapter 2 is the most perceptive insight to the value of personal papers that I have seen. If personal communication declines, where will the future researcher find motivations in the past? We are confronted with this question when researching ancient civilizations, when we know what happened but do not have any supporting information about cause. Is history to become a documentary Stonehenge or Easter Island?

And, if the future *is* to depend on digitized records as its source for knowledge of the past, what will be the means of verification of authenticity? Perhaps Judge Richey's metadata will be the key to separate out the bogus from the real, and we should not worry about it. After all, researchers are forever coming across forged documents relating to important events. They look at the writing material, the ink, the handwriting and the use of language to assist in the uncovering of forgeries, but their common tests of the base material, the impression substance, the graphic representation, and the text do not apply to digitized information—will a personal identification number be sufficient proof of authenticity in the future?

The researcher one hundred years hence may view us through picture and sound, but is reality captured on the CBS Evening News? Are the minor manifest events reported each day sufficient to add up to the long-range evolutionary changes that take place in society? On the other hand, we, too, look at the minutia without really seeing that it is but one strand of the interconnecting threads that make up the fabric of history. When we look at the struggles between the Serbs, Croats and Bosnians in 1995, do we shrug and attribute it to the Turkish capture of Constantinople in 1453?

I opened this book with quotes from two letters from William J. Calhoun some eighty-five years ago. How have things changed? State Department communications have become "status reports," and are supplemented by communications from the intelligence agencies, the military attachés, and representatives of other government units on the scene. The language has been structured, and one would most likely not find a "big, fat and burly" reference to the leader of another country among the messages in the "cable traffic." Nor, I suspect, would there be the disparaging remarks about their diplomatic skills expressed in uncouched terms. Such things might be found in later "background" reports and de-briefings, once the agent has returned home. But those then become reflections, rather than observations, and are colored by time and discretion.

The other Calhoun letter, to Harriet Monroe, remains a touchstone for the quality of personal letters as historical documents. Not only are the sentiments the same, verbatim, as those expressed to the State Department, but they are enhanced by reports of first impressions, observations, mood settings, and near-poetic rhetoric. It is an interesting letter because, although personal, it discusses nothing of a personal nature except impressions of what is happening. It thus brings international affairs and intrigue down (or perhaps up) to human scale, and makes the reader eighty-odd years later feel that *this* is probably the truth, whereas official correspondence often conveys the sense of veiled half-truths, reported for a purpose.

Do the William Calhouns of the world still exist? Are they today writing to family and friends, who will donate those letters to an institution for further research? Perhaps, but with rapid air transportation, home leaves, E-mail, and the camcorder one has the impression that such personal observations will be held until the traveler returns and can reveal all in small parties over cocktails at home or in a presentation at the local club. Will those verbal revelations make it into the collections at the Library of Congress?

Perhaps, but if they do, they would have to have been recorded, and the tape would go to the audiovisual collection, not the manuscript collection.

It is dangerous to take a personal experience and project it as universal, but I believe that three personal experiences over the past four decades may be instructive, and illustrate my point.

In 1953 I sent a twelve-page letter home describing the last leg of an auto trip from New York to Fairbanks, Alaska. The trip was harrowing: the three-year-old Studebaker was on its last legs by the time we got to Spokane; the road north of Whitehorse was flooded and we had to take a five hundred-mile detour through muskeg and ruts; tires went, brakes gave out, and the engine consumed a quart of oil every one hundred miles. I related the whole tale. This was only one of a regular series of letters that I wrote home, and the family made certain that they were passed around to relatives and friends, and then deposited in a shoebox.

Reading that letter today invokes a sense of the past, the primitive conditions of the Canadian Northwest, the then exotic names such as Watson Lake, Fort Nelson, Carmacks, Minto, Kluane Lake (which had flooded, causing the detour), Dawson, Sixtymile, Chicken, and Tok, the never-ending daylight (it was August), the total lack of accommodations for hundreds of miles, the gas pumps at roadhouses reeking of stale beer and cigarette smoke. The letter told it all, but it was one of the few ways to communicate with home before easy and inexpensive telephones and the camcorder.

The second example comes from a nephew who, in the 1960s, joined the Peace Corps, and later other international assistance organizations, and has spent his life since in Kenya, Uganda, Sri Lanka, Estonia, Latvia, Ukraine, Albania, and other locations. His letters of twenty years ago were full of news, impressions, opinions, and points of debate, to which I tried to respond. They tell of youthful enthusiasm, tribal affairs, local political intrigue, news of his new and growing family, and the idealism of the Camelot generation. Somewhere along the way they stopped coming, and instead were replaced by telephone calls, usually about plans to visit on the next home leave, where his experiences were related verbally, condensed and suffering from the time lag from event to report. Is it that he has become so cosmopolitan that there seems no need to report what I can read in the *New York Times* or the *Washington Post*? or, indeed, see live on CNN? Is this an isolated case, or a trend?

The third example concerns a girlhood friend of my wife, who married and moved to Southeast Asia. In parallel time both my wife and her friend had children and developed active family lives. They corresponded regularly about the children, about conditions in their respective families, the struggles of their respective husbands climbing up through or being stymied in their careers, comments on other common friends and their activities, and all of the chitchat that goes on between old acquaintances meeting new experiences.

A few years ago the communications slowed down. After a number of attempts to get the friend to write, a package came, containing a ninety-minute home video. It took us through the city, the university where a son studied, into a wedding ceremony, on an auto trip through the countryside, and to a gathering of friends at a houseparty. The video showed the girlhood friend well (apparently) and enjoying the life with family and friends (apparently), and it put her in the physical context of her existence. But, at the end, we were both disappointed because, all in all, it was an impersonal document that left us with impressions and assumptions, told us what and where, but provided very little insight *about* one who had matured through an entirely different culture from that of her youth.

It is probably true that the generational changes in personal communication are to be neither welcomed nor deplored, but accepted as marks of the transit of civilization. Our experience in the twentieth century has been to receive our signals from the past through the plastic and literary arts, from the vases and monuments, the cave paintings and architectural ruins, as well as from papyrus and clay fragments, the confetti of the Dead Sea Scrolls, the rubricked and lapis lazulied sheets of lamb underbellies inscribed in Carolingian uncial script, the oak gall-inked prose on high-rag-content paper, and the faded typewriter carbon or purple hectograph copy of a letter of state. And in all of those writings and representations of the past we look for the *persona*, the individual to whom we can somehow relate and who will, perhaps, help us make sense of who we are and what we are doing here.

The change in human communication can be surmised from the recent appearance of a book that gathers together letters for their own sake.[9] These are not years of correspondence of an individual that will give us a perception of a life, nor are they letters on a subject trying to enlighten us about how the correspondents reacted to world or local events. These are letters that provide us with examples of the letter-writing art or craft, containing "328 items of highly varied character"[10] from Elizabeth I to Groucho Marx. The book celebrates the art of putting ink to paper and expressing, describing, reveling in and deploring the human condition. A 1995 exhibition at the National Archives, commemorating the fiftieth anniversary of the end of World War II, displayed letters from servicemen to families and friends. Since these letters were not official documents they were not in the holdings of the National Archives, but had to be solicited from veterans. Will such an exhibit come out of any near-future war? Or will such an exhibition consist mainly of photographs and videotapes? Could life in Peking, the "processions of men, women and children; of carriages, carts, rickshas and wheelbarrows; of camels, horses, mules, donkeys and dogs; of funerals and weddings, which are ever winding their way through the city streets," be depicted on videotape? Of course, but they would have little meaning without the comment that "we foreigners go about the streets, the shops, walls and temples as before . . . as though no hoary old empire was dying, as though one of history's great tragedies was not being enacted around us, as though no sound of the war and rumble of a great revolution was heard." It is that commentary that connects us with William J. Calhoun.

Will future researchers have these human conditions available to them in the collections of personal papers of *fin de siècle* individuals? Possibly, but it might be more difficult to predict what will reflect society fifty years hence. Perhaps historians and biographers will be able to catch much of the past and play it back for the momentous as well as mundane *events*. But for the life of the individual they may find only literary shards, and will have to go poring over moldy antiquities to piece together the psyche of past generations. We, therefore, are blessed, in that there are those 72,000-plus collections of personal papers already safely stored, mostly processed, described and ready for us to use, and, we hope, for others after us. What happens when those others look back at the twenty-first century is anyone's guess, and it may be that researchers will turn to the official records, the census and military records, the tax lists, old health and medical files, videotapes and sound recordings, oral histories, Barbara Walters interviews, and the printed word to probe the civilization that succeeds us. In this scenario, the personal papers will have been replaced by the official records in archives, and tomorrow's progeny may find that they are well aware of *what* happened in history, but that they have to work hard to find out why. David Mearns unknowingly transcended the generations of archivists and manuscript curators when he observed that they are faced with a "phenomenon consorting with a quandary."[11] Only tomorrow the phenomenon may be a significant increase of information about the world and society, but the quandary will be trying to perceive the human dimension in it all.

NOTES

1. "The Written Word Endures." Motto of the National Archives and Records Administration.

2. Miss Manners, "Stay Close to Your Pen, Pal," *Washington Post*, (February 25, 1996), F2.

3. At one of my retirements, I received a personal letter sent to my home from a person of position whom I admired and respected. Unfortunately, the well-meaning organizers of my retirement celebration solicited a letter from the same person. He was gracious enough to send one, which was then bound in with others that had been solicited. Long after the ceremony and my departure, I substituted the first received for the one solicited.

4. Dan Beyers, "Students Ride High on New Technology. Computer Know-How Alters Balance of Power in School," *Washington Post* (October 2, 1995), A1.

5. Raymond W. Smock, "What Promise Does the Internet Hold for Scholars?" *The Chronicle of Higher Education* (Sept. 22, 1995), B1–B2.

6. Dennis Burton, *A Guide to Manuscripts in the Presidential Libraries*, entry 3188, p. 231.

7. Marshall McLuhan and Quentin Fiore, *The Medium Is the Message: An Inventory of Effects* (New York: Bantam Books, 1967).

8. Smock, ibid., B1.

9. Frank Kermode and Anita Kermode, eds., *The Oxford Book of Letters* (New York: Oxford University Press, 1995).

10. S. Schoenbaum, review of *The Oxford Book of Letters*, *The Washington Post Book World*, September 19, 1995, 9.

11. Mearns; see chapter 4, note 15.

APPENDIX

Text of the exemptions to the Freedom of Information Act. Sect. (a)(6)(C)(b). This section does not apply to matters that are—

(1)(A) specifically authorized under criteria established by an Executive order to be kept secret in the interest of national defense or foreign policy and (B) are in fact properly classified pursuant to such Executive order;

(2) related solely to the internal personnel rules and practices of an agency;

(3) specifically exempted from disclosure by statute (other than section 552b of this title), provided that such statute (A) requires that the matters be withheld from the public in a manner as to leave no discretion on the issue, or (B) establishes particular criteria for withholding or refers to particular types of matters to be withheld;

(4) trade secrets and commercial or financial information obtained from a person and privileged or confidential;

(5) inter-agency memorandums or letters which would not be available by law to a party other than an agency in litigation with the agency;

(6) personnel and medical files and similar files the disclosure of which would constitute a clearly unwarranted invasion of personal privacy;

(7) records or information compiled for law enforcement purposes, but only to the extent that the production of such law enforcement records or information (A) could reasonably be expected to interfere with enforcement proceedings, (B) would deprive a person of a right to a fair trial or an impartial adjudication, (C) could reasonably be expected to constitute an unwarranted invasion of personal privacy, (D) could reasonably be

expected to disclose the identity of a confidential source, including a State, local, or foreign agency or authority or any private institution which furnished information on a confidential basis, and, in the case of a record or information compiled by criminal law enforcement authority in the course of a criminal investigation or by an agency conducting a lawful national security intelligence investigation, information furnished by a confidential source, (E) would disclose techniques and procedures for law enforcement investigations or prosecutions, or would disclose guidelines for law enforcement investigations or prosecutions if such disclosure could reasonably be expected to risk circumvention of the law, or (F) could reasonably be expected to endanger the life or physical safety of any individual;

(8) contained in or related to examination, operating, or condition reports prepared by, on behalf of, or for the use of an agency responsible for the regulation or supervision of financial institutions; or

(9) geological and geophysical information and data, including maps, concerning wells.

GLOSSARY OF TERMS

ACRL	Association of College & Research Libraries
AHA	American Historical Association
ALA	American Library Association
ArchivesUSA	World Wide Web and CD-ROM compilation of DAMRUS, NUCMC, and NIDS information
BRISC	Baltimore Regional Institutional Studies Center
CD-ROM	Compact Disk Read-only Memory
DAMRUS	Directory of Archives and Manuscript Repositories in the United States
DDC	Dewey Decimal Classification
DTD	Document Type Definition
EAD	Encoded Archival Description
Eureka	On-line reference tool of RLIN
FirstSearch	On-line reference tool of OCLC
FOIA	Freedom of Information Act
FSA	Farm Security Administration
GOPHER	a menu-based way to retrieve information hierarchically
HTML	Hypertext Markup Language
ISOO	Information Security Oversight Office
MARC	Machine Readaable Cataloging
MARC/AMC	Machine Readable Cataloging/Archives-Manuscripts Control (sometimes Archives Mixed Collections)
NARA	National Archives and Records Administration (1985–)
NARS	National Archives and Records Service (1952–85)
NHPRC	National Historical Publications and Records Commission

NIDS	National Inentory of Documentary Sources
NIDS-US	National Inventory of Documentary Sources in the United States
NUCMC	National Union Catalog of Manuscript Collections
OCLC	On-line Computer Library Center
OPAC	On-line Public Access Catalog
PCC	Papers of the Continental Congress
RG	Record Group
RLIN	Research Libraries Information Network
SAA	Society of American Architects
SGML	Standard Generalized Markup Language
WLN	Western Library Network
WWW	World Wide Web

BIBLIOGRAPHY

Archival Records

National Archives and Records Administration. General Records of the Department of State, 1910–1929. RG59

National Archives and Records Administration. Pacific-Sierra Region, San Bruno, CA, Farm Security Administration. RG96

National Archives and Records Administration. Office of General Counsel. General Services Administration. RG269

National Archives and Records Administration. Office of the Archivist of the United States. RG64

Manuscript Collections

Gunther, John. Papers. Regenstein Library. University of Chicago.

Jefferson, Thomas. Papers. Library of Congress Manuscript Division.

McLean, Evalyn Walsh. Papers. Library of Congress Manuscript Division.

Monroe, Harriet. Papers. Regenstein Library. University of Chicago.

Patton, George S., Jr. Papers. Library of Congress Manuscript Division.

Riley, Edith Dolan. Papers. University of Washington Library (Seattle).

Simons, Hi. Papers. Regenstein Library, University of Chicago.

Strauss, Herbert R. Papers. Theodore Roosevelt Papers. Correspondence of Theodore Roosevelt and Lemuel E. Quigg, 1894–1919. Regenstein Library. University of Chicago.

Books

Association of College & Research Libraries (a division of the American Library Association). *Standards for Ethical Conduct for Rare Book, Manuscript, and Special Collections Librarians.* Chicago: ACRL, 1994.

Avrin, Leila. *Scribes, Script and Books: The Book Arts from Antiquity to the Renaissance.* Chicago: American Library Association, 1991.

291

Bailyn, Bernard. "The Peopling of British North America: Thoughts on a Central Theme in Early American History—A Working Paper." In *The Past Before Us*. Edited by Michael Kammen. Ithaca: Cornell University Press, 1980.

Baker, Richard A. *The United States Senate: A Historical Biography.* Washington, D.C.: The Senate, 1977.

Barzun, Jacques. *Clio and the Doctors.* Chicago: University of Chicago Press, 1974.

Bellardo, Lewis J., and Lynn Lady Bellardo. *A Glossary for Archivists, Manuscript Curators, and Records Managers.* Archival Fundamentals Series. Chicago: Society of American Archivists, 1992.

Berner, Richard C. *Archival Theory and Practice in the United States. A Historical Analysis.* Seattle: University of Washington Press, 1983.

Bintliff, Barbara, and Al Coco. "Legal Aspects of Library Security." *Security for Libraries.* Chicago: American Library Association, 1984, 83–107.

Brichford, Maynard. *Archives and Manuscripts: Appraisal and Accessioning.* Chicago: Society of American Archivists, 1977.

Carlyle, Thomas. *On Heroes, Hero-Worship, and the Heroic in History.* Garden City, N.Y.: Dolphin Books, Doubleday & Company, Inc., n.d.

Fisher, David Hackett. *Historians' Fallacies: Towards a Logic of Historical Thought.* New York: Harper and Row, 1970.

Flower, John. *Moonlight Serenade: a Biodiscography of the Glenn Miller Civilian Band.* New Rochelle, N.Y.: Arlington House, 1972.

Fukuyama, Francis. *The End of History and the Last Man.* New York: The Free Press, 1994.

Garraty, John A. *The Nature of Biography.* New York: Alfred A. Knopf, 1947. Also published by Vintage Books, 1964.

Gasaway, Laura N., and Sarah K. Wiant. *Libraries and Copyright: A Guide to Copyright Law in the 1990s.* Washington, D.C.: Special Libraries Association, 1994.

Gottschalk, Louis. *Understanding History.* New York: Alfred A. Knopf, 1950.

Hamilton, Ian. *Keepers of the Flame.* Boston: Faber & Faber, 1994.

Heat-Moon, William L. *Blue Highways.* Boston: Little, Brown, 1982.

Iggers, Georg G., and Konrad von Moltke. "On the Character of Historical Science." *The Theory and Practice of History: Leopold von Ranke.* Translated by Wilma A. Iggers and Konrad von Moltke. New York: The Bobbs-Merrill Company, Inc., 1973.

Kaminski, John P., ed. *Citizen Jefferson: The Wit and Wisdom of an American Sage.* Madison, WI: Madison House, 1994.

Kane, Joseph N. *Famous First Facts.* 4th ed. New York: H.W. Wilson Company, 1981.

Kemp, Edward C. *Manuscript Solicitation for Libraries, Special Collections, Museums and Archives.* Littleton, CO: Libraries Unlimited, 1978.

McLuhan, Marshall. *Understanding Media.* 2d edition. New York: Signet Books, 1964.

Milton, George Fort. *The Eve of Conflict: Stephen A. Douglas and the Needless War.* Boston: Houghton Mifflin Company, 1934.

National Center for Education Statistics. *Digest of Education Statistics, 1993.* Washington, D.C.: National Center for Education Statistics, 1993.

National Historical Publications and Records Commission. *Historical Documentary Editions.* Washington, D.C.: NHPRC, 1993.

Nesmith, Tom. *Canadian Archival Studies and the Rediscovery of Provenance.* Metuchen, N.J.: The Scarecrow Press, 1993.

Peterson, Gary M., and Trudy Huskamp Peterson. *Archives and Manuscripts: Law.* SAA Basic Manual Series. Chicago: Society of American Archivists, 1985.

Posner, Ernst. *Archives of the Ancient World.* Cambridge: Harvard University Press, 1972.

Quist, Arvin S. *Security Classification of Information.* Vol 1. Introduction, History, and Adverse Impacts. Oak Ridge, TN: Oak Ridge Gaseous Diffusion Plant, operated by Martin Marietta Energy Systems, Inc. Report K/CG-1077/VI, September 1989.

Schellenberg, T. R. *Modern Archives: Principles and Techniques.* Chicago: University of Chicago Press, 1956.

———. *The Management of Archives.* New York: Columbia University Press, 1965.

Society of American Archivists. *Code of Ethics for Archivists.* Chicago: SAA, 1992.

Spragge, Shirley C. "Old Wine in Old Bottles: Renovating an Old Building for an Archives." *The Archival Imagination*, Barbara L. Craig, ed. n.p.: Association of Canadian Archivists, 1992.

Stearns, Peter N. "Toward a Wider Vision: Trends in Social History." *The Past Before Us: Contemporary Historical Writing in the United States.* Edited by Michael Kammen. Ithaca: Cornell University Press, 1980, 205–230.

Steinbeck, John. *The Grapes of Wrath.* New York: The Viking Press, 1939.

Taylor, Hugh. "Transformation in the Archives: Technological Adjustment or Paradigm Shift?" in Nesmith, *Canadian Archival Studies and the Rediscovery of Provenance.*

Thucydides. *History of the Peloponnesian War.* Translated by Richard Crawley. London & Toronto: J.M. Dent & Sons, Ltd., 1914.

Using the Nation's Documentary Heritage: The Report of the National Historical Documents Study. Washington: D.C.: National Historical Publications and Records Commission in cooperation with the American Council of Learned Societies, 1992.

Yates, JoAnne. *Control through Communication: The Rise of System in American Management.* Baltimore: Johns Hopkins University Press, 1989.

Articles

American Library Association. "ALA Code of Ethics." *American Libraries* (July/August 1995), 673.

Babcock, Phillip H. "Insure Against Employee Theft." *History News* 36, no. 9 (September 1981): 19.

Bradsher, James G. "We Have a Right to Privacy." *Constitutional Issues.* Edited by Mary Boccaccio. n.p.: MARAC, 1988, 11–20.

Brand, Katharine E. "Developments in the Handling of Recent Manuscripts in the Library of Congress." *American Archivist* 16 (April 1953): 99–104.

————. "The Place of the Register in the Manuscripts Division of the Library of Congress." *American Archivist* 18 (January 1955): 59–67.

Campbell, Ann M. "Reports from Weedpatch." *Agricultural History* 48, no. 3 (July 1974): 402–404.

Campbell, Edward G. "Functional Classification of Archival Material." *The Library Quarterly* 11 (1941): 431–441.

Cappon, Lester J. "American Historical Editors before Jared Sparks: 'They Will Plant a Forest.' " *William and Mary Quarterly* 30 (1973): 374–400.

Chesnutt, David R. "Presidential Editions: The Promise and Problems of Technology." *Documentary Editing* 16, no. 3 (September 1994): 70–77.

Desnoyers, Megan Floyd. "The Journey to the John F. Kennedy Library." in "Ernest Hemingway: A Storyteller's Legacy," *Prologue: Quarterly of the National Archives* 24, no. 4 (winter 1992).

Galvin, Theresa. "The Boston Case of Charles Merrill Mount: The Archivist's Arch Enemy." *American Archivist* 53 (summer 1990): 442–450.

Geselbracht, Raymond H. "The Origins of Restrictions on Access to Personal Papers at the Library of Congress and the National Archives." *American Archivist* 49 (spring 1986): 142–162.

Greenberg, Douglas. "Get Out of the Way if You Can't Lend a Hand: The Changing Nature of Scholarship and the Significance of Special Collections." *Biblion: the Bulletin of the New York Public Library* 2, no. 1 (fall 1993): 5–18.

Greene, Mark A. "Moderation in Everything, Access in Nothing?: Opinions About Access Restrictions on Private Papers." *Archival Issues: Journal of the Midwest Archives Conference* 18, no. 1 (1993): 31–41.

Hite, Richard W., and Daniel J. Linke. "A Statistical Summary of Appraisal during Processing: A Case Study with Manuscript Collections." *Archival Issues* 17, no. 1 (1992): 23–29.

Jackanicz, Donald. "Theft at the National Archives: The Murphy Case, 1962–1975." *Library and Archival Security* 10, no. 2 (1990), 23–50.

Lemisch, Jesse. "The American Revolution Bicentennial and the Papers of Great White Men." *American Historical Association Newsletter* 11 (1971): 7–21.

Lytle, Richard H. "Intellectual Access to Archives: I. Provenance and Content Indexing Methods of Subject Retrieval." *American Archivist* 43 (winter 1980): 64–75.

————. "II. Report of an Experiment Comparing Provenance and Content Indexing Methods of Subject Retrieval." *American Archivist* 43 (spring 1980): 191–208.

McNeill, William H. "Mythistory, or Truth, Myth, History, and Historians." *American Historical Review* 91, no. 1 (February 1986): 1–10.

McWilliams, Ruth. "Preparing for the Biographer: A Widow's Task." *Manuscripts* 36, no. 3 (summer 1984): 187–196.

Mearns, David C. "The Lincoln Papers." *American Library Quarterly* 4, no. 8 (December 1947): 369–385.

———. "He Had Nothing, Only 'Plenty of Friends.' The Story of the Long-awaited Abraham Lincoln Papers." *New York Herald Tribune Weekly Book Review* 24, no. 25 (8 February 1948): 1–2.

———. "Personal Papers, Including Manuscripts." *Library Trends* 5, no. 3 (January 1957): 313–321.

Rhoads, James B. "Alienation and Thievery: Archival Problems." *American Archivist* 19 (January 1966): 197–208.

Shelley, Fred. "Ebenezer Hazard: America's First Historical Editor." *William and Mary Quarterly* 12 (January 1955): 44–73.

Spindler, Robert P., and Richard Pearce-Moses. "Does AMC Mean 'Archives Made Confusing?': Patron Understanding of USMARC AMC Catalog Records." *American Archivist* 56 (spring 1993): 330–341.

Stender, Walter W., and Evans Walker. "The National Personnel Records Center Fire: A Study in Disaster." *American Archivist* 37 (October 1974): 521–550.

Documentary Editions

Adams, Abigail, and John Adams. *Letters of Mrs. Adams, the Wife of John Adams.* Edited by Charles Francis Adams. 2 vols. Boston: Charles C. Little and James Brown, 1840.

———. *Familiar Letters of John Adams and His Wife Abigail Adams, during the Revolution.* Edited by Charles Francis Adams. Boston and New York: Houghton Mifflin Company, 1876.

Adams Family. *Adams Family Correspondence.* Edited by Lyman H. Butterfield. Cambridge, MA: The Belknap Press of Harvard University Press, 1963.

———. *The Book of Abigail and John: Selected Letters of the Adams Family, 1762–1784.* Edited and with an introduction by L. H. Butterfield, Marc Friedlaender, and Mary-Jo Kline. Cambridge, MA: Harvard University Press, 1975.

Burr, Aaron. *Political Correspondence and Public Papers of Aaron Burr.* Edited by Mary-Jo Kline. 2 vols. Princeton: Princeton University Press, 1983.

Calhoun, John C. "Correspondence of John C. Calhoun." Edited by John Franklin Jameson. *Annual Report of the American Historical Association for 1899*, vol. 2. Washington, D.C.: GPO, 1900.

Chesnut, Mary. *Mary Chesnut's Civil War.* Edited by C. Vann Woodward. New Haven: Yale University Press, 1981.

Cormany Family. *The Cormany Diaries: A Northern Family in the Civil War.* Edited by James C. Mohr and Richard E. Winslow, III. Pittsburgh: University of Pittsburgh Press, 1982.

Doehla, Johann Conrad. *A Hessian Diary of the American Revolution.* Translated and edited by Bruce E. Burgoyne. Norman: University of Oklahoma Press, 1990.

Franklin, Benjamin. *The Memoires of the Life and Writings of Benjamin Franklin.* Edited by William Temple Franklin. 6 vols. London: Henry Colburn, 1818–1819.

Freedom: A Documentary History of Emancipation, 1861–1867. Edited by Ira Berlin and Leslie Rowland. Series I, 3 vols.; Series II, 1 vol. Cambridge, MA: Cambridge University Press, 1982–1993.

Gallagher, Gary W., editor. *Fighting for the Confederacy: The Personal Recollections of General Edward Porter Alexander.* Chapel Hill: The University of North Carolina Press, 1989.

Garvey, Marcus. *Marcus Garvey and Universal Negro Improvement Association Papers.* Edited by Robert A. Hill. 10 vols. Berkeley: University of California Press, 1983– .

Grant, Ulysses. *The Papers of Ulysses S. Grant.* Edited by John Y. Simon. 20 vols. Carbondale: Southern Illinois University Press, 1967– .

Hamilton, Alexander. *The Papers of Alexander Hamilton.* Edited by Harold C. Syrett. 27 vols. New York: Columbia University Press, 1961–1987.

Harwell, Richard, and Philip N. Racine, eds. *The Fiery Trail: A Union Officer's Account of Sherman's Last Campaigns.* Knoxville: The University of Tennessee Press, 1986.

Jay, John. *The Papers of John Jay.* Edited by Richard Morris. 2 vols., with a third and final volume in progress. New York: Harper and Row, 1975–1980.

———. *The Correspondence and Public Papers of John Jay.* Edited by Henry P. Johnston. 4 vols. New York: Burt Franklin, 1890; reprint, Lenox Hill Publishing and Distribution Co. [Burt Franklin], 1970.

———. *John Jay, the Making of a Revolutionary.* Edited by Richard B. Morris. Vol. 1, Unpublished Papers, 1745–1780. New York: Harper and Row, 1975.

Jefferson, Thomas. *Memoir, Correspondence and Miscellanies, from the Papers of Thomas Jefferson.* Edited by Thomas Jefferson Randolph. 4 vols. Charlottesville: F. Carr and Company, 1829.

———. *The Writings of Thomas Jefferson.* Edited by Henry A. Washington. 9 vols. Philadelphia: J. B. Lippincott and Company, 1864.

———. *The Works of Thomas Jefferson.* Edited by Paul Leicester Ford. 12 vols. New York: G. P. Putnam's Sons, 1904–1905.

———. *The Papers of Thomas Jefferson.* Edited by Julian Boyd, Charles Cullen, John Catanzariti. Series I, 26 vols. Princeton: Princeton University Press, 1950– .

Johns Hopkins University. *Records of the Johns Hopkins University Seminary of History and Politics.* Edited by Marvin M. Gettleman. New York: Garland Publishing Company, 1987–1990.

Johnson, Andrew. *The Papers of Andrew Johnson.* Edited by LeRoy P. Graf, Ralph W. Haskins, Paul Bergeron. 12 vols. Knoxville: University of Tennessee Press, 1987– .

Lafayette, Marie Joseph Paul Yves Roch Gilbert du Motier, Marquis de. *Lafayette in the Age of the American Revolution: Selected Letters and Papers, 1776–1790.* 6 vols. Edited by Stanley J. Idzerda, Linda Pike, Robert Rhodes Crout. Ithaca, N.Y.: Cornell University Press, 1977– .

Latrobe, Benjamin Henry. *The Papers of Benjamin Henry Latrobe.* Edited by Edward C. Carter, II. 8 vols. New Haven: Yale University Press, 1977–1988.

Laurens, Henry. *The Papers of Henry Laurens.* Edited by Philip M. Hamer, George C. Rogers, David R. Chesnutt. 13 vols. Columbia, SC: University of South Carolina Press, 1968– .

Olmsted, Frederick Law. *The Papers of Frederick Law Olmsted.* Edited by Jane Turner Censer. Vol. 4, Defending the Union: The Civil War and the U.S. Sanitary Commission, 1861–1863. Baltimore: Johns Hopkins University Press, 1986.

Plymouth, Massachusetts. *Plymouth Court Records, 1689–1859.* Edited by David Thomas Konig. 16 vols. Wilmington, DE: Michael Glazier, Inc., 1978–1981.

U.S. Congress. *Circular Letters of Congressmen to Their Constituents, 1789–1829.* Edited by Noble E. Cunningham, Jr. 3 vols. Chapel Hill: University of North Carolina Press, 1978.

———. *Documentary History of the First Federal Congress of the United States of America, March 4, 1789–March 3, 1791.* Edited by Linda Grant De Pauw, Charlene Bangs Bickford, Helen E. Veit, Kenneth R. Bowling. Baltimore: Johns Hopkins University Press, 1972– .

U.S. Constitution. *The Documentary History of the Ratification of the Constitution.* Edited by Merrill Jensen, John P. Kaminski, Gaspare Saladino. Madison: State Historical Society of Wisconsin, 1976– .

Washington, Booker T. *The Booker T. Washington Papers.* Edited by Louis B. Harlan, Raymond W. Smock. 14 vols. Urbana: University of Illinois Press, 1972–1989.

Washington, George. *The Diaries of George Washington.* Edited by Donald Jackson, Dorothy Twohig. 6 vols. Charlottesville: University of Virginia Press, 1976–1978.

Wilson, Woodrow. *The Papers of Woodrow Wilson.* Edited by Arthur S. Link. 69 vols. Princeton: Princeton University Press, 1966–1993.

Government Documents

U.S. Department of State. *Classification of Correspondence.* (Adopted August 29, 1910.) Prepared by the Division of Communications and Records. Washington, D.C.: GPO, 1910.

U.S. Library of Congress. *National Union Catalog of Manuscript Collections.* Washington, D.C.: Library of Congress, 1959/61–93.

U.S. National Archives. *Seventh Annual Report of the Archivist of the United States.* Washington, D.C.: GPO, 1942.

U.S. National Archives and Records Administration. *Life Cycle Systems Data Elements Manual ("Data Elements 800").* Washington, D.C.: NARA, August 4,
1988.

————. *Reference Report. "Inquiry: Records Relating to Amelia Earhart."* Washington: NARA, n.d., 5 pp.

U.S. National Archives and Records Service. *Staff Information Circular* 15 (July
1950).

U.S. Office of Government Ethics. *Standards of Ethical Conduct for Employees of
the Executive Branch.* Washington, D.C.: U.S. Office of Government Ethics
(August, 1992).

U.S. Senate. Judiciary Committee. "Statement of Peter A. Jaszi, Washington
College of Law, American University, on S. 483, the Copyright Term Extension Act of 1995, September 20, 1995, before the Senate Judiciary Committee 1995." Distributed at the hearing.

Finding Aids, Guides, and Catalogs

Burton, Dennis A., James B. Rhoads, and Raymond W. Smock, comps. *A
Guide to Manuscripts in the Presidential Libraries.* College Park, MD: Research
Materials Corporation, 1985.

Butler, John P. *Index: The Papers of the Continental Congress. 1774–1789.* 5 vols.
Washington, D.C.: NARS, 1978.

California State Archives. Records of the Secretary of State. *Inventory no. 6.*
Compiled by W. N. Davis, Jr. Sacramento, 1978, rev. 1980.

Hamer, Philip M., comp. *A Guide to Archives and Manuscripts in the United States.*
New Haven: Yale University Press, 1961.

Hinding, Andrea, comp. *Women's History Sources: a Guide to Archives and Manuscript Collections in the United States.* New York: Bowker, 1978. 2 vols. Vol. 2,
Index, edited by Suzanna Moody.

National Historical Publications and Records Commission. *Directory of Archives
and Manuscript Repositories in the United States.* Phoenix: Oryx Press, 1988.

Tennessee State Library and Archives. Manuscript Section. Archives Division.
Jacob McGavock Dickinson. A Register of His Papers (Revised). Register Number 1. Nashville, TN: 1959/1964.

U.S. Library of Congress. Manuscript Division. *The American Colonization Society: A Register of Its Papers in the Library of Congress.* Washington: Library of
Congress, 1979.

————. *Felix Frankfurter: A Register of His Papers in the Library of Congress.*
Washington: Library of Congress, 1971.

————. *Papers of James Monroe: listed in chronological order from the original manuscripts in the Library of Congress.* Washington: GPO, 1904.

————. *Robert Wilson Shufeldt: A Register of His Papers in the Library of Congress.*
Naval Historical Foundation Collection. Washington: Library of Congress,
1969.

————. *W. Averell Harriman: A Register of His Papers in the Library of Congress.* Washington: Library of Congress, 1991.

U.S. National Archives and Records Administration. *Inventory of the General Records of the Department of State 1789–1949*, Inventory No. 15, RG59 (Microfiche Edition). Washington, D.C.: NARA, 1992.

Washington State Historical Records Advisory Board. *Historical Records of Washington State: Records and Papers Held at Repositories.* Olympia, WA, 1981.

Legal Decisions and Statutes

Am Jur 2nd Charities ss5.

15 Am Jur 2nd Charities ss3.

U.S. Copyright Act, 1909. 17 U.S. Code. 1(5)

U.S. Copyright Act, 1978. 17 U.S. Code. 101, 102.

U.S. Copyright Act, 1991. U.S. Code. Vol. 17.

Harper and Row v. Nation Enterprises, 471 Sup. Ct. 542 (1985)

Hebrew University Association v. George D. Nye et al. 169 A.2d 641.

New Era Publications International v. Henry Holt and Co., SNY No. 88 Civ/ 3126 (PNL), 8/9/88; 695 F. Supp, 1493, at 1498; and 873 F. 2d 5767 (2d Cir. 1989).

Salinger v. Random House, Inc. (650 F. Supp. 413 S.D.N.Y. 1986 and 811 F.2d 90), reh'g denied. (818 F2d 252 (2d Cir.), cert. denied (56 U.S.L.W. 3207 Oct. 6, 1987).

Wright v. Warner Books, 748 F. Supp. 105 (S.D.N.Y. 1990); and 953 F. 2d 731 (2d Cir. 1991), 734.

Unpublished Papers

Braddock, Alan. "A Gopher in the Repository." Typescript November 30, 1993. 15 pp.

————. "Teaching an Old Gopher New Tricks, or How to Improve Internet Access to Archives and Manuscripts Information." Typescript, fall 1994. 27 pp.

Mahoney, Timothy J. "The Impact of 'New' Social History on American Manuscript Collections as Reflected in The National Union Catalog of Manuscript Collections, 1959–1991." Typescript, fall 1993. 28 pp.

Rosenthal, Robert. "The Minotaur Among the Manuscripts." Typescript. Paper presented at the annual meeting of the Society of American Archivists, October 14, 1971. 12 pp.

Ruth, Janice. "Women's Diaries: A Draft Guide to the Holdings of the Library of Congress Manuscript Division." Typescript, 1988, 77 pp. In the Manuscript Division.

Songster-Burnett, Jennifer. "Charities & Gifts: An Overview of Some of the

Laws Affecting Manuscript Repositories." Typescript. October 14, 1991. 17 pp.

Electronic Messages

Maier, Pauline. MIT. (1994, December 8). "Re Documentary Editions" [Discussion]. Scholarly Editing Forum [On-line]. Available from listserv @ SEDIT-L@UMDD.UMD.EDU.

Meyer, Daniel. (1995, February 6). University of Chicago Library, Special Collections. Re the Papers of Harriet Monroe. E-mail to author.

Sheehan, Mike. (1994, December 15). "Re Presidential Papers" [Discussion]. Scholarly Editing Forum [On-line]. Available from listserv @ SEDIT-L@UMDD.UMD.EDU.

Index

About the Author

Frank Burke is a graduate of the University of Chicago, where he was awarded the M.A. and Ph.D. degrees in history. Over the past thirty-five years he has held positions of responsibility at the University of Chicago Special Collections, the Library of Congress Manuscript Division, and the National Archives. At the Archives between 1967 and 1988 he was, among other positions, executive director of the National Historical Publications and Records Commission for fourteen years, and acting archivist of the United States for three years. In 1974 he began teaching part-time at the University of Maryland College of Library and Information Services, and in 1988 he assumed a full-time faculty position there. In June 1996 he retired from the University as professor emeritus, but will continue to teach courses occasionally. He has written and lectured on archival topics since his first article was published in 1967 in the *American Archivist*.

Dr. Burke is past president of the Association for Documentary Editing and the Society of American Archivists, and a fellow of the latter. He is a member of most of the professional archival societies in the United States.